OUTDOOR LIFE®
DEER
HUNTER'S
YEARBOOK

Outdoor Life® Books
MEREDITH® PRESS
Des Moines, Iowa

Cover photo: Len Rue Jr.

Published by Outdoor Life® Books
150 East 52nd Street
New York, New York 10022

Meredith® Press is an imprint of *Meredith® Books*
President, Book Group: Joseph J. Ward
Vice President and Editorial Director: Elizabeth P. Rice

For Meredith® Press:
Executive Editor: Maryanne Bannon
Editorial Project Manager: Kay M. Sanders
Production Manager: Bill Rose

Produced by Barbara G. Tchabovsky
Consulting Editor: George H. Haas
Book Designer: Jeff Fitschen

Special thanks to:
Vin T. Sparano, editor of *Outdoor Life* magazine
Laurel Kurnides, Production Director, *Outdoor Life* magazine
Donald Callum, Production Manager, *Outdoor Life* magazine
Trish Majka, Associate Art Director, *Outdoor Life* magazine

©1993 by Meredith Corporation, Des Moines, Iowa
Distributed by Meredith Corporation, Des Moines, Iowa

ISBN: 0-696-20000-7

Printed in the United States of America

10 9 8 7 6 5 4 3 2 1

Contents

4   CONTENTS

PREFACE

Hunting: The Future

Hunting has become a political issue in the United States. This was made absolutely clear in November 1992 in Arizona when a referendum known as Proposition 200 was put before the voters of that state. The proposition was not enacted into law. But, if it had been, all trapping, hunting, and fishing on state public lands—which make up 85% of the total land area of Arizona—would eventually have become illegal. Not only deer hunters but all hunters would have been deprived of their sport.

The referendum was couched in terms that seemingly would only have banned trapping by outlawing all forms of traps and snares. The intent of the law, however, was stated as "It is the intention and desire of the people of Arizona to make our public lands safe and humane for all creatures found on Arizona public lands. We desire to manage our wildlife and protect our property by humane and nonlethal means." If that all-inclusive wording had become law, other laws and state regulations could have been enacted that would have banned any consumptive use of wild creatures, even including fishing by a barefoot boy in a pond.

This was the first time that a ban on all outdoor hunting and trapping was proposed in any state. What the authors of the proposition meant by "nonlethal" means of controlling wildlife has not been explained—animal contraception, which seems impossible, or perhaps, the reintroduction of large numbers of predators—but then, we are left to wonder if the originators of the proposition believe that wolves and mountain lions kill humanely.

The petition for the referendum was presented with the signatures of 170,000 registered voters in Arizona, and after the proposition was accepted as the basis for a referendum, scientific polling of the electorate indicated that the referendum would pass if the vote were taken immediately. However, sportsmen groups and interested—and contributing—parties from all over the United States mounted a quick education campaign. Radio, television, and print were used to tell the voters what the proposition really meant.

The vote came in November 1992, and 62% of the voters turned it down. But, it is important to note that 38% of Arizona voters voted for the Proposition—and that 38% may be more active next time.

"I used to be a hunter, but now I'm a food gatherer." Illustration by Leo Cullum

That 38% of the electorate voted for Proposition 200 in a western state is astonishing. The large influx of retirees from the East and from California may have affected the results. However, the close vote made it clear that cooperation and coordinated efforts by hunters, fishermen, and trappers nationwide are the only things that stand between them and similar enactments in any state.

As every reader of the *Deer Hunter's Yearbook* knows, it consists mostly of narratives and articles from *Outdoor Life*. The last few editions have started with an article concerning an "issue" of interest and concern to sportsmen. The Arizona referendum was decided by the vote in November 1992, and though the issue was discussed in excellent *Outdoor Life* articles before and after the vote (July 1992 and February 1993), these articles are not included in this *Yearbook*

edition because the issue in Arizona is settled—at least for the time being. But I felt that the referendum should be mentioned in this Preface. Why? Because it can happen in your state, too. No issue could interest deer hunters more than the possible extinction of their sport.

In this edition of the *Deer Hunter's Yearbook*, Part I includes a single "issue" article—"Why I Taught My Sons To Be Hunters" by the late Archibald Rutledge, who was the Poet Laureate of South Carolina. In the article, the venerable author describes how he taught his sons to hunt small game and then deer. Rutledge wrote the article over 50 years ago, but the *Outdoor Life* editors reprinted it in December 1992, and for very good

Photograph by Len Rue Jr.

reason. Nowadays, in many crowded states, it is becoming more and more difficult to teach youngsters to hunt and to learn firsthand the principles of sportsmanship and safety. Many youngsters no longer grow up with nature and outdoor sports because they no longer live in rural areas. Teaching youngsters under these circumstances takes a lot more work than it did 50 years ago, but sportsmen who exercise as much good sense as Rutledge did 50 years ago can still do a good job, though they often have to rely on plinking, paper targets, and claybirds, rather than field shooting. Open seasons are much shorter, and since most Americans now live in large towns or suburbs, taking a budding sportsman afield involves getting up early and driving long distances—something Rutledge never had to do. But, if you don't make the effort, you're selling the sport short—and you are making it much easier for antihunters to propose—and perhaps, someday enact—laws like Proposition 200.

The Rutledge article is also interesting because Rutledge was such a linguistic traditionalist. His writing style is reminiscent of the 1890s or early 1900s. If you want to know how most narratives and articles for *Outdoor Life* were written then, you can't do better than reading Rutledge.

Related in spirit are the two articles in Part II—The Spirit of the Hunt. These are classic hunting stories—one a sportsmen's delight about an old pro and a tyro who go out of their way to be fair to each other, and the other a tale in which an old-timer allows a young hunter a true trophy—a lesson in extraordinary sportsmanship

Part III—Tips on Preparation and Safety—includes articles on basic techniques and precautions that are important for all hunters—whether they hunt for whitetails, mule deer, or bigger game.

Other parts of this edition are similar to those in previous editions—but with a few changes. This year, we do not have two separate parts—one on whitetail deer hunting and one on mule deer hunting. Instead, whitetail and mule deer hunting are included in one section—Hunting Whitetail and Mule Deer. This change reflects a change in American hunting. As mule deer have

The techniques for hunting whitetail deer like this are increasingly being used for mule deer. Photograph by Len Rue Jr.

been more intensively hunted, they have become more and more wary, and Western hunters are increasingly using Eastern whitetail techniques. This is being done almost to the exclusion of the old-fashioned scout, glass, and stalk method that was once really the only way to hunt mule deer. Why? Because mule deer are very seldom found in open country nowadays, and they appear to be much smarter than they used to be. If the trend continues, hunting both kinds of deer will be much the same in the future, no matter where you hunt. Putting whitetail and mule-deer hunting techniques together in one section therefore seemed appropriate. It would not have been only a few years ago.

As usual, there's a section on Hunting Bigger Game, because I've never known a deer hunter anywhere who didn't want to hunt these larger antlered animals.

We've added a section on This Happened to Me this year. Readers of *Outdoor Life* are familiar with these illustrated cartoon items that appear in each issue. Surveys reveal that more than 90% of subscribers read these items each month. These true incidents—the editors check—are interesting, of course, but most also have a message, commonly about safety afield. The editors

have always felt that This Happened To Me presents a continuing worthwhile safety message. If anything, the ones included in this *Yearbook* present the message that deer and other antlered game can be truly dangerous and that hunters should exercise great care. That's worthwhile if it prevents a single serious accident.

The *Yearbook* ends with two sections on techniques—one on Bowhunting and one on Firearms and Shooting. *Outdoor Life* no longer publishes *Hunting Guns* (nor *Deer and Big Game*), but we were able to include two excellent articles from previous editions of *Hunting Guns*, which were never reprinted in the *Yearbook*. Articles several years old can be—and are—still very informative and interesting. In fact, I'm looking forward to selecting a few classic stories from older issues of *Outdoor Life* for future editions of the *Deer Hunter's Yearbook*.

One very important thing hasn't changed at all. The reader will still find that both very informative articles and interesting narratives are included. You may not learn many facts from the hunting narratives, but they are simply a pleasure to read—or at least they are to me. I hope you agree.

George H. Haas
Consulting Editor, *Deer Hunter's Yearbook*

PART 1

AN ISSUE FOR HUNTERS

Why I Taught My Boys To Be Hunters

By Archibald Rutledge

In the realm of outdoor literature, few have captured the Southern tradition as sweetly as Archibald Rutledge. South Carolina's first poet laureate, Rutledge was an avid hunter and wrote often of the virtues found in a life lived close to nature. In "Why I Taught My Boys To Be Hunters," Rutledge explores the unique bond forged when the hunting tradition is passed from father to son. It's a call for the preservation of the hunting heritage written in words that ring as true today as they did upon their first printing 55 years ago.—*Outdoor Life*

I have said that my hunting has often been solitary, but that was chiefly in the early days. During the last twenty-five years, I have rarely taken to the woods and fields in the shooting season without having one or more of my own sons with me. Few human relationships are closer than those established by a mutual contact with nature, and it has always seemed to me that if more fathers were woodsmen and would teach their sons to be likewise, most of the so-called father-and-son problems would vanish.

Providence gave me three sons, only about a year and a half apart. Since it was not possible for me to give them what we usually call the advantages of wealth, I made up my mind to do my

Illustration by Randy Mack Bishop

best by them. I decided primarily to make them sportsmen, for I have a conviction that to be a sportsman is a mighty long step in the direction of being a man. I thought also that if a man brings up his sons to be hunters, they will never grow away from him. Rather, the passing years will only bring them closer, with a thousand happy memories of the woods and fields. Again,

Illustration by Randy Mack Bishop

a hunter never sits around home forlornly, not knowing what in the world to do with his leisure. His interest in nature will be such that he can delight in every season, and he has resources within himself that will make life always seem worthwhile.

Hunters should be started early. As each one of my boys reached the age of six, I gave him a single-shot .22 rifle, and I began to let him go afield with me. For a year or so, I never let him load the gun, even with dust shot, but I just tried to give him some notions of how to handle it, of how to cross a ditch or a fence with it, and in what direction to keep the muzzle pointed.

It was a great day for each youngster when he shot his first English sparrow with a .22 shotshell.

From the time when the first one was six years old, I could never get into my hunting clothes without hearing, "Dad, take me along!" Sometimes an argument was added: "I will shoot straight. I will put it on him!" To these winning pleas I have always tried to give an affirmative answer, even when I had to alternate carrying a played-out boy and a played-out puppy. But I knew that I was on the right track when I was trying to impress on the younger generation the importance of shooting straight. I directly

applied to my own children that old copy-book maxim, "Teach the young idea how to shoot." I think the rod and gun better for boys than the saxophone and the fudge sundae. In the first place, there is something inherently manly and home-bred and truly American in that expression, "shooting straight." The hunter learns that reward comes from hard work; he learns from dealing with nature that a man must have a deep respect for the great natural laws. He learns also, I think, in a far higher degree than any form of standardized amateur athletics can give him, to play the game fairly.

Most of our harmless and genuine joys in this life are those which find their source in primitive instincts. A man who follows his natural inclinations, with due deference to common sense and moderation, is usually on the right track. Now, the sport of hunting is one of the most honorable of the primeval instincts of man. What human thrill is there in lounging into a grimy butcher shop and sorrowfully surrendering a hard-earned simoleon for a dubious slab of inert beef? Certainly any true man would far rather trudge 15 miles in inclement weather just for a chance at a grouse. Even if he gets nothing, he will be a younger and better man when he gets home, and with memories that will lighten the burden of the days when he cannot go afield.

A lot of good people, seeing me rearing my sons to be woodsmen, have offered me advice. "How can you love nature and yet shoot a deer?" "How can you bear to teach those children to kill things?"

These parlor naturalists and lollipop sentimentalists, whose knowledge of nature is such that they would probably take a flying buttress for a lovely game bird, are incapable of understanding that it is far less cruel to kill a wild deer than it is to poleax a defenseless ox in a stall. The ox has no chance, but the deer has about four chances out of five against even the good hunter. Besides, I have a philosophy that teaches me that certain game birds and animals are apparently made to be hunted, because of their peculiar food value and because their character lends zest to the pursuit of them. It has never seemed to me to be too far-fetched to suppose that Providence placed game here for a special purpose.

Hunting is not incompatible with the deepest and most genuine love of nature. Audubon was something of a hunter; so was the famous Bachman; so were both John Muir and John Burroughs. It has always seemed to me that any man is a better man for being a hunter. This sport confers a certain constant alertness and develops a certain ruggedness of character that, in these days of too much civilization, is refreshing; moreover, it allies us to the pioneer past. In a deep sense, this great land of ours was won for us by hunters.

Again, there is a comradeship among hunters that has always seemed to me one of the finest human relationships. When fellow sportsmen meet in the woods or fields or the lonely marshes, they meet as friends who understand each other. There is a fine democracy about all this that is a mighty wholesome thing for young people to know. As much as I do anything else in life, I treasure my comradeships

with old, grizzled woodsmen. Hunting alone could have made us friends. And I want my boys to go through life making these humble contacts and learning from fellow human beings, many of them very unpretentious and simple-hearted, some of the ancient lore of nature that is one of the very finest heritages of our race. Nature always solves her own problems, and we can go far toward solving our own if we will listen to her teachings and consort with those who love her.

In the case of my own boys, from the .22 rifle they graduated to the .410 shotgun; then to a 20-gauge; then a 16; then a 12. I was guide for my oldest son, Arch, when he shot his first stag. We stalked him at sundown on Bull's Island, in the great sea marsh of that magnificent preserve, creeping through the bulrushes and the myrtle bushes until we got in a position for a shot. And that night at the clubhouse, when I went to bed late, I found my young hunter still wide awake, no doubt going over our whole campaign of that memorable afternoon.

I was near my second son, Middleton, when he shot his first five stags. I saw all of them fall—and these deeds were done before he was eighteen.

I followed the blood-trail of the first buck my youngest son, Irvine, shot. He had let drive one barrel of his 16-gauge at this great stag in a dense pine thicket. The buck made a right-about-face and headed for

Illustration by Randy Mack Bishop

the river, a mile away. He was running with a doe, and she went on across the water. The buck must have known that he could not make it, for he turned up the plantation avenue, actually jumped the gate, splashing it with blood, and fell dead under a giant live oak only 80 yards from the house!

It's one thing to kill a deer, and it's another to kill one and then have him accommodate you by running out of the wilds right up to your front steps. That kind of performance saves a lot of toting. This stag was an old swamp buck with massive antlers. Last Christmas my eldest son had only three days' vacation, but he got two bucks.

Yes, I have brought up my three boys to be hunters, and I know full well that when the wild creatures need no longer have any apprehensions about me, my grandchildren will be hard on their trail, pursuing with keen enjoyment and wholesome passion the sport of kings. While other boys are whirling in the latest jazz or telling dubious stories on street corners,

Illustration by Randy Mack Bishop

I'd like to think that mine are deep in the lonely woods, far in the silent hills, listening to another kind of music, learning a different kind of lore.

This privilege of hunting is about as fine a heritage as we have, and it needs to be passed on unsullied from father to son. There is still hope for the race when some members of it are not wholly dependent upon effete and urbane artificialities for their recreation. A true hunter will never feel at home in a nightclub. The whole thing would seem to him rather pathetic and comical—somehow not in the same world with solitary fragrant woods, rushing rivers, and the elegant highborn creatures of nature with which he is familiar. Hunting gives a man a sense of balance, a sanity, a comprehension of the true values of life that make vicious and crazily stimulated joy a repellent thing.

I well remember the morning when I took all three of my boys on a hunt for the first time. I had told them the night before that we were going for grouse and had to make an early start for Path Valley. There must have been a romantic appeal in the phrase "early start," for I could hardly get them to sleep that night. And such a time we had getting all the guns and shells and hunting clothes ready, and a lunch packed, and the alarm clock set! And now, nine years after that memorable day, we still delight in making early starts together.

That day, before we had been in the dewy fringes of the mountain a half hour, as we were walking abreast about 50 yards apart, we had the good fortune to flush a covey of five ruffed grouse. It was the first time that any of my boys had had a shot at this grand bird, which to my way of thinking outpoints every other game bird in the whole world, bar none. An old cock with a heavy ruff fell to Middleton's gun. A young cock tried to get back over Irvine's head. It was a gallant gesture, but the little huntsman's aim was true, and down came the prince of the woodland.

Arch and I were a little out of range for a shot on the rise, but ere long we flushed other birds and I had the satisfaction of seeing him roll his first *Bonasa umbellus*. We were walking through some second growth which was fairly thick. I had just been telling him that in such cover a grouse is mighty likely to go up pretty fast and steep to clear the treetops, where, for the tiniest fraction of a split second, it will seem to pause as it checks its rise and the direction of its flight, which is to take it like a scared projectile above the forest. I had been telling Arch that the best chance under such circumstances was usually offered just as the grouse got above the sprouts and seemed to hesitate.

I had just taken up my position in line when

out of a tangle of fallen grapevines that had been draping a clump of sumac bushes a regal grouse roared up in front of Arch. I could see the splendid bird streaking it for the sky and safety. At first I was afraid that Arch would shoot too soon, then that he would shoot too late; either one would be like not shooting at all. But, just as the cock topped the trees and tilted himself downward, the gun spoke, and the tilt continued, only steeper and without control. With a heavy thud the noble bird dropped within my sight on the tinted leaves of the autumnal forest floor.

Fellow sportsmen will appreciate what I mean when I say that was a great day for me. When a father can see his boy follow and fairly kill our most wary and splendid game bird, I think the Old Man has a right to feel that his son's education is one to be proud of. I'd far rather have a son of mine able to climb a mountain and outwit the wary creatures of the wilderness than to be able to dance the Brazilian busybody.

When Arch was thirteen, I had him up at daybreak with me one morning in the wilds of the Tuscarora mountains. From the crest of the wooded ridge on which we were standing, we could see over an immense gorge on either side and beyond them, far away over the rolling ridges, northward and southward. It was dawn of the first day, and there were many hunters in the mountains. The best chance at a turkey in that country at such a time is to take just such a stand and wait for one to fly over or perhaps to come walking warily up the slope of one of the leaf-strewn gullies. We had been standing together for about fifteen minutes and had heard some shooting to the north of us, three ridges away, when I saw a great black shape coming toward us over the treetops.

"Here he comes, son!" I told my youthful huntsman. "Hold for his head when he gets almost over you."

Three minutes later my boy was down on the slope of the gorge, retrieving a 19-pound gobbler, as proud as a lad could be, and entitled to be proud. It was all he could do to toil up the hill with his prize.

Irvine shot his first turkey on our plantation in Carolina. He was on a deer stand when this old tom came running to him through the huckleberries. The great bird stood almost as tall as he did.

Middleton killed his first under peculiar circumstances. We walked into a flock together, at daybreak, and they scattered in all directions, but were too drowsy to fly far. He wounded a splendid bird, and it alighted in a tall yellow pine about 100 yards from us. There was not enough cover to enable him to creep up to it, and the morning was so very still that I was afraid his first step would scare the gobbler from his lofty perch.

"I know what to do," he whispered to me as I stood at a loss to know what to advise. "Don't you hear that old woodpecker hammering on that dead pine? Every time he begins to rap I'm going to take an easy, soft step forward. Perhaps I can get close enough."

"Go ahead," I told him and stood watching this interesting stalk.

The woodpecker proved very accommodating and every other minute hammered loudly on the sounding tree. Step by cautious step Middleton got nearer. At last he raised his gun, and at its report the gobbler reeled earthward. I thought the little piece of woodcraft very neatly executed.

If the sentimentalist were right, hunting would develop in men a cruelty of character. But I have found that it inculcates patience, demands discipline and iron nerve, and develops a serenity of spirit that makes for a long life and long love of life. And it is my fixed conviction that if a parent can give his children a passionate and wholesome devotion to the outdoors, the fact that he cannot leave each of them a fortune does not really matter so much. They will always enjoy life in its nobler aspects without money and without price. They will worship the Creator in his mighty works. And because they know and love the natural world, they will always feel at home in the wide, sweet habitations of the Ancient Mother.

This article is reprinted from *Hunting & Home in the Southern Heartland: The Best of Archibald Rutledge* by Archibald Rutledge, edited by Jim Casada; published by the University of South Carolina Press, Columbia, South Carolina, 1992.

PART 2

THE SPIRIT OF THE HUNT

The Big Deer Bet

By Larry Dablemont

Coach Wilkens came to Texas County when I was only 13; he made an impression on me that will last forever.

The Coach was a pretty fair pool shooter and an educated man who could sit down and tell hunting stories with the best of the front bench regulars.

The front bench regulars were a dozen or so old-timers who had spent their lives hunting and fishing the Ozarks of southern Missouri. In their later years, they spent time on the front bench of my father's pool hall, remembering. It was a small country pool hall, the kind of place where a 13-year-old kid could fit right in. In fact, I ran the place much of the time.

When I wasn't too busy, I liked to sit near the big front bench on my three-legged stool listening to Ol' Bill and Ol' Jim and Jess Wolf and Virgil Halstead and anyone else who wanted to tell tall stories about hunting and fishing in Big Piney River country.

Coach Wilkens fit in with the front bench regulars like a bow-tie salesman at a cockfight. But he was the only teacher I ever knew who came into the pool hall, and that alone made him my hero. My other teachers were constantly urging me to spend more time doing homework and less time in the pool hall. In fact, some went so far as to say that a 13-year-old boy shouldn't even be allowed in such a place.

But Coach Wilkens didn't feel that way. He said there were lots of ways to be smart, and in their own way Ol' Bill and old-timers like him had a lot to teach the world if only someone would listen.

It was something how he earned a spot on that front bench, an outsider with an education, somehow accepted and appreciated for what he was. In time it was obvious that the old men liked Coach Wilkens, and he liked them.

In fact, he even went trotline fishing with Ol' Bill one night during the summer, and Virgil Halstead let him go bowhunting on his back forty, even though all the front bench regulars hooted at the idea of a grown man out there chasin' deer with a bow and arrow.

There were some jaws that dropped a bit when Coach killed a forkhorn buck a half-dozen days into October. But deer season was deer season, not a time for playin' Indians, as Ol' Bill often said. And firearms deer season in the Ozarks took place in mid-November, when the bucks were in the rut and a man nearly froze to death before the first rays of sun hit the forest floor.

Coach Wilkens and Ol' Bill argued over that quite a bit. Coach said he figured the only thing easier than killing a deer during gun season was gigging fish in a rain barrel or maybe huntin' house cats with a shotgun.

Ol' Bill would never forget that. He propped one foot on the spittoon, shifted his chaw of tobacco, and ran a leathery hand over his stubble of beard.

"I didn't say it was hard to get a deer, young feller," he said with an air of indignation. "But

I knew Coach as a schoolteacher, but one deer season long ago, he and Ol' Bill taught me something not found in any book. Illustration by Randy Mack Bishop

some of us don't hunt a deer; we hunt them ol' veteran, thicket-sneakin, brush-huggin' rascals with antlers the size of ax handles." All the front bench regulars laughed at that. Ol' Bill had pretty much put this upstart in his place. Everyone knew that Bill had taken some nice bucks. He was a good hunter, no question about that. He always got his deer, and it was usually a dandy with antlers that anyone would be proud to set over the fireplace.

Coach wasn't offended by such talk. He was smiling too, but there was a gleam in his eye as he answered Ol' Bill's boast.

"Maybe things are different here in the Ozarks," he said. "Back in Ohio we had quite a few more big bucks."

Ol' Bill started to say something, but Coach wouldn't let him get a word in. "I remember once when I was a kid how my dad bet some windbag deer hunter that he could get a better buck in three days than the other feller could get in a week."

Coach paused a minute, and Ol' Bill jumped in, "How much did he lose?"

"He didn't lose," Coach said, "and the name 'Wilkens' still causes folks to think of big bucks back home. It grieved my poor ol' daddy somethin' terrible that I didn't carry on in his shoes, but I'd feel terrible betting with some ol' timer who had spent most of his life hunting bucks the size of billy goats."

Ol' Bill stood up to walk around the spittoon, and I knew the fur was about to fly. Unfortunately, I had to go rack up a back table and collect the money, and when I returned it was all over. Coach and Ol' Bill had $20 bet on who could bring in the best buck. Jess Wolf, Virgil Halstead, and Ol' Jim were to be the judges. It wasn't a situation that favored the coach, but he didn't seem concerned. If he lost $20 he could afford it, and the whole thing was a lot of fun for him.

Ol' Bill didn't have that kind of attitude. He meant to take Coach Wilkens' money with no mercy shown.

News of the bet spread around town like wildfire over the next few days. Most of the front bench regulars were of the opinion that Coach had lost his money.

Ol' Bill was more than just a good story teller. He was an honest-to-goodness outdoorsman with more big bucks to his credit than any hunter in the county.

Back in the days when there were hardly any deer in the Ozarks, just after they opened a limited season, Bill would bring bucks to the check station that would attract bigger crowds than a parade.

My Grandpa Dablemont told me all about that, but he told me too that Ol' Bill wasn't able to hunt the Ozark hills as he once did. Grandpa and Ol' Bill were trapping partners in years past and my granddad was one of his closest friends. Sometimes when Bill would be telling a big story about hunting or fishing, he'd point to my grandpa there on the front bench and say, "Ain't that the way it was, Fred."

Of course grandpa would smile and nod his head and come back with another story.

When we were fishing for black perch one afternoon on Brushy Creek, I asked my granddad if all those stories were gospel truth. "In a gen'ral sort a way I reckon," he answered. "Sometimes as the years roll on, fish get a mite bigger and antlers get a bit wider."

Grandpa stared awhile at the bobber sitting stone-still on the surface, and he told me something I'd always remember.

"Ol' men like me an' Bill come to the time they can't do what they once could," he said. "Then all they got left is mem'ries an' stories to make 'em feel a bit younger an' more important in the eyes of a young sprout like you. Don't begrudge 'em that boy, it's all they got left to keep 'em goin'."

Illustrations by Randy Mack Bishop

Still and all, I couldn't help but pull for Coach. Ol' Bill was just doing too much blowing and bragging about how he had that bet won. I couldn't see it at the time, but Ol' Bill wanted to sound a good deal more confident than he was.

It started showing a little, though, just before the deer season opened. Ol' Bill mentioned on occasion that one leg was giving him problems, and he wasn't going to be able to hunt his old territory. Then he went on something terrible about how there were so many greenhorns from the city these days that they were spooking the big, older bucks into heavy cover, making night dwellers out of them.

Bill would have been seriously worried if he knew about Coach's grandmother's farm. It wasn't big, but it joined my Grandpa McNew's farm and there were several deer that crossed back and forth between the farms.

Along one wooded ridge there was a natural passageway from one farm to another, with the kind of heavy vegetation that gave big bucks the security they needed.

Coach had a stand built there, and it was a good one. By bowhunting in October he had the advantage over Bill. There were two or three bucks using that ridge that were real eye-poppers. I didn't see them, but Coach showed me their tracks and told me all about them.

One afternoon in November, he showed me the fresh scrapes near his tree platform.

"This is where I'll be hunting," he told me. "You're welcome to use the one I've got built over next to your granddad's farm. The same buck that made these scrapes probably made one or two over that way, I would suppose."

As I remember it, the opening day of deer season that year dawned cold and clear and still, close to perfect if it hadn't been so cold. When you're 13 years old, it's tough to sit in a tree stand very long, and 30 F makes it next to impossible.

That's all compounded by the fact that 13-year-old boys rarely have much confidence—at least I didn't. I had never killed a deer, and I didn't figure I ever would.

Nevertheless, I may have played a part in Coach Wilkens' success because when I climbed

down from my stand just hours after I climbed into it, I heard a deer snort, then two. I never saw them, but the deer turned back toward the Coach, and it wasn't 10 minutes later that three does trotted past him.

It's a wonder how smart bucks are most of the time. The big ones are harder to find than chiggers in a redbone hound. But during the rut, bucks aren't normal, and behind those three does, 100 yards or so, was an 8-point buck that some men hunt for a lifetime.

I heard Coach shoot when I was almost to my grandmother's farmhouse—the first report followed by a second—the two shots only four or five seconds apart.

Coach was back at my grandparents' house in 30 minutes. The buck had been hit hard, then turned back toward my stand, and had crossed onto my grandparents' property. When he discovered I wasn't on my stand, Coach returned to his pickup and came to ask permission to trail the buck on neighboring land. It was permission he didn't need, of course, but Coach was ahead of his time during that era in the Ozarks.

I went along to help find the buck, the excitement building as Coach described the deer, at least an 8-pointer he figured, one of the two big bucks he had seen before.

If I had stayed on stand, I probably would have seen the wounded buck pass by me within 80 yards or so. The blood trail was easy to follow; in a few minutes, we trailed the buck into a cedar thicket where he had gone down for good.

I knew at first glance that Coach had won his bet with Ol' Bill. Not that it was any kind of record or anything, but the antlers were wide and heavy, well-proportioned with eight strong points, maybe a ninth projecting low off the left beam just over the forehead.

As Ozark bucks go, it was a good one. Most any hunter would have wanted that set of antlers to hang over his fireplace or front porch. It was the kind of buck that most of the front bench regulars would remember in years to come, a little bigger after each season added some glory to the memory.

Coach field-dressed the buck, and I watched

and helped and went on something awful about how I couldn't wait to see the look on Ol' Bill's face that night. As I remember it, Coach was elated with that buck.

But later, Coach seemed more subdued. On the way in to the check station, he asked me if I reckoned Ol' Bill had ever killed a buck that big. Of course he had, and several at that. I told Coach about pictures of big bucks in my grandpa's album.

"Ol' Bill has probably hung as many big bucks in the smokehouse as any hunter in the county," I told him.

As the pickup bounced over the gravel road toward town, I said something that caused Coach Wilkens to become quiet and somber.

"Ol' Bill is gonna lose more than just $20 because of this here buck," I told him cheerily. "This might stop all his bragging about being the best deer hunter in Texas County."

We stopped at the pool hall late in the morning. No one had seen Ol' Bill, but several of the front bench regulars were there and everyone pretty much agreed that this buck made Coach a winner.

"He'll likely not bag one at all now," Jess Wolf said of his old friend. "Ol' Bill ain't likely to bring in a buck smaller'n that'n, an he ain't apt to see a better one."

I don't rightly remember how I spent the afternoon, but I was there in the pool hall that evening. I took over while my dad went home for supper. It was a busy Saturday evening as always on opening day of deer season. Several hunters were anxious to tell about bucks they had bagged or missed. A few others talked about the one they only saw. But the conversation eventually got around to the nice 8-pointer that hung in Coach Wilkens' garage that night.

Though subdued, Ol' Bill was not ready to surrender. He said he hadn't seen the big buck that everyone claimed Coach had killed, but he figured he had passed up one bigger that very morning.

There were a few chuckles and Ol' Bill even grinned a little as he cut off a plug of tobacco.

"I'll say this fer that Coach feller," Bill went on, "he's a dang poor deer hunter if he hauled in a buck like I hear he did and he ain't down here braggin' about it."

While everyone laughed I went to answer the phone. It was Coach Wilkens, and he wanted to know if I had said anything about helping him find his buck. I told him I had tried several times, but a 13-year-old kid sometimes has trouble getting a word in edgewise. Coach told me that what he was about to do would seem a bit strange to me, but he'd explain things later.

I don't guess anything ever puzzled me more—especially when Coach walked in and acted like he had bent the barrel on his best deer rifle. You've never seen such a long face on a man that was so happy only eight or nine hours before. Amid all the congratulations and back slapping, Coach just reached in his pocket, pulled out a $20 bill and handed it to Ol' Bill. It grew quiet in the pool hall and Ol' Bill nearly swallowed his tobacco. He had come to the pool hall ready to eat crow and try to hang onto his dignity for awhile, hoping for a miracle later in the week. But everyone in that pool hall thought Ol' Bill had given up any hope of winning the bet.

Coach sat down on the front bench, and the snooker game on the front table stopped for awhile as he explained why he had decided to concede. I couldn't believe what I was hearing.

"It was Friday evening just after school," he said. "I was on my way over to Edgar Springs to see about a rifle a fellow had for sale, when two does jumped out in the highway and crossed in front of me. I slowed down a bit and some salesman from St. Louis came roarin' around me about 60. About that time, a big buck came across the ditch behind those two does and that salesman slammed on his brakes hard.

"Well the darn fool was a little late, and he hit that buck just hard enough to roll him a time or two. For a moment or so I thought the buck wasn't hurt bad, but then I saw he was having a hard time climbing the embankment going up into the woods, one leg broke for sure."

Everyone was really caught up in the story, and Coach acted like he'd rather kiss the local librarian than confess to what he did.

"Well to make a long story short, I helped the St. Louis feller look over his car, and he went on with little more than a bent fender. I bought that rifle, and on the way back I stopped to see if that buck had made it very far."

Coach paused for a moment, shook his head and stared at the floor. "He hadn't," he said sadly. "So I put him out of his misery and called the game warden, and he said the situation being what it was he didn't see why I couldn't dress him out, hang him up and go back this morning and put my tag on him, so that's what I did. But it isn't right to claim some crippled buck as a trophy, and I'm here to pay up."

I stood there listening with my mouth open, knowing better than to protest, but wishing more than anything that I could say something.

The front bench regulars admitted that some of the local hunters might have never owned up to such a thing, but it was admirable of a man to not let good venison go to waste. Coach had done an unselfish thing, sacrificing his deer tag and telling the truth even if it cost him $20.

Ol' Bill wouldn't take the money, though. He said that before he could win it fair and square, he'd have to bring in a buck of his own. He said Coach should keep his fingers crossed, but with the rest of the week left, his chances weren't good.

In school on Monday, Coach explained everything. "It was a dumb thing I did, Larry," he told me. "I caused Ol' Bill to put more than $20 on the line. He was betting his self-worth, his stature in the eyes of his friends. If I had won that bet, that old man would have lost the thing that meant the most to him—his reputation as a deer hunter."

I told him I understood, and I would help him keep his secret.

"Everyone deserves to have something he can brag about when he grows old," Coach told me. "I'm not ever going to forget that again."

Coach couldn't have stood taller in my eyes than he did right then. And I suppose if it had ended that way, I would have had quite a story to tell someday. But it didn't end there because on Wednesday morning Ol' Bill drove his battered old red International pickup into town with a buck in the back of it. For two or three hours, folks gathered along Main Street to look at what Jess Wolf said was "the damnedest set of horns I ever seen."

It was an atypical set of antlers that had two long tines growing straight down and others sticking up and out like thorns on a honey locust tree. Some said it had 14 points; some said it had better than 20. I was in school so I never saw it, except for the pictures

Ol' Bill and his three judges made a big thing of taking Coach's $20 the following Saturday night with all the front bench regulars there looking on.

Coach looked awful humble, but I knew he was enjoying himself. He had more friends in that pool hall that night than any Northerner had a right to expect.

But at the right time, Ol' Bill sat down and propped his feet on a spittoon and told Coach he wasn't much of a liar.

"Half a dozen fellers I know that saw your buck said he didn't have no broke leg," Bill grinned. "An' damn, boy, we all know the game warden roun' here."

Before long, Coach sheepishly admitted he had made the whole thing up and there was a good deal of knee-slapping and ribbing going on.

Bill said he was gonna forgive him for all that. "It's a good thing I didn't believe that story though, or it woulda ruint my whole dad-blame deer season."

Coach looked at Ol' Bill with question marks all over his face. "How could I ..."

Bill didn't let him finish. "If I'd a believed that yarn of yours," he said as he shifted his tobacco, "I'd a shot me a 6-pointer on Monday mornin!"

I don't know. It could be that Ol' Bill had his most memorable deer season because he was so intent on winning that $20 bet fair and square. But I doubt he passed up a 6-pointer—a spike maybe, but not a 6-pointer. The front bench regulars were still talking about both bucks in late winter. Coach came in once or twice a week to argue with Ol' Bill about what made the best coonhound or what shot size was best for duck hunting.

Just before spring, they really got carried away over who was the best river fisherman and before it was over, Coach and Bill had bet $20 on who could catch the biggest brownie before July. Ol' Jim, Jess Wolf and Virgil Halstead were to be the judges. I don't think Coach would have had it any other way.

First Trophy

By Jim Spencer

The woods around me were in the middle of the morning shift change. The night prowlers were beginning to drift toward their nests, and the daytime creatures were taking over. A big boar coon, making his way home to some hollow tree in eastern Arkansas' White River bottoms, ambled along the bottom of the steep-sided draw below me. He had been feeding all night in the harvested rice fields farther up the ravine where it flattened out onto the prairie. He passed so close I could see one ear was tattered, a souvenir of some long-forgotten battle.

He wasn't in any hurry, and I watched with interest as he waddled down the draw and out of sight. I was idly imagining what the other fellow must have looked like when I heard something to my left, back up the draw in the direction of the rice fields. I cranked my head around slowly, scrutinizing the area, trying to will something to move. Nothing did.

I stayed alert, though. Much better hunters than I have learned the hard way that a seasoned, gun-shy old buck can seem to disappear from the face of the earth by doing nothing more elaborate than freezing in place. I had made that mistake before. I wasn't about to make it again.

The seconds stretched into minutes. My neck began to ache gently, insistently, but I was sure I had heard something, and I was slow to give up. Five minutes went by, then 10, before I convinced myself that the noise had been a squirrel. I slowly turned back to continue watching the downslope side of the ravine, and there stood the old man.

To this day I don't know where he came from. The woods were dry as a cactus garden, and the leaves were six rustly inches deep, but he came so quietly I never heard a thing. When I first saw him, he was no more than 30 feet from me, but apparently he hadn't seen me inside the heavily leafed treetop I was using for a blind.

I could see the creases and seams in his weather-beaten face. He had on a hat of no particular description, and he peered intently from under its battered brim. He wore no glasses, and I got the distinct impression from the unsquinting way he scanned the woods that he didn't need any.

I kept waiting for him to spot me in my treetop, but his attention was focused on the ravine below, and he never glanced my way. After a while he shoved away from the post oak he'd been leaning against and made his way down the bank to the bottom of the ravine. He crossed

As the big buck stepped within gun range, the sudden memory of the old man across the ravine slammed into me like a blind-side tackler. Did the buck come into the first-come, first-served category, or did the first chance belong to the old man? Illustration by Dick Lubey

the narrow flat at the bottom of the draw and eased up the other slope.

Going uphill or downhill in dry leaves is, for me, an awkward business at best. Not so for this old man. He was ramrod straight on both slopes, negotiating each with no visible difficulty, and if he made a sound, I missed it. He carried his gun, a wear-silvered Model 94, at halfport, so that it could be pressed into service in an instant.

He moved silently along the hogback ridge across the way until he was about 80 yards below my stand. A thicket of young cane grew there, and he sort of backed into it and sat down. He

cut two or three stalks of cane with his pocketknife and stuck them up in the soft soil in front of him to break up his outline. This was before the days of mandatory safety colors, and in his faded brown-and-green plaid shirt, he was very nearly invisible.

The November sun sent its first blade of light stabbing into the new day. That's when I saw how wisely the old man had chosen his stand. While the sun was bright in my face, making me squint and strain to see into the gloom of the deep ravine, my opponent across the way had the sun at his back, and a deer in the wash below him would have the same disadvantage I had.

I debated whether to change locations and decided against it. The sun would soon be high enough to cease being a nuisance, I reasoned, and the old man's presence wasn't worrying me. I had him cut off in the direction the deer were most likely to come from. In my youthful arrogance (I was 18), I figured nothing shootable would make it by me. So I waited.

Deer hunting is by turns one of the dullest and one of the most exciting sports, and usually the transition from drowsiness to heart-thudding anticipation comes so swiftly it catches the hunter off guard. That's the way it was this time.

I was fighting hard to keep my eyes open, watching a chickadee standing on its head in the fork of a sapling in front of me, when a blur of motion up the ravine to my left jarred me back to the business at hand. The movement became a slipping deer, keeping to the brush in the bottom of the ravine.

Just like a smart old buck will do, I thought smugly, glancing down to be sure the breech of my automatic rifle was closed. The deer came on, but I couldn't get a look at its head because of the brush. I raised my gun to look through the scope, and when I did, the barrel banged into one of the branches of my natural blind. The dry leaves buzzed like a sackful of rattlesnakes, and that was the end of that chance. The still-headless whitetail melted into the brush and went wherever it is that deer always go in situations like that.

I was furious, and if anyone ever calls me the names I called myself right then, he's going to have to fight. Fifteen minutes later I was still mad, but there was a lot of time left for hunting. Plenty of time, as it turned out.

A half-hour after the dry-leaves fiasco, another blur of movement in the ravine caught my eye. There was no question of identity this time. Two smallish does picked their way gingerly past me and on to the south past the old man's stand. I could make him out in the cane blind, but I couldn't tell if he saw the deer or not. He was so still he appeared to be asleep.

More time passed uneventfully, and I was getting drowsy again when a pack of hounds struck a cold trail a mile to the south of us, away off in the bottoms toward the river. The dogs trailed falteringly for a while, bawling mournfully every so often to let the world know they were earning their keep.

Suddenly the tempo of the chase changed. One of the dogs had evidently pushed the deer out of its bed and was running it by sight; his voice held too much excitement and the pace was too fast for him to be trailing. By the time the rest of the pack joined the jump dog, the pace had slowed a little, but it was still one hot chase.

From the direction and distance of the sounds, I was pretty sure where the action was taking place—in a long, narrow strip of nearly impenetrable cover we called the bear thicket. I was pleased at this turn of events, because one arm of the thicket ran almost into the mouth of my ravine. It was one of the most-used escape routes for thicket deer harassed by dogs. The only thing worrying me was the old man; he had me effectively cut off in that direction.

The chase wandered up and down the bear thicket for some time before the deer tired of it and beelined for the river. The hounds' yodeling grew fainter and fainter and then faded out altogether, but through it all I kept watching the downstream side of the ravine.

The buck appeared as suddenly and quietly as the old man had appeared three hours earlier. One second he wasn't there and the next second he was, as if he had been there all along, standing in the classic pose at the edge of a small cane patch and looking over his shoulder in the direction of the bear thicket. His ears were the only thing in motion, monitoring all directions at once for sounds of possible danger.

It was the ear movement that caught my eye, but it was his rack that held my attention. Even at 200 yards I could tell that I was looking at the best head I'd ever seen. The main beams looked as thick as an ax handle, and the points rising from them were 10 inches long and stiletto-straight.

Satisfied that he wasn't being followed, the big fellow lowered his head and started slipping

The old man smiled, his faded blue eyes twinkling, as the young hunter knelt, excited, jabbering nonstop.
Illustration by Dick Lubey

toward me. From the front his headgear was just as beautiful, just as impressive. The tips of his main beams were more than 1 foot apart. There looked to be at least 12 points on his rack, and even the brow tines were long.

I could have killed him without any trouble. I was above his level and 150 yards away. He had his head low, and he was walking straight at me—perfect conditions for a neck shot. I had the rifle to my shoulder and was smoothing out the wrinkles in the sight picture when the sudden memory of the old man slammed into me like a blindside tackler. The crosshairs wavered.

Indecision kept my finger off the trigger. Did the buck fall into the first-come, first-served category, or did the first chance belong to the old man across the ravine? I glanced in his direction. He hadn't moved a muscle. The buck came

steadily on, now only 100 yards from me and almost directly in front of the old man.

I never considered myself a noble person, but there must have been a little bit of residual Boy Scout still in me waiting to be used up. I lowered my rifle and waited for the old man to down the monster deer, hating myself for doing it and hating the old man for being there.

The buck passed in front of the old man, and he moved for the first time since he had sat down, bringing his saddle rifle up in a slow, smooth swing. I held my breath, watching with mixed emotions. The hunter in me wished for a quick, merciful kill, but my selfish side hoped for a miss so that I might have a chance.

Neither possibility took place. The old man cheeked his rifle and tracked the buck in his sights as it made its way toward me, but the shot never came. Finally he lowered his rifle and settled back into the cane blind, still watching the buck .

Puzzled, but too excited to worry about it just then, I shifted ever so slightly as the buck came abreast of me. I didn't think I made any noise, but when I moved, the heavy-headed old fellow froze in his tracks and swung his head to look directly into my treetop.

The rifle was already at my shoulder. I settled the wildly gyrating crosshairs on his neck and squeezed the trigger, and the buck wilted where he stood.

The heavy boom of the .30/06 was still rolling down the ravine when I let out a whoop and charged out of my blind and down the slope, like a Comanche brave bent on collecting scalps.

That deer made a picture I won't ever forget, Iying there in a little patch of dusty sunlight in the bottom of that ravine. His rack was perfect. There were not 12 points, but 14, all just as long and straight as they had appeared. The main beams were even heavier than I had thought. I never did weigh him, but he looked as big as a Poland-China brood sow .

I was standing there admiring him when a quiet voice behind me said, "He's mighty pretty, ain't he?"

I nearly jumped out of my skin. In the excitement of the past minute I had completely forgotten the old man, and he had ghosted to within 10 feet of me before speaking.

"Didn't mean to startle you," he said. He watched with mild amusement as I struggled to regain my composure.

"You didn't . . . I mean . . . I sort of forgot you were around," I stammered, my eyes gravitating once more to my first trophy.

The old man walked a slow circle around the buck, looking at him from every angle. "I expect so," he said.

He knelt and ran his hands over the rack as if he were blind, letting his fingers linger on the huge, rough-textured butt swells. For a long time he crouched there looking at my buck. Finally, he stood up.

"Need some help with him?"

"Yes, sir," I answered, "if you don't mind. He looks pretty heavy to me."

The old man smiled, his faded blue eyes twinkling. "I expect so," he said again.

We set to work at the field-dressing chore. Adrenalin-fortified, hyperventilated, too excited to sleep for at least a week, I jabbered nonstop while we worked. The old man smiled and nodded and answered whenever I asked him a question, but mostly he kept quiet and let me have the floor.

His name was Earl Bennett, he said, and he was a retired forester from south Arkansas, down around Lake Village.

We finished gutting the buck, and Mr. Bennett helped me drag him out of the ravine. This was no easy task and we were winded when we reached the top of the bank.

While we were catching our breath, the old man squeezed my shoulder. "You've got a fine buck here, son," he said.

I couldn't stand it any longer. The question was eating holes in me: "Why didn't you shoot when he came by you?"

The old man was quiet for a long time, so long that I nearly asked him again. But then he started to speak.

"I'd tell you the answer if I knew how to say it," he said. "But even if I did, you're too young to understand."

"How do you know that?"

Earl Bennett smiled at me again, and his voice was as gentle as the expression on his face. "If you could understand the answer, son, you wouldn't need to ask the question."

I never saw Mr. Bennett again to tell him this, but he was right.

In the first place, I'm pretty sure the old man knew I was in that treetop all along. Maybe he wanted something more to remember than another set of horns. If that's what he was after, I gave it to him—I was hopping around like a toad on a hot plate that day. Thinking back on it, remembering his quiet little smile, I believe that's what he wanted.

I know one thing for sure: I owe somebody a trophy. And one of these days, when the opportunity arises, I intend to pay my debt.

I'd like to keep this thing going.

PART 3

TIPS ON PREPARATION AND SAFETY

Getting Permission

By Jim Zumbo

There aren't a whole lot of hunters who enjoy asking for permission to hunt on private land. Most of us are basically shy and are reluctant to walk up to a door and talk to a stranger.

Whenever I'm with pals, we normally take turns or flip a coin to see who will knock on the farmhouse door. My favorite method of determining who gets out of the truck is to start off in alphabetical order. Naturally. I'm always last because my name begins with a "Z." When I'm lucky, the pesky chore of eyeballing a farmer or rancher face-to-face never gets to me.

I absolutely dislike asking for permission—just as I was hesitant to ask a pretty girl to dance when I was a lad. Maybe I'm afraid of rejection. Whatever the reason, I'd rather go to the dentist's office than knock on a stranger's door.

In farm country, deer may find a favorite food—and you a chance to hunt on private land. Photo by Outdoor Images/Tom Huggler

No matter what type of hunting you do—small or big game—be sure to get permission to hunt private lands. Photograph by Outdoor Images/Tom Huggler

I hunted once with a guy who was a salesman. He started selling by going door-to-door. That guy had a lot of nerve, and when we were looking for hunting places, he'd bounce right up to a house and make a pitch. He seemed to enjoy it. I liked it immensely, because all I did was sit in the truck and let my buddy do all the work.

Perhaps one of the reasons we don't like asking is because of the unfortunate stereotype that hunters must live with. Because of the bad press, which is almost always spotlighted by the media, we're often considered irresponsible. All of us—even preachers once they don hunting garb—must share the burden.

Common arguments suggest that hunters shoot livestock, windows, houses, and just about everything else that's loose or nailed down. Rumors have it that they leave gates open, litter areas with beer cans, and generally act like bums.

Sorry, but I don't believe that these allegations are well-founded. Granted, there are some bad actors out there, but it's my opinion that the majority of hunters indeed respect the property on which they hunt.

Land is being posted for several basic reasons. Rural properties are commonly purchased by city folks, many of whom don't hunt, don't want strangers with firearms on their land, or reserve their land for friends and relatives. Given the increasing crime problems in rural areas, even landowners who have been around for generations are becoming distrustful of strangers. Some property owners close their lands and either charge fees or lease to outfitters, sportsmen's clubs, or groups of hunters. And finally, some hunters are truly inconsiderate or just plain vandals, prompting landowners to put up posted signs.

This discouraging situation is now common across America, and it is quickly gaining popularity in the West. Since the 1970s, many people owning private land in prime big-game states have made a transition to fee hunting or are simply posting their property against all hunting.

More landowners are posting their land, but with the right approach, you could find yourself crossing the line to great hunting. Photograph by Charles S. Alsheimer

The landowners can't be blamed for charging fees. As business people, they're entitled, like anyone else, to monetary benefits from wildlife that consume feed on their property. Many of the things that were free years ago must now be purchased. Who ever thought we'd have to pay for air to inflate a low tire at a gas station? Or pay to bring garbage to the town dump? Everything in our society has a price tag on it nowadays, including hunting rights.

Happily, there are still plenty of landowners who allow free hunting these days, and there are ways to get permission to hunt these properties. All it takes is perseverance and a positive attitude.

First, remember that the landowner is a human being, not an escaped convict who will shoot you on sight. Of course, if he or she has a couple of pit bulls sitting on the front porch, or signs up saying something like "Hunters will be shot; survivors will be prosecuted," give that place a wide berth. Otherwise, muster up your courage and give it a try.

I'm amused by a humorous story told by Ralph Stuart, senior editor of *Outdoor Life*. Stuart was driving along a country road looking for a place to hunt turkeys, when he was particularly attracted to one piece of ground. A lone farmhouse sat at the end of a long driveway, and it took Stuart some time before he screwed up enough nerve to drive down the lane.

He parked his rig near the house and had barely started for the front door, when an ominous-sounding voice from the garage said, "If you're looking for trouble, you've found it." Dumb-founded, Stuart hesitantly headed to the garage and saw an old man peering at him.

"I was just looking for a place to hunt turkeys," Stuart said nervously, "and was wondering if you own these fields back here."

The old man's face changed from a scowl to a smile, and he said, "Hunt turkeys? Is that all you want?" With that, the man started up a friendly conversation, and the two spoke for quite some time.

As it turned out, they had some mutual friends, and Stuart was granted permission. A new turkey spot was added to his list simply because Stuart had stopped to talk. Most other hunters would have driven by, intimidated by the chore of asking a favor from a stranger.

Here are some ways to break the ice if you have a hard time getting those first words out.

Remember that it's tougher to ask if you walk in stone-cold, having no idea what the name is of the person you're speaking with. Stop at a country store or gas station and inquire about area landowners. Locals will quickly weed out unlikely property owners, and they might point you in the right direction.

Get a haircut and talk to the barber, or visit

DO'S AND DON'TS

- When you walk up to knock on a door, don't be dressed in hunting clothing. Some landowners may be intimidated by a camo-clad visitor and would be more receptive to an individual in street clothes.
- Don't approach a landowner for permission the day before or during the season, as this will put undue pressure on him/her to make a quick decision (a decision that will likely be negative as a result) .
- If you are given permission and the landowner asks how many people are in your party, be precise. Don't say there will be three and show up with five.
- Contact the landowner every time you hunt his/her property. If you're told that you can hunt the following Saturday and Sunday, don't show up two weekends later and hunt without asking again.
- Never assume that permission granted one year automatically means permission granted the next.
- Be certain of any special instructions that you are asked to follow. If a farmer tells you to stay out of a particular field, make sure that you know which one he is talking about. If you're asked not to cross the third fence behind the barn, pay attention to which fences you do cross.

- Make sure that you understand what game you are allowed to hunt. For example, you may be permitted to hunt rabbits, squirrels, and ducks, but not pheasants or geese. If you're hunting deer and your license allows for an either-sex animal, check with the landowner first. He/she may not want you to take does.
- Remember that hunting someone else's land demands propriety. Respect the property as if it were your own.
- Follow up after your hunt. A thank-you note is in order, and a Christmas card wouldn't hurt. A small token of your appreciation, such as a bushel of apples or a ham, is sometimes nice (though be sure not to insult a non-drinking landowner with the gift of a bottle). If you want to offer the landowner some of your game, clean it in the field and deliver it ready for the oven. Since most farmers have access to all the meat they want, it might be an unwelcome chore to have to clean game that well-meaning hunters toss on the porch. (Also, there are often regulations regarding the donation or transfer of game animals, so check state laws before giving wild meat to anyone.)

with the local game warden or forest ranger.

Stop at farms that have roadside stands and buy some fresh fruits and vegetables. Ask about hunting opportunities on the farmer's land or the neighbors'.

If you see livestock along the road and the animals appear to be escapees, stop at the nearest ranch or farmhouse and report them. Volunteer to help round up the animals—your good deed might be rewarded with permission to hunt.

If you're scouting on a weekend, attend a local church. Some have a social coffee after services—a great way to meet people in rural areas.

If there's a county fair or 4-H function going on, participate and chat with farmers. Buy some homemade jam, jelly, or maple syrup while you're at it.

If you're a member of a national fraternal organization, such as Elks, Moose, Eagles, or others, visit the local chapter and get acquainted. The same is true with civic groups, such as Lions,

Kiwanis, and Rotary chapters. Fellow members will often give you info on where you might hunt.

Contact the regional office of the state wildlife agency. These offices often compile lists of landowners who allow hunting.

A work-trade agreement is a unique way to get a green light from a farmer. I know an enterprising guy who struck a great deal. My friend, who is a house painter by profession, agreed to paint a farmer's house in return for hunting permission for himself and two of his pals. The three men pitched in and painted the house on a few summer weekends. Now, they have permanent permission to hunt a fine piece of land.

If a landowner does give you permission, it's also a nice idea to return during the off-season and offer your services for a day or two. Farmers often need help mending fences, and I've never heard any turn down assistance when it's time to bring in a crop.

Conditioning Yourself To Hunt

By Jim Zumbo

We called the mountain Big Top. It was a steep-sided chunk of real estate, timbered from bottom to top. To get to its highest elevation, we had to leave camp about 5:00 A.M., and by taking our time and not straining ourselves, we could be at the top just as daylight began breaking. The two-hour climb was brutal, but the hunting opportunities on top of the mountain were worth it.

About half of the hunters in our camp never made it to the top. They were in poor physical condition, not because of age or disability, but because they simply hadn't cared enough to get in shape before the hunt. They didn't expend much effort to get to areas used by game, and when they scored, it was pure luck.

If you're assuming that this mountain is in the West, high up in the Rockies, you're wrong. Big Top is in New York's Catskill Mountains, just a two-hour drive from New York City.

There's a common belief that whitetail hunting doesn't require much physical outlay. To be sure,

plenty of record-book bucks have been taken in the Back 40 or just a short walk from a barn or cornfield.

Though there are ways to hunt whitetails if you're in poor shape, many successful hunters beat the odds because they're literally willing to go the extra mile. This pertains to hunting not only whitetails but other species as well. Because of topography and large tracts of roadless country, hunting in the West usually requires much more physical conditioning than does hunting in other areas.

If you hunt from a tree stand close to a road, watch trails from a ground blind, act as a stander on a drive, or take short walks from the road, you won't be placing many physical demands on your body. This is especially true in well-roaded areas or farmland.

Unfortunately, the energy requirements of the hunt don't stop at reaching your stand. If your quarry is big game, and you score, you're faced with the chore of transporting your prize from where it fell to a road. If you're alone and the carcass is large, a Herculean effort might be required to get the animal out. You can always leave the carcass and go get help, but in crowded woods on public land, many hunters are unwilling to leave their animal behind.

Getting an animal out of the woods ranks as one of the toughest physical challenges you'll ever face. Think about it. Say that you kill a whitetail in Pennsylvania that dresses out at 130 pounds. That might not seem like much, but if you're alone, or even with a pal, and the nearest road is uphill, that carcass will seem to weigh a half-ton by the time you reach your destination.

Bird hunting in broken terrain can be as physically challenging as many big game pursuits. Photograph by Jim Zumbo

Certain factors may cause you to hurry the transporting process. Hot weather, flies, the presence of bears, or the need to return home are just some of the things that could encourage you to put yourself at serious physical risk by picking up the pace. You tend to forget the health hazards in your enthusiasm for getting an animal out. My advice is to very carefully consider every possible way of making it easier on yourself.

If you intend to penetrate mountainous country, whether you're after whitetails, elk, small game, or birds, you should be up to the task of negotiating rugged terrain without bringing on serious health problems.

Don't be fooled into thinking that only big game requires that you be in good shape. I recall a tough hunt for quail in broken Arizona desert terrain where we had to hike over some nasty rimrock country in 95F heat, trying to keep up with a fast-paced pointing dog. A number of duck hunts in boot-sucking mud come to mind as well, as do numerous snowshoe hare outings in elk country.

Sound logic dictates that we use good sense when we design our hunts, but hunting is an unpredictable sport. There's always the possibility that something unforeseen will happen— something that requires more physical effort than anticipated. The bottom line is that we should be as physically prepared as we can be to meet the rigors of the hunt.

Therein lies the big problem. Becoming physically prepared isn't something you can buy, win in a contest, or wish for. To be successful at getting in shape, you must first convince yourself that you will alter your lifestyle accordingly. Diet and exercise are the two primary considerations, and they happen to be two activities that most human beings detest.

Getting in shape isn't a uniform activity that applies to everyone. A 35-year-old man may be able to train much more vigorously than a 60-year-old. Certain physical limitations may restrict the degree of conditioning, as well. A person with heart or lung problems obviously must be much more careful in exercising than a healthier individual.

The average hunter heads out into the woods a couple of weekends a year or maybe a week, at the most. For that amount of time, the majority aren't willing to undergo a major lifestyle change to get in shape. Trouble is that these are usually the people who suffer fatalities in the woods, just as the unfit person who has a heart attack while shoveling snow.

Obviously, if you're going on a hunt of a lifetime, such as a long-awaited Western hunt in the high country, you'll have more motivation to condition yourself. Amazingly enough, I see plenty of hunters who arrive in camp in terrible condition, especially those who have signed on for what they assume is a relatively easy horseback hunt. What

Hauling game in rough terrain or bad weather is hard work. Be sure you are in good physical condition.
Photograph by Charles J Alsheimer

SHAPING UP

The answer to meeting hunting's physical requirements is to get in shape long before the hunt. Exercise and diet are mandatory, but plenty of folks have problems disciplining themselves in both categories. Try to work seriously at one of them, at least.

As an outdoorsmen with fish and game in your freezer, you have a headstart on a good diet. Both are wonderful foods from a health standpoint, provided you cook them with low fat and cholesterol in mind. Plenty of cookbooks tell you how to prepare these healthy foods.

The following workout program is recommended by *Outdoor Life* Sports Medicine Editor Paul Gill, M.D. According to Gill, there are four elements to a S.A.F.E. physical fitness program: Strength, Ability, Flexibility, and Endurance. To a considerable extent, ability is something you're born with, but you can do something about the other three.

Gill says to stretch for at least 15 minutes prior to any exercise program. This will improve your flexibility. Warm up first by jogging, walking, or cycling for a few minutes. When you stretch, hold the stretch for 20 to 60 seconds. Do the exercise slowly, and don't bounce.

Four good stretching exercises that should be done daily are:

- Alternate-toe stretches: Stand with your legs apart, bend at the waist, and reach out and touch first your right foot with your left hand, and then twist at the waist and touch your left foot with your right hand.
- Wall push-up: Stand facing a wall, about 4 feet away. Lean forward and place your palms on the wall. Keeping your back straight and feet flat on the floor, bend your elbows so that your body moves toward the wall. Hold this position for 20 seconds.
- The plow: Lie flat on your back and lift your legs over your head. Keep them straight as you try to touch the floor behind you with your toes. Hold them there for 20 seconds.
- Hurdler's stretch: Sit on the floor with one leg stretched out in front of you and the other behind you. Grasp the forward leg with your hands and pull your head down until it touches your knee. Hold for 20 seconds.

To build strength, Gill recommends that you work with a given weight until you can perform several repetitions, or reps, and then add weight or resistance. If you are interested in developing pure strength, lift heavy weights for less repetitions; if you're concerned with muscular endurance, stick with low weights and more repetitions. Endurance is best improved by aerobic activity such as jogging, brisk walking, swimming, cross-country skiing, cycling, tennis, and rowing.

The following guidelines should assist you in designing a daily workout program:

Monday, Wednesday, Friday

- Light warm-up for 15 minutes.
- Stretching exercises for 15 minutes.
- Strength exercises for 45 minutes: Bench presses, four sets of 10 reps; squats or leg presses, four sets of 10 reps; arm curls, four sets of 10 reps; lat pulldowns, four sets of 10 reps; bent-leg sit-ups, two sets of 30 reps. Start with a weight that you can handle easily for 10 reps, then work up to a final set that requires an intense effort to complete 10 reps. Try to handle more weight in the next workout. Cool down: Stretch for 15 minutes.

Tuesday, Thursday, Saturday

- Light warm-up for five minutes.
- Stretching for 15 minutes.
- Aerobic activity for 30 to 60 minutes.
- Cool down: Walking, then stretching for five or so minutes allows the body to clear lactic acid and other metabolic wastes from the muscles.

they have failed to realize, of course, is that you can't ride a horse everywhere you hunt; plenty of hiking is required in most cases.

Many hunters who come West will be competing with plenty of other hunters in crowded woods. This demands even tougher hunting, requiring them to work much harder to get away from other hunters or to be the first one to the basin or the top of the mountain.

In practically every case, you can alter your lifestyle to meet the challenges of a hunt. There is one exception, however—an ailment caused by altitudes above 5,000 feet, which may strike even fit people. Technically called acute mountain sick-

COPING WITH HIGH ALTITUDE

Sources for the following information on acute mountain sickness were the Colorado Altitude Research Institute and *Outdoor Life* Sports Medicine Editor Paul Gill, M.D.

Symptoms of High Altitude Sickness

- Mild to moderate headache
- Loss of appetite
- Occasional nausea and vomiting
- Fatigue
- Unusual shortness of breath
- Difficulty sleeping

Prevention and/or Adjustments

- If possible, arrive in high country about three days before the hunt to acclimatize yourself.
- Several days before your climb, switch to a diet of 70 percent high-carbohydrate foods, such as pasta, grains, fruits, and vegetables.
- Travel to high country in stages, never going higher than 8,000 feet the first day, then climbing 1,000 to 2,000 feet on subsequent days. (If possible, drop to lower elevations to sleep.)
- Exercise in moderation the first few days.
- Drink more water and juices than usual.
- If you use alcohol or coffee, do so in moderation.
- Avoid salty foods.
- Take one 500mg tablet of Acetazolamide each day. Acetazolamide increases ventilation and blood-oxygen content and will prevent high-altitude sickness in most cases. (For tough trips, start taking tablets the same day or one day prior to your climb.)
- If your guide is traveling too quickly, don't try to keep up with him. Ask him to slow down.
- If symptoms appear, descend several thousand feet to where they desist. If this isn't possible, stop, and don't exert yourself for at least three days.
- If symptoms intensify, consult a doctor.

(Note: Individuals with heart or lung disease or who are overweight and smoke are much more susceptible to altitude sickness.)

---

ness, this illness is also known as altitude or high-country sickness, and it is the result of decreased amounts of oxygen getting into your blood because of lower atmospheric pressures.

According to the Colorado Altitude Research Institute (CARI), one out of every four visitors to Colorado's high country has an ailment caused by high altitudes. Though CARI is basically referring to skiers, hikers, and backpackers, hunters no doubt suffer the same symptoms, perhaps more so because of the demands of negotiating steep, heavily timbered terrain and of getting a heavy-bodied mule deer or elk out of the woods.

A common problem among hunters is back pain. I suffer from it, and when it hits, I'm usually out of business for several weeks. I'm told by my doctor pals that I'm not unusual. Back problems are routine human ailments no matter what lifestyle we lead. I'm also told that exercise is the best way to prevent back pain from occurring. It took some time for me to become a believer, but I'm sold on it now.

You'll be glad you're in shape when it comes time to pack that trophy out of the high country. Photograph by Jim Zumbo.

One recent summer while loading cases of my books from the printing plant, my back went out. The pain lasted for several weeks, extending into the fall hunting season. I recovered shortly thereafter, and when my daughter-in-law, who is a physical therapist, scolded me severely, I heeded her advice. Now, I exercise and wear an orthopedic back brace, a corsetlike contraption that allows me to do practically anything.

You've heard this advice before, and I'll say it again: Consult your physician long before you embark on a diet or exercise program.

The bottom line is that you should get in the best shape you possibly can before you take off on your next hunt. It's mighty nice to be able to climb that mountain and feel good when you reach the top. And it's also mighty nice to beat the hunting odds and tie your tag to a prize animal. That's more than enough reason to take a good hard look at your lifestyle and think health. Every other aspect of your life will be cheerier, as well.

Blaze in the Woods

By Bob Gooch

Hmmm, I guess it works," I said to myself, a smile coming to my face. It was the week after Christmas, and a few days were left in the late dove season. But the deer season was also at its peak, and a new Virginia law required all hunters to wear hunter orange during the firearms deer season.

Wait a minute, even in the dove fields? What's hunting coming to? Had the regulation makers even considered that the late dove season ran concurrent with the firearms deer season?

But there it was: in the books, in black and white. No doubt about it.

Fortunately, I recognized a solution that might minimize the possible problem for dove hunters such as myself. Unlike most states, Virginia allows hunters to meet the color requirement by displaying hunter orange at shoulder level within body reach and visible from 360°.

I complied with the law by simply removing my orange vest and wrapping it securely around a utility pole. Seated with my back to the pole, I was visible to the occasional deer hunter that stalked past. The secured vest did not flap in the autumn breeze, so movement wasn't a problem, and I could only hope that the hunter orange didn't serve as a warning signal to approaching birds.

The true test came soon enough. A dove circling the harvested grainfield winged by, and my light field load dropped it cleanly.

Satisfied with the arrangement, I went to recover my downed bird. But wait! If I walked away from the orange-wrapped pole, I would be violating the law. I wore no hunter orange clothing.

This time, I was able to correct the problem by digging out the orange cap I had worn into the field. To better conceal myself, I had swapped the orange cap for a camouflage cap once the vest was attached to the pole.

With these two adjustments to my usual hunting method, I had seemingly solved the hunter orange dilemma—at least for dove hunting during the deer firearms season. There was, of course, no problem during the early dove season because the deer season was not yet open and the hunter orange mandate was not in force.

Don't get me wrong. I have no quarrel with the hunter orange regulation in any state. It has saved lives across America. I pushed for the regulation in Virginia for years and actually hunted in hunter orange clothing long before it was a law. It can, however, handicap the hunter by

HUNTER ORANGE—WHAT IS IT?

Now that you're aware of the many and varied ways to cope with hunter orange in the woods, a simpler thought might occur to you: Just what is hunter orange? What separates the color from plain orange, or fire red, or even the old stalwart red/black plaid pattern, for that matter?

According to the Maine Department of Inland Fisheries and Wildlife regulations summary, hunter orange is defined as a "daylight fluorescent orange color with a dominant wave length between 595 and 605 nanometers, excitation purity not less than 85 percent, and luminance factor of not less than 40 percent." And you thought handloading was complicated.

In another colorful twist, Arkansas currently offers hunters the option of wearing "fluorescent chartreuse," a hue most familiar to buzzbait bass fishermen. Apparently, the color is more visible than hunter orange in low-light conditions. No word from Arkansas on the definition of fluorescent chartreuse, but if you need clarification, just visit your local tackle shop.

HUNTER ORANGE IN MOTION

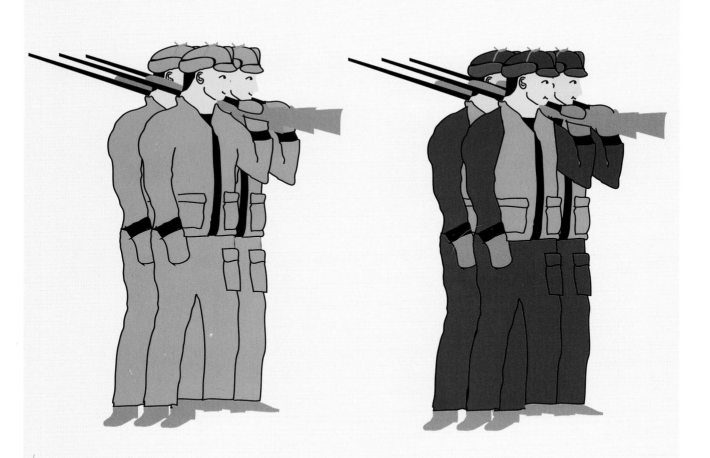

Hunters looking to minimize the hunter orange handicap should avoid wearing orange pants and gloves. Both garments accentuate movement and alert game to your presence. Hunter orange hats or caps are required in some states, but if not mandated, hunters should consider wearing a vest instead.

forcing him to rethink hunting as he has known it for years. Orange-emblazoned hunters must rethink concealment and camouflage, the very essence of successful hunting for deer and most other game species.

So how do you deal with the hunter orange regulation, enjoy the protection it offers, and still have a successful hunt? Let's consider a few options.

Hunter orange was almost certainly proposed with deer hunting in mind. After all, deer were supposed to be color-blind, and therefore the hunter would not be handicapped by the bright color. This is debatable, but it's generally agreed that movement, not color, is the real problem for the whitetail hunter, and a bright shade of clothing, such as hunter orange, does accentuate movement.

Knowing that, we hunters can work toward taking full advantage of the protective color regardless of whether it's the law—in some states it's not—while trying to minimize the potential handicaps it presents. That's why I wrapped my vest around the utility pole instead of wearing it. Stationary, it didn't seem to bother the doves, but wrapped around my turning and twisting body it might have had the birds flaring off all afternoon.

The obvious solution is to limit movement of the bright color as much as possible. Selecting the right hunter orange clothing helps in this respect. Varying state regulations tend to limit this option, but knowing what to wear, in what situations, is a helpful step toward minimizing the hunter orange handicap.

Let's consider clothing. Thumbing through hunting clothing catalogs or browsing through gun shops across America, you're likely to see hunter orange gloves for sale. Well, common sense says that hunter orange gloves certainly are not an essential piece of hunt-

ing garb. Gloves of this color do little to help the hunter comply with most state regulations, and no other part of the body moves more than the hands. Covering the hands with hunter orange greatly telegraphs movement.

Years ago I owned a pair of bright orange hunting gloves, but I was mostly a rabbit hunter then, and the color caused little or no handicap. In fact, the gloves probably made me more conspicuous to my companions who might otherwise unknowingly swing in my direction trying to get on a fleeting bunny. In other situations, however, such as stillhunting, bright gloves only warn deer of your presence.

And what about caps or hats? "I would think a cap or hat would be the worst choice in orange clothing," said my son-in-law, an avid hunter. He's also an engineer given to analytical thinking. Take, for example, the hunter on a deer stand. He's constantly moving his head—listening and looking—probably more so than his

During drives, it's important that hunters are visible to their partners. The hunter in the best shooting position should wear the least amount of orange. Photograph by Charles S. Alsheimer

hands. Wearing an orange hat, the hunter's movement is telegraphed in every direction.

Several state game agencies, however, require the hunter to wear a hunter orange cap or hat, and in other states it's a convenient way to comply with the law, especially when the requirement is only 100 to 150 square inches of hunter orange clothing. In either case, a hunter orange hat can be a blessing or a curse.

Years ago I was a member of a small deer hunting party, and as a precaution I was wearing a bright orange cap, the only item of my clothing in that color. The law did not require it then. I had filled my permit early and was assigned to driving duty. "We could see you coming just about every step of the way," one of my fellow hunters told me when I had completed the drive—one incidentally that produced a trio of whitetails.

So you see, in such situations a hunter orange cap can be effective protection, but many other times, the hat spooks game, as well. I no longer wear an orange cap afield, except in those states where it is required. Good hunters must move their heads frequently, and the movement is too visible to quarry when the hunter's head looks like a bright orange beacon. Instead, when permitted by law, I prefer to display orange on some other part of my clothing.

Next let's look at trousers—or even socks or boots—in hunter orange. On a stand, the feet and legs probably don't move as much as the hands and head, but they certainly get plenty of motion when the hunter is walking—again, a good example is while stillhunting. Besides, nearly all state regulations specify that the color must be worn above the waist. So hunter orange trousers and footwear do not, in most instances, meet the hunter orange square-inch requirements. In that case, they are a detriment to a hunter's chance of success.

OK, we've seen why hunter orange gloves, caps and hats, trousers, and footwear ward off wildlife as well as other hunters. But where's the happy medium? To many hunters, the answer is a jacket or vest, depending upon the weather.

Several Christmases ago, my wife gave me a beautiful wool hunting jacket. It's roomy, warm, and comfortable—and bright orange. "I'll have to put on my sunglasses to look at you, Da," said my 5-year-old granddaughter when I modeled it that Christmas morning.

I love that jacket, and I've gotten plenty of mileage out of it. I've worn it on many successful deer hunts and took a nice elk in Arizona while wearing the jacket. And I suspect I'll wear it for seasons to come, now that my old red plaid wool jacket has been rendered illegal by hunter orange regulations.

In retrospect, however, I would make one change if I could. I would limit the orange color to the body of the jacket and have the sleeves in camouflage or some drab color. Why? Because the arms, like the hands and head, are constantly moving on a stand.

This didn't occur to me until several years after I got the jacket, and obviously the manufacturer hadn't considered it. I may yet have the jacket altered. The change would make it a more practical hunting jacket.

Sorting through various items of hunter's clothing, it becomes obvious that a vest is the least expensive and probably the overall easiest way to comply with hunter orange regulations. In fact, a scan of state-by-state regulations reveals that hunter orange vests comply with the regulations in just about every state.

A vest can be functional—with shooting patches, cargo pockets, shell loops—and flexible enough to allow the hunter to adjust for the weather. If the weather's warm, for example, you can wear a vest over just a shirt. I prefer vests made of soft cotton. They're quiet and fit well over other clothing. Those made of plastic or other hard-finished material tend to be too noisy.

That about covers hunter orange clothing. However, there are other options for coping with hunter orange requirements that deal with the use of clothing in unconventional ways or employing hunter orange accessories.

For example, the Virginia "shoulder-level-within-body-reach" option described earlier is not allowed in many other states, but it can be used effectively in states where hunter orange is not yet mandatory. (Surprisingly, there are a number of states not requiring hunter orange, including some of the best hunting states in America. However, authorities strongly recommend the use of hunter orange even where it is not mandatory.) The method can also be employed when hunting in seasons outside of the periods during which hunter orange is mandatory. Generally, hunter orange is required during firearms big-game seasons only. When the Virginia option can be used, it opens up a great variety of possibilities. For instance, suppose a hunter has a permanent tree stand along a hot deer trail. Several weeks before opening day he can wrap a sash of orange cloth around the tree at shoulder level and let the animals become accustomed to it before the season begins.

Wildlife will soon accept the orange sash as part of the environment and ignore it, but it still serves to flag other hunters. Orange must be worn to and from the stand, but it can be removed once on the stand.

A number of states require the use of hunter orange during upland bird and other small-game seasons. This is not much of a problem when hunting cottontails with beagles or bird hunting, but it sure can interfere with a squirrel hunter's chances—and it's a handicap

THE ORANGE CAMO DEBATE

How much better, or worse, is hunter orange in a camouflage pattern as opposed to the solid color? This is a question some state game enforcement departments have not come to grips with, though other states have answered the question by banning the use of colored camo altogether.

The different shades of opinion stem from the comparatively different shades, or brightnesses, of colored camo and solid hunter orange garments. Many officials believe that camouflage hunter orange is duller and less visible than the solid color, offering less protection for the hunter.

There is currently no conclusive evidence indicating whether hunter orange camo helps or hurts a hunter. However, all hunters should carefully check state regulations before donning colored camo clothing. Colorado and Virginia are but two states that have outlawed camouflage hunter orange.

David Croonquiest, assistant director of law enforcement for the Colorado Division of Wildlife, said that studies show that solid hunter orange provides better protection simply because it is easier for hunters to see.

Similarly, Ron Groener, information assistant for the Wisconsin Bureau of Fisheries and Wildlife Management, said that his agency has not prohibited camouflage hunter orange, but the state doesn't recommend it. Groener pointed out that because of

the way deer see, they may more easily pick out the shaded camo pattern than the solid color.

In Pennsylvania, where turkey hunters are required to wear hunter orange, the debate on hunter orange camo takes on added significance. Undoubtedly, many turkey hunters will opt for colored camo to comply with the upcoming hunter orange mandate. Bruce Whiteman of the Pennsylvania Game Commission said that the

Camo hunter orange is outlawed in some states because it is deemed less visible than the solid color. Photographs by Charles S. Alsheimer

department feels the solid color is best, but it has not moved to ban colored camo. As he explains it, camouflage clothing must have sufficient amounts of hunter orange color to be legal. "There must be enough solid color in the [camouflage] garment to meet the minimum hunter orange requirement," Whiteman said. In Pennsylvania, that requirement is 100 square inches of hunter orange for spring turkey hunters and 250 square inches in the fall.

that's not easy to minimize.

Probably the best approach to squirrel hunting when faced with the hunter orange requirement is to take a stand at a den tree in winter or at a nut tree earlier. This means some scouting to locate active den trees or nut-bearing trees where the animals are feeding. Limiting hunter orange to the torso helps, too. Shouldering a gun with orange-clad arms could send a bushytail scurrying before you ever get off a shot.

Stalking is more difficult. About the only solution is to limit the hunter orange to a vest (if it meets the regulations) and to move slowly and quietly, hoping that you can spot a squirrel before it sees you. Then, keep the trunk of a big tree between you and the squirrel until you are within range.

Certainly, such squirrel hunting practices can be applied to many other kinds of hunting for both big and small game.

A more controversial subject is hunter orange requirements during the spring turkey season. Hunter orange in the spring turkey woods is considered blasphemous by some. But is it?

In recent years, few forms of hunting have been plagued more by accidents than turkey hunting—accidents caused by gobbler hunters misidentifying their targets. The result can cause serious, or even fatal, injury.

Still, spring turkey hunters generally are not ready to embrace hunter orange. After all, concealment and stealth are the essence of the sport. Hunters use complete camouflage clothing, camouflaged guns, gloved hands, grease-painted faces or faces concealed by masks. It seems that hunter orange would violate the basic approach to this popular spring hunt.

"Not so," said Kit Shaffer, a well-known Virginia turkey hunter and for years the top turkey biologist for the Virginia Department of Game and Inland Fisheries. "I wear a hunter orange vest all the time, but take it off and wrap it around a tree trunk just above my head when I start to work a bird. And I've recently called a half-dozen gobblers within range. Movement is the key. Don't move, and the turkeys are not alarmed."

Shaffer tells about a test that the game department conducted. "[The department] selected a test area, baited it, and set up a hunter orange mannequin. The feeding turkeys flocked all around it. They then tied an orange handkerchief to the mannequin. With the handkerchief fluttering in the breeze, the birds wouldn't come near."

In Pennsylvania, hunters are required to wear 100 square inches of hunter orange to and from stands during spring turkey season. The color is not required when the hunter is set up to call birds. Though it's doubtful that hunter orange will be required for spring turkey hunting in every state in the near future, it can nonetheless help prevent hunting accidents. And it's not necessarily a burden to the hunter.

For example, Hunter's Specialties of Cedar Rapids, Iowa, has produced a turkey-carrying bag in hunter orange. The successful hunter can place his gobbler in the bag, sling it over his shoulder and head out of the woods reasonably confident that the turkey on his back won't be mistaken for a live bird.

Hunters can also make use of the hunter orange sash mentioned earlier, or an orange headband worn over a camo cap or hat.

Spring gobbler hunters move about the woods considerably, listening for gobblers or trying to provoke a gobbler with crow calls or an owl hoot. Hunters are rarely within range of a bird at that point, and they can protect themselves with the sash or headband. Then, when a turkey gobbles, and they begin to work the bird, hunters can remove the protective color. Or hunters can wrap the sash around a tree where they set up—as Kit Shaffer does with his vest.

Keeping in mind that hunter orange in combination with movement is the real handicap, the innovative hunter can enjoy the protection of the color and still minimize its effect on a great variety of hunting situations. It's largely a matter of rethinking, or slightly altering, successful techniques.

Above all, remember that such simple, common sense adjustments in hunting methods can prevent tragic accidents. As Kit Shaffer said, "I don't want to trade [my life] for a turkey."

Finding Your Way

By Tom Huggler

The woods of the Huron-Manistee National Forest are as familiar to deer hunter Glen Haglund as Route 31, which splits the small city of Manistee, Michigan, where Haglund grew up and now lives.

The many roads and forest trails, and the Manistee River, make it hard for anyone who knows north from south to get lost in the nearly 1-million-acre forest. However, a friend who Haglund invited along on a deer hunting trip knew little about directions and less about finding his way out of the woods. Haglund made the mistake of figuring that his pal carried a compass, always the first item to pack on any camping, hunting, or fishing trip.

Shortly after splitting up, Haglund heard rifle shots from the direction where his friend had gone. Thinking that a deer could be down, he changed course to offer help. Haglund's friend needed help, all right. He was lost.

"I suspected it when more shots were fired and then thought I could hear him hollering," Haglund said. "But when I got to that spot, the hollering was fainter than ever."

Haglund began to jog, then flat-out ran as he tried to intercept the now obviously panicked hunter. The man was so disoriented that he didn't hear Haglund's shouts or rifle shots, and he ran blindly in the kind of mindless flight that can turn an animal into the teeth of the raging forest fire it's trying to escape.

The man was strong and in good physical shape. Luckily he kept hollering or Haglund might not have been able to run him down. When Haglund finally reached the exhausted and weeping man, he was sitting on the ground, his face and hands scratched and his clothing torn. He no longer carried his gun.

Getting lost—really lost and not just turned around—is a frightening, humiliating experience. I was only 7 years old when I followed a black squirrel into the forest behind my uncle's cabin and became an instant panic case when the squirrel didn't lead me home again as Walt Disney had indicated it would. I was so scared I messed my pants. Luckily my dad had a loud voice; within minutes I was saved. That may have been the first time I was lost, but it probably won't be the last.

Becoming lost is a rite of passage that every woods-wise outdoorsman has experienced, whether or not he admits it. The alternative, though, is never learning to orient yourself, and you know what that means: a lifetime of hunting along familiar roads and trails, of never pitching a tent on some top-of-the-mountain stream, of never venturing onto a good bass lake when the stars come out.

So, if you have yet to experience finding your way out of the woods, my advice is to get lost—on purpose—but in a controlled situation. Find a wooded area, for example, that is bounded by mile-section roads so that no matter how turned around you become, you will find the

Always plot a course using a map. Here, the author sketches a stick map to outline a backwoods landmark. Photograph by Randy Carrels

way out. The experience will teach you to use a compass correctly and how to read a map.

Then, the next time you're outdoors you'll remember to take a bearing and to look over your shoulder so that you can recall landmarks later when retracing your steps. You'll become more familiar with the woods, too, and in the event that you must spend a night outdoors, you'll be better prepared to handle it.

The first rule of being lost is not to panic. Take several deep breaths and get control of yourself. Unless you're in the Arctic or deep in some Amazonian jungle, you can't be more than a few hours from help. Sit down and assess the situation, calmly. (Standing, you're more inclined to run in blind fear.) Eat a candy bar. Relax. Go over the travel route in your mind. Now, how far is it from that last landmark?

Once you've settled down, retrace your line of travel as you remember it. If you have a compass and took a bearing before departing, walk back in the opposite direction until you come out to famil-

iar surroundings. Always believe your compass. The top of the map in your pocket will probably be north. Not sure? Use the position of the sun as a guide, or make a simple direction-finder by holding a twig across your palm and looking at the shadow. From either of these methods, you should be able to determine east and west. If that fails, and you have no map or compass, and are certain you're lost, then get as comfortable as possible and stay put until help arrives.

One recent October, a 74-year-old man who hunts grouse in the same enormous clearcuts where I camp and hunt in Michigan's Upper Peninsula got lost and spent the night outdoors. The man had no matches and no food, but he did not panic and run off. He spent the night warm between his two setters. When a search party found the man the next morning, he was in good health, except for being hungry and a bit embarrassed by his predicament.

You can hedge against getting lost by always carrying a map and compass. You should also tote stick matches and a good knife and tell someone where you are going and when you expect to return. Leave a note in your vehicle so authorities will know when you left and where you were heading.

A map and compass are valuable tools only if you know how to use them. For years I have used county maps such as those put out by the DeLorme Mapping Company to find camping and hunting spots. Satellite imaging and infrared photography have provided outdoor recreationists with new and helpful maps that are actual photographs, many of which are overlain with a scale and identification.

Topographic maps, though, are the most popular because they contain a wealth of information, as any backpacker or wilderness canoeist will attest to. The typical hunter and angler, however, doesn't study them and few practice using them. Topo maps give elevations in contours of brown print, but they also point out rivers and lakes (blue), key roads (red), vegetation (green), and manmade objects such as dams and buildings (black). Popular scales are 1 inch to 250,000 inches (1:250,000) or 1 inch equals 4 miles; 1:62,500 or 1 inch equals 1 mile; and 1:24,000 or 1 inch equals 2,000 feet.

Larger and smaller scale topo maps are also available. Each allows you to use an orienteering or "map" compass (one containing a travel arrow, 360° gradation and an inch ruler—don't settle for compasses that have only N, E, S, and W imprinted on them). With a good map compass, you can determine exact distances between locations and chart an accurate course.

For many outdoorsmen, second only to the fear of getting lost is the fear of having to learn how to use a compass. Yet nothing could be simpler: Point the direction of travel arrow at a land-mark; turn the rotating dial until the magnetic arrow (usually red in color) lines up with the travel arrow; read the bearing in degrees.

To illustrate: Let's assume your travel course is north/northeast at 40° (40° east of north). To find the way back, add 180° (half of a circle). In this example, the way out then is 220° south/southwest.

When walking, let nature be your guide—pick out a landmark, such as a big pine tree, walk to that spot, check your bearing and pick out additional landmarks, one at a time, until you reach your destination. With a little practice, you should be able to find hunting hotspots and return to good fishing holes.

Remember, too, to calculate declination, which is the angle of difference between true north and magnetic north (the direction a compass actually points). The declination may vary by as much as 20° west for someone living in Maine to as much as 30° east for a resident of Alaska. All topo maps explain declination with a simple diagram.

A good place to practice orienteering is on a golf course where the various greens and their flags serve as landmarks. A well-equipped sport-

MAP AND COMPASS SOURCES

The U.S. Geological Survey has divided each state into quadrangles. For a free "Topographic Map Index Circular" and a pamphlet called "Topographic Map Symbols," write the National Cartographic Information Center, 507 National Center, Reston, VA 22092.

To order maps, write U.S. Geological Survey Map Sales, Box 25286, Denver, CO 80225. For Canadian maps, write the Department of Energy, Mines and Resources, Maps Distribution Office, 615 Booth St., Ottawa, Ontario KlA OE9.

The video "The ABCs of Compass and Map" can be ordered postpaid from Brunton U.S.A., 620 E. Monroe Ave., Riverton, WY 82501 (307-856-6559). The video "Finding Your Way in the Wild" is available postpaid from Quality Video Inc., 7399 Bush Lake Rd., Minneapolis, MN 55439 (612-893-0903).

For more information about the GPS NAV 5000, contact Magellan Systems Corp., 960 Overland Court, San Dimas, CA 91773 (714-394-5000).

The following companies make orienteering or map compasses:

B.C.B. International
1510 N.W. 74 Ave.
Miami, FL 33126
(305-477-7031)

Brunton U.S.A.
620 E. Monroe Ave.
Riverton, WY 82501
(307-856-6559)

Buck Knives Inc.
Box 1267
El Cajon, CA 92022
(800-326-2825)

Coghlan's Ltd.
121 Irene St.
Winnipeg, Manitoba
R3T 4C7
(204-284-9550)

Compass Industries Inc.
104 E. 25th St.
New York, NY 10010
(800-221-9904)

Selsi Company Inc.
40 Veterans Blvd.
Carlstadt, NJ 07072
(800-ASK SELSI)

Silva Compasses
Johnson Camping Inc.
Box 966
Binghamton, NY 13902
(800-847-1460)

Texsport
Box 55326
Houston, TX 77255
(800-231-1402)

COMPASSES AND MAPS TO FIND YOUR WAY

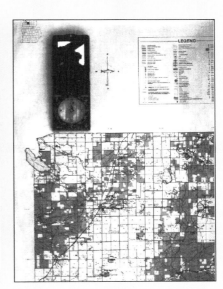

Aerial photographs make helpful maps for outdoorsmen. Use compasses, such as the ones shown here, to help chart your travel route. Photographs by Outdoor Images/Tom Huggler

ing-goods outlet will have a selection of compasses as well as books and videos. Two excellent videos are "The ABCs of Compass and Map" by Brunton U.S.A. or "Finding Your Way in the Wild," produced for Johnson Camping.

The latest development in orienteering taps into the Global Positioning System (GPS) that depends on satellites designed primarily for the nation's defense. Handheld GPS receivers such as the Magellan NAV 5000 weigh mere ounces yet allow boaters, hikers, campers, hunters, and fishermen to use satellite data to figure out current location,

altitude, and speed. Once you have a position fix, information can be computed in less than a minute and is updated every second. Think of a GPS unit as an electronic compass that constantly records your speed and direction as you walk.

In the wilderness, the shortest distance between two points is not always a straight line, especially when navigating lake and mountain areas. Knowing how you got into the woods is the key to knowing the way out, and it takes on added importance when you have a canoe or heavy pack on your back. 🦌

Safety in the Trees

By Paul G. Gill Jr., M.D.

It was the blood that caught Steve's eye. Not a pool of blood as you would see after a hunter has dressed out a deer, but a smattering of splotches on the snow under the old tree stand.

The stand didn't look strong enough to support a squirrel, much less a man. It sagged badly on one side, and its rotten boards were covered with bracket fungi. A single set of footprints led to and from the stand, and the snow had been brushed off the steps leading up the tree. When Steve saw the bolt-action rifle lying in the snow, he knew whoever had been using the stand was in trouble. He slipped on his snowshoes and followed the tracks.

A few minutes later, he found a man lying in the snow, barely breathing. His clothing was wet and covered with snow. His face was ashen, and beads of sweat dappled his brow. In a hoarse, scarcely audible voice, he told Steve his story: He had fallen out of the stand earlier that morning and was knocked out when he hit his head on a stump. When he regained consciousness, he had terrific pain in his back, shoulder, and chest. He didn't think he had much chance of being rescued, because he hadn't told his friends or family where he was going, so he tried to walk out of the woods on his own. But he collapsed after a few hundred yards and had been lying in the snow for an hour.

Steve made the hunter as comfortable as possible and then went to get help. By the time he returned with the emergency medical technicians, the man was dead.

Any deer hunter will tell you that tree stands are the greatest invention since the rifled barrel. A stand gives the hunter a commanding field of vision, makes him less visible to the deer, and decreases human scent dispersion at ground level.

But deer stands have a down side. National

SPLIT-COIL CARRY

Step A   Step B

One person can carry an injured hunter with the split coil carry. The coil of rope is knotted, separated into two coils and worn on the hunter's back like a backpack (Step A). The victim puts his legs through the lower part of each coil and holds on with his arms (Step B). Illustration by Chris Armstrong

Would you know what to do if you stumbled upon an injured hunter deep in the woods? Simply running to get help is not enough. You should render whatever assistance you can to your fellow sportsman, starting with first aid.

The first thing you should do for a hunter who has fallen out of a stand is check his ABCs (Airway, Breathing, Circulation) without moving him. Then examine him from head to toe, looking for injuries. Control bleeding by applying firm pressure to the wound with sterile gauze pads or any bulky, clean material, and then apply compress dressings. Splint obvious fractures and cover the injured hunter with a sleeping bag to keep him warm.

Next comes the tough part: getting the injured hunter out of the wilderness. Whether and how you evacuate him depends on a number of factors, including his condition, the time of day, the weather, the available equipment, the terrain,

statistics on deer stand-related injuries are unavailable, but the experience in Georgia during the period 1979-1989 is sobering. During that 10-year period, 214 deer stand-related injuries were reported, including 17 fatalities; 111 of the injuries resulted from falls.

Doctors at the Medical College of Georgia interviewed 17 hunters who survived their falls from deer stands and found that 83 percent of them had fallen from hunter-constructed stands. None of the hunters had been wearing safety belts at the times of their accidents. The Georgia researchers reported that the four most common causes of deer stand-related injuries were: structural failure of the stand, carelessness, falling asleep in the stand, and medical problems (asthma, passing out).

A fall from a 15-to-20-foot-high deer stand can produce severe injuries. Fractures of the long bones of the arms and legs and spinal injuries are especially common, and many victims suffer long-term disability and permanent paralysis.

TWO-PERSON POLE CARRY

In the two-person pole carry, the two rescuers don backpacks, and then pass a pole or branch between their backs and the lower straps of their packs. The victim sits on the pole and holds onto their shoulders. Illustration by Chris Armstrong

SAFER DEER STANDS

Here are some ways to keep your deer stand from becoming a diving platform.

• If you've built your own stand, inspect it carefully before deer season. Check the steps, supports, and floor, and replace any cracked or rotten boards. The stand may have been solid last year, but tree growth can easily rip out or shift nails or screws, and the limbs supporting the stand may have rotted in the interim. Dismantle any stand that is beyond repair so that other hunters won't get hurt using it.

• Check the nuts, bolts, and welds on climbers and lock-on stands. They can loosen or weaken over time.

• Use both hands to climb up into the stand and haul your gun or bow up with a cord.

• Use a safety restraint while in the stand.

• Carry a whistle so that you can summon help if you get hurt.

• Tell your family or friends where you will be hunting and when you expect to be back.

• Remember that there is safety in numbers. Go into the woods in groups of two or more and split up to hunt, but be sure to plan to meet later at specific times and places.

• Don't use a tree stand if you have a serious medical condition (for example, epilepsy, diabetes or heart disease) that could lead to a fall.

Photograph by Tom Tietz

and the number of rescuers. If the injured person is able to move under his own power, escort him out of the woods. If he cannot walk because of a leg injury and the road is not too distant, consider carrying him with one of these techniques:

• Piggyback: If his name isn't Tiny Tim, you'll only be able to carry the victim for short distances with this back-breaking technique.

• Backpack carry: The victim rides in the pack with his legs hanging out of the bottom.

• Split-coil carry: Coil 30 to 40 feet of rope, tie a knot in it, and split it into two equal coils. Slip the coils over your shoulders as though you were putting on a knapsack and then have the victim put a leg through the lower part of each coil and wrap his arms around your shoulders.

If the hunter's condition is deteriorating, he does not have a spinal injury or multiple fractures, and there are at least two rescuers, consider evacuating him using one of these two methods:

• Two-person carry: The rescuers stand on either side of the victim, join hands under the victim's back and knees and carry him out.

• Two-person pole carry: The rescuers don backpacks or knapsacks, stand side-by-side, and pass a long pole or branch between their backs and the lower straps of their packs. The victim sits on the pole between his rescuers and hangs onto their shoulders.

The above methods are inappropriate for the seriously injured hunter. If the hunter is seriously injured and does not have a spinal injury or multiple fractures, two rescuers can fashion a pole litter by tying a series of sticks across two parallel poles or branches set 18 inches apart. If a blanket or tarp is available, that can be used to cover the sticks and make a blanket or tarp litter.

If you believe that the injured man is too badly hurt to be moved, and you are the only rescuer, you have no choice but to stabilize him as well as you can and then go for help.

Whitetail U.

By John E. Phillips

Traditionally, deer hunting as a sport has been passed down from generation to generation. Like many other hunting enthusiasts my age, I learned the old way from men who had spent their lifetimes in the woods studying the habits and haunts of whitetails.

Unfortunately, those men are gone now, as is the abundance of land that I once hunted. Today, many large tracts of public and private land have been broken up and leased to hunting clubs— and when someone pays a high price for a lease, he's not exactly thrilled about teaching anyone else how to hunt and take deer on that lease. The same goes for the fellow who's learned to successfully hunt public lands—he's understandably reluctant to show you how and where he finds deer, seeing as you're likely to become his competition for those animals.

Nowadays, finding men who have invested the time necessary to learn to consistently take deer is not nearly as easy as it was 30 years ago. Getting those individuals to teach you the tricks of the trade is even more difficult.

However, there *are* some men out there who are willing to school you on how to locate and take deer each season on the lands that you hunt.

A number of hunting lodges and guides are now offering a new service—one-on-one deer hunting instruction, similar to the personalized fitness programs set up for individuals at many health centers. For many, it is the quickest, least expensive, and most cost effective and efficient way to become a deer hunter.

With this method of deer hunting instruction, the student has his own instructor who teaches him how to read deer sign, find deer, determine deer movement patterns, and pinpoint the most productive places to take stands. These instructors are not as concerned with their students actually bagging deer during the course as they are with teaching the students the woodsmanship and deer knowledge that they need to find and take deer anywhere they hunt. The knowledge gained through one of these courses will improve any hunter's ability.

"At our lodge, we set aside 400 to 500 acres of land where the deer are plentiful," explained Bo Pitman of White Oak Plantation, near Tuskegee, Alabama. "Then we teach hunters how to read the land and find where and how the deer are moving, as well as where they are bedding and feeding." Pitman is a master

Whereas learning about deer behavior—such as when and where bucks are likely to rub or where they're apt to bed—would normally take years, instructors can now school hunters on the finer points in only a short time. Full-page photograph by Charles S. Alsheimer; inset photograph by John E. Phillips

woodsman who has a teacher's heart and a love for the sport of deer hunting.

"My goal is to teach hunters how to hunt more effectively when they return home," Pitman said. "I'm not as concerned about someone taking a deer while he is here as I am about teaching him how to hunt deer. Then he can apply that knowledge to any area he hunts and drastically increase his odds for bagging more bucks."

Certain tactics always produce bucks no matter what area of the country you hunt. "Two of the strategies I teach outdoorsmen are to hunt thick-cover regions as well as open woods and green fields," said Larry Norton, a soft-spoken woodsman and a guide at Bent Creek Lodge near Jachin, Alabama. All of his life, Norton has pursued deer where he lives in deer-rich central Alabama. "Big bucks stay in thick cover. To take these animals, you either must know how to get in the cover with the deer, how to lure the deer out of the cover to enable

and often take better bucks by stalking. But most hunters move too quickly through the woods to effectively take deer. They don't know how to place their feet to keep from making noise as they walk. They don't understand when to walk and when to stand still. Stalking is an art form requiring practice and skill, and it is a deadly deer tactic that many successful hunters can learn to use."

Dr. Bob Sheppard of Carrollton, Alabama, typically spends more than 100 days a year hunting whitetails and often takes bucks with bows and blackpowder rifles, as well as with modern firearms. With his analytical, scientific mind, Sheppard has studied and learned the details of deer hunting, and he shares his findings with his students. He believes that hunters can bag more deer by learning how to read aerial photos and topographic maps to locate possible food sources and stand sites.

"I teach my students to do most of their scouting before the season with maps," Sheppard said. "I begin a course by having the hunter study maps, including a topo map, of the land we will hunt. Students learn to distinguish pine trees from hardwood trees on aerial photos. We pinpoint where the hardwood bottoms and the funnel areas occur and locate thickets and edges on the photos. From our map work, we will pick 8 to 20 possible sites to ground

Instructors concentrate on teaching hunters techniques that will work anywhere. One such method is learning to analyze aerial photographs and topographic maps to best determine productive sites to help you intercept deer. Photographs by John E. Phillips

you to get a shot, or how to set up near the cover and catch the deer moving into or out of these thick-cover refuges. Once you learn how deer move in these regions and understand how to set up in these places, you can take bucks in thick-cover areas wherever you hunt.

"Stalking, or what many individuals call still-hunting, is another skill I want my students to learn. You can cover more ground, find more deer,

check." Once Sheppard and his students study the maps of the areas they intend to hunt, they next go to those spots and scout to see how accurate their assumptions about the stand sites are.

"If we find four or five productive-looking stand sites with plenty of trails and droppings," Sheppard continued, "we next try to determine where the deer are going, why they are moving to certain areas and what time of day they are traveling. I'm convinced that if a hunter concentrates 80 percent of his time learning about the deer he is trying to take and 20 percent of his time hunting, he will bag more bucks more often than if he spends 80 percent of his time hunting and only 20 percent scouting."

Chris Yeoman, a hunting guide and outfitter from Rapid City, South Dakota, enjoys teaching hunters how to bag Western whitetails. Yeoman knows the mind of a whitetail and often can predict what a deer will do and where a deer will go almost before the deer knows itself. "Driving river-bottom habitat is one of the most productive tactics a Western deer hunter can learn," according to Yeoman. "Positioning the standers to keep their scent from contaminating an area is critical to ensuring that bucks come within shooting range of the standers. Learning to properly execute drives is a skill that can and will produce more bucks for you."

In the West, whitetails may travel as much as 15 miles in a day when they are rutting, especially if the population of does is small. Knowing how and where to set up on the major travel trails can increase your odds of taking more and bigger bucks.

"One afternoon I set up in a good spot along a travel trail I had located," Yeoman recalled. "I had spotted a big buck on this same trail 10 miles away the day before. Late in the afternoon, I had a chance to take that same buck.

"Unless hunters know how to find and follow travel trails and where to set up on these trails, they will usually be taking stands where the deer were the day before instead of setting up where the deer may appear. Although we may hunt

With the help of an instructor, a hunter can learn the preferred deer foods in his area, and at what time those foods will be utilized. Photograph by John E. Phillips

whitetail deer somewhat differently here in the West, many of the tactics that I teach are applicable for hunting whitetails in the East."

One of the primary methods of hunting whitetail deer in any part of the country—whether you are bowhunting or gun hunting—is to set up over a food source. Although you may know how to find a food source, to be consistently successful in taking a buck every season, you must understand how to locate the one food source the deer are favoring when you are hunting.

"By having a well-defined area to study for three or four days, we can teach students how to read deer sign and not only determine what foods the deer on a section of land are feeding on, but also what food source they prefer to come to on the days the hunter is in the woods," said Craig Hawkins, a guide at Hawkins Ridge Lodge in Eufaula, Alabama. "For example, if deer are feeding on acorns, some individual trees will produce better-tasting acorns than other trees of the same species. By pinpointing these preferred trees, you can increase your odds for bagging a buck. I teach students how and where to find these magic trees."

Ronnie Groom, a veteran instructor of many deer hunting schools from Panama City, Florida, believes that teaching hunters to pick the most productive stand site is one of the most important subjects that he covers with his students.

"When deer hunting, you must learn to read the wind and let the wind conditions determine where you can take a stand," Groom said. "I teach a student that even if he has a spot where

COURSE SELECTION

The lengths, dates, and costs of various deer hunting courses vary, but, as of 1992, you could expect to pay about $500 per day for food, lodging, and instruction. Details are worked out with the individual instructors, and when you call, be specific about what you want to learn.

Following are the addresses of the instructors mentioned in the article.

Ronnie Groom
C&G Sporting Goods
137 Harrison Ave.
Panama City, FL 32401
904-769-2317

Craig Hawkins
Hawkins Ridge Lodge
Rte. 4, Box 167
Eufaula, AL 36027
205-687-6820

Ed McMillan
Cedar Creek Lodge
Box 1337
Brewton, AL 36427
205-867-2696

Larry Norton
Box 293
Pennington, AL 36916
205-654-2667

Bo Pitman
White Oak Plantation
Rte. 1, Box 40-H
Tuskegee, AL 36083
205-727-9258

Bob Sheppard
Box 148
Carrollton, AL 35447
205-367-8915

Chris Yeoman
2904 W. Saint Anne
Rapid City, SD 57702
605-348-4973

he is certain he can take a buck, and the wind is wrong to hunt that place, then he shouldn't go to that spot on that day. Knowing when to hunt what stand site may be the most important aspect of the hunt that you can learn."

Groom shows students how to find multiple stand sites in the same region. Then, regardless of the way the wind is blowing on the day they plan to hunt, they still have stand sites that they can hunt. During his courses, Groom uses a specific block of land to hunt on, which he feels helps his students learn to find and take the most productive stand sites on a particular piece of property. Then, Groom teaches students how to apply this knowledge wherever they hunt.

Trophy bucks are difficult to find and even harder to hunt. But Ed McMillan, a guide at Cedar Creek Lodge near Selma, Alabama, who has hunted deer all of his life, specializes in teaching hunters how to take trophy deer. He also instructs hunters on how to produce trophy bucks in their area through management.

"To hunt trophy bucks, you must know that the land you're hunting has older age-class deer on it," McMillan said. "If the land doesn't have these older age-class deer, you can often manage that land to produce trophy bucks for you to hunt. But remember, once you have a three-to eight-year-old buck on your property, he will be much smarter and much harder to hunt than the younger age-class bucks. You will have to use different tactics to bag a trophy buck than you do when hunting younger bucks. Although trophy deer hunting is not for everyone, the techniques I teach can help you to understand the mind of a trophy whitetail, if you can find one to hunt."

McMillan teaches a student to locate and hunt one particular buck in a woodlot and to concentrate all of his efforts on learning all that he can about that trophy deer. McMillan's students learn to pass up any bucks that are not the trophies they are hunting. At the end of McMillan's course, the student has developed a blueprint of how to find and hunt a trophy buck anywhere in the nation.

The best way to maximize the knowledge that you gain from your personal deer hunting instructor is to carry a microcassette tape recorder with you and record all of the information that you're given. Also, take a note pad and pen to draw diagrams and illustrations. Then when you arrive home, you can utilize this knowledge to solve many of your deer hunting problems.

If you learn from a personal deer hunting instructor, your chances of bagging a buck every season are greatly increased. The knowledge that you gain from this one-on-one experience will last you a lifetime.

PART 4

HUNTING WHITETAIL AND MULE DEER

Three Bucks Three Ways

By Jim Shockey

The silence. It's the first thing you notice when you hunt the Northern bush country in Canada. The snow muffles all sound. It hangs thick on the evergreen branches, bending them downward, enveloping every noise in cold cotton batting.

Nothing was stirring that particular morning. I reached out and touched the tip of a snow-laden spruce bough, giving it just enough of a shake to separate the snow from the branch in a small avalanche. The clump dropped silently to the ground.

As I stepped under the bough, sure now that I wouldn't end up with snow down my back, I felt pressure under my foot. I slowly lifted my boot back up and stepped out farther. Too many times I'd snapped a branch under the snow and frightened a big buck into flight.

My legs were now scissored in an awkward stance, but some sixth sense stopped me from stepping again. For several minutes I waited in

Illustration by David Taylor

that position. Though my eyes told me that there was nothing ahead or beside me and the track I was following gave no indication of being any fresher than it had been, I knew enough to trust my instincts.

Sometimes your senses pick up a clue so subtle that your mind fails to register the information. Perhaps it's a flickering ear or the glint of an antler tine; other times it's less concrete, like the whisper of hair against a branch or the foggy hint of exhaled breath. It's easy in the deep, impenetrable silence of the Northern timber to feel your pulse jump and breath quicken. It's easier to believe that there's something close.

I waited.

Then, suddenly, he was there, standing massively before me. The buck had risen silently from his hidden bed, his impossibly thick neck thrust high—defiant. As the deer had risen, so too had the rifle in my hands risen to my shoulder. For seconds we stood facing each other at a scant 50 yards. Then I squeezed gently on the trigger and ended the most unusual hunting season of my life.

You see, that buck was my third trophy whitetail in three days of hunting. Each was taken in the bush, and each was harvested one-on-one by a different hunting method. The first, a nontypical 5×6 from Alberta, I'd taken while still-hunting; the second, a massive 8×8 nontypical from Saskatchewan, I'd taken from a tree stand; and the third, the high-racked Saskatchewan 10-pointer just described, I'd taken while tracking.

Now, I remember finding a $20 bill once, and another time I threw double sixes on four consecutive casts of the dice, but I've never really been lucky to speak of. My luckiest day was the day my wife agreed to marry me. And though I may never be that lucky again, never in my wildest imagination did I believe that I might take three trophy whitetail bucks in one hunting

season—let alone in three days of hunting.

Still, lucky or not, every year for five years I'd made the pilgrimage from my home in British Columbia to Saskatchewan and Alberta to try my hand at taking the whitetail of a lifetime. Though I'd met with some success in the past, never had I even seen more than two trophy-class animals in one season.

The year 1991 was different!

My annual hunt started, as it usually did, with an all-night treacherous drive across the continental divide into Alberta. By leaving my house Saturday after work, I was able to reach my destination a couple of hours northeast of Edmonton by Sunday afternoon. As expected, guide Larry Miller was waiting for me when I arrived, and just as predicted, within minutes we were in Miller's half-ton and scouting. (Provincial regulations prohibit Sunday hunting in the area we were in.)

A few years before, Miller had taken me on a similar tour and had pointed out two spots where he'd said a buck might show up. The first spot had looked good, but the second had appeared as unpromising as any I'd ever seen.

"You should sit there," Miller had said, motioning to the hopeless-looking spot. "I saw a huge set of tracks crossing there last week."

After I'd quizzed him for a few minutes and discovered that he'd never actually seen a buck at the spot—and in fact didn't even know if the buck that had made the tracks sported a large rack or a small one—I'd declined his offer.

"Thanks, anyway," I'd replied, smiling my best patronizing smile. "But I'll take the other spot."

To make a long story short, Miller had shot a 14-pointer with a 30-inch-wide spread the next day at the spot I'd turned down. Now when he tells me to sit at a spot, I do just that.

Our scouting tour took us through some beautiful timbered country, much of it capable of hiding a fleet of Boeing 747s, and certainly a whitetail buck. Eventually, though, Miller stopped the truck on a snow-covered dirt road overlooking a stubble field. The field was nestled up against a deep, forested ravine. Because it was the beginning of the third week of the hunting season, neither one of us expected to see any deer until minutes before dark—and we didn't.

"Tomorrow morning I'm going to drop you off here in the dark and you're going to sneak down to the ravine," Miller told me. "At first light you'll start stillhunting back toward the top end of the ravine, but always make sure you stay within shooting distance of the field." He looked at me to see if I intended to protest. "I'll see you at noon."

"Why noon?" I asked with a frown. (I like to be in the bush all day.)

"You'll have your big buck by then," he said. He smiled and waited to see if I had any comment. "That is unless, of course, you have other ideas?"

"Nope." I wasn't about to make the same mistake twice.

Of course, that's not to say that I believed him. I'd never taken an Alberta buck scoring more than 140 Boone and Crockett Club points in any of the previous four seasons, and I certainly didn't believe that I would do so by noon the following day.

Regardless, the graying dawn the next morning found me deep in the ravine. I wasn't sure whether I would freeze to death or get lost first, but I had no doubt that stillhunting would be no easy chore. The forest floor was covered with a 2-inch layer of frozen snow. It was like walking over a million cornflakes, each with its own tiny megaphone.

Still, I had had success under similar conditions before. The deer had to walk through the snow, too, and when they did, they wouldn't be able to hear for their own noise. I knew that if I took it slow enough, there'd be a chance.

Two hours later and only a couple of hundred yards from my starting position, I was beginning to think that there was less of a chance than I'd

originally thought. I took a careful look around and then stooped to examine an old set of tracks.

I was still looking at the tracks a minute later when a squirrel chattered just out of sight around a knob to my right. Instantly, I was alert. From where the squirrel had sounded off, it would have been very difficult to see me, and I figured that if it wasn't me that the squirrel was scolding, then it had to be something else just on the other side of the knob.

As quietly as my frozen joints would allow, I rose high enough to see over the knob. The buck must have been aware that something wasn't right as well, because just as I was craning my neck to see over the hill, so, too, was he. As soon as we made eye-to-antler contact, he was gone.

Any deer hunter knows that a running whitetail in thick timber doesn't present much of a shot, so making what was to prove to be a fortuitous decision, I opted to hold my fire and instead keep my eyes peeled for glimpses of the buck as he made his way through the trees.

Once out of sight, the buck angled to circle around me. Unfortunately for him, however, I had anticipated the move and was watching with my binoculars as far back into the forest as I could see.

Nearly five minutes later, my vigilance—or gamble, rather—paid off, and I was rewarded with the barest glimpse of antler and hide through a tiny gap in the trees far beyond where my unassisted eyes could have ever picked up movement. By kneeling down and bobbing my head around for the best view, I managed to pick out another clear channel about 100 yards ahead of where I'd spotted the sneaking buck.

Minutes later I was beginning to believe that the buck had changed course and was heading directly away, but just then the telltale nose and rack of the big whitetail filled the 3-inch gap I had my rifle scope trained on. This time when the buck's shoulder entered the gap, I squeezed a shot off.

I lost the sight picture immediately, but was confident that the bullet had flown true as I made my way the 150 yards to where I'd last seen the deer. I found the heavy-racked buck lying within yards of where he'd been when I'd shot. He was my first true trophy Alberta whitetail—with eleven scorable points and a field-dressed weight of nearly 220 pounds.

It was 10:30 A.M.

Because the limit in Alberta is one deer, I was tagged out; so three days later, I bid adieu to Miller and made my way east to Saskatchewan. I intended to hunt in the southern half of the province where the year before I had taken a tremendous 13-point buck with my muzzleloader. Unfortunately, I had to wait until the beginning of the following week to hunt, so I decided that a tour of the northern half of the province was in order in the meantime.

In this area the season was already open, and the whitetail limit is two per year. This is the region that sportsmen from the United States are limited to for deer hunting, and it is also home to some of the largest whitetails in the world. Coincidentally, the northern portion of Saskatchewan also happens to be some of the most difficult country to hunt. Almost every square mile of the region is covered with timber, swamps, or lakes, and without farmland to draw the deer out, it is basically futile to try to pattern a big buck there. One advantage, however, is that with tens of thousands of square miles to get lost in, a hunter can head out for days and never see another hunter's track.

Never having had the chance, much less the reason, to bother hunting in the North Country, I must say that I was impressed. Everywhere I looked I saw deer tracks. Every road I walked down I found sign in the form of large rubs.

I also found the locals more than accommodating with information, and from them I learned that, for the most part, the American hunters who ventured into the area each year seldom went home empty-handed. I was also told about a rancher in the area who seldom denied permission to hunt. I was at his place first thing in the morning.

I'm happy to report that the locals hadn't steered me wrong, and after gaining permission, I walked the perimeter of one corner of the 10-square-mile forested ranch. (It was Sunday, which means no hunting in Saskatchewan.) During my walk, I saw several does and a small buck—nothing big—but what I did find was a spot between two small lakes that seemed to serve as a natural funnel. More importantly, I found several sets of fresh tracks belonging to at least one large buck.

In principle, my plan was easy enough: All I had to do was set up my portable tree stand and wait for a big buck to show up. In practice, however, in the sub-zero temperature, pulling off the plan proved to be a real test of endurance.

By 10 the next morning, I was cold; by 11, I was positively frozen. But that didn't worry me nearly as much as how I started to feel by noon. After that, I started to warm up and feel drowsy. For an

The author took this massive 5×6 nontypical while stillhunting on crusted snow in the Alberta bush. The buck field-dressed at close to 220 pounds. Photograph by Jim Shockey

instant I believed that I was suffering from hypothermia, but then I realized that snow, which had begun falling early in the morning, now covered the quilted blanket I was wrapped in like a big fluffy overcoat. Great insulation and not bad camouflage, I thought, as long as the deer didn't get suspicious of a 220-pound snowy owl sitting in a tree.

Eight hours after I'd put up my stand, I saw my first deer—a doe. She crossed in front of me within 40 yards. Several minutes later, another doe and two fawns walked by, and then a third mature doe. This last

The author's whitetail trophy triple consisted of (from left) a Saskatchewan 16-pointer, an Alberta 11-pointer, and a Saskatchewan 10-pointer. Photograph by Jim Shockey

year off his land. The next morning I stopped at another ranch house 20 miles away and received permission to hunt. Snow had continued falling until first light, and I knew that conditions would be perfect for tracking.

As luck would have it, I hit fresh tracks shortly after entering the woods. The buck had evidently crossed in front of me less than an hour earlier. For three more hours, I followed as stealthily as I was able. The buck was obviously in full rut, his tracks veering from one side to the other as he

doe was constantly looking behind her as she walked.

I wasn't surprised when the buck appeared a short time later, his nose thrust out toward the doe and his head slightly cocked to one side. What did surprise me, though, was the buck's size. He dwarfed the doe. And his rack! I stopped counting typical points at 10 and started counting sticker points. At 6 points, I decided it was time to move. The buck stopped in his tracks 30 yards away when the snow that had been covering me fell to the ground with a loud oomph. And at the rifle report, I had my second trophy whitetail of the season.

This second buck was the largest-bodied whitetail I've ever taken, weighing nearly 300 pounds field-dressed. The bases of his 16-point rack measured 6 inches in circumference. He was a real wall-hanger.

I thanked the farmer as I left, respecting his wish that no hunter take more than one buck per

checked out deer beds long since vacated. Eventually, he must have tired of his travels and decided to bed for a few hours. And it was at his bed, tucked into the underbrush at the top of a small knoll, that I found him, as I recounted at the beginning of this story.

This last buck completed my most memorable hunting season to date, rounding out what I call my whitetail trophy triple. He weighed upward of 250 pounds on the hoof, and sported a near-perfect, 22-inch-wide 10-point rack. Only a broken brow tine kept his heavy rack from scoring well into the 150s (by Boone and Crockett standards).

Now, I realize that my odds of finding another $20 bill are pretty slim, and I'll probably never roll double sixes four times in a row again, but there is no doubt that the odds of either of these things happening are a whole lot better than are my chances of ever again shooting three trophy bucks, in three days, by three ways.

Secrets of the Bog Bucks

By Jeff Murray

It was the only time Frank Hanson had nodded off while on a deer stand. Like other victims of buck fever, Hanson rarely dozes in the field. Fortunately, this nap was a light one. A familiar noise jarred him back to hair-trigger consciousness, and the drama he was dreaming of moments before began to unfold in the bog around him.

Slosh, slosh, slosh. Slosh, slosh, slosh.

The sweet sound of a heavy animal in the marsh grew louder, and Hanson drew a nocked arrow to the corner of his mouth. Instinctively, the bow pointed in the direction where the deer was likely to emerge.

Hanson had every reason to believe that history would repeat itself. For five consecutive seasons, he had an 8-point or better buck within range at this cherished hotspot. Three of them ended up on the meat pole, with one making the record books.

Slosh, slosh. Thump, thump, thump.

A whitetail appeared with panting breath and mud-coated legs. Just a few more steps and Hanson would be in bowhunter heaven—the deer would be standing broadside at 20 paces.

Suddenly Hanson relaxed. This was not the deer he was after. Its neck was sleek and streamlined, and its headgear sported three, maybe four, thumb-sized points on each side. After nibbling on a few dogwood shoots, the young buck curled up under a nearby cedar.

Though Hanson would not draw his bow again that morning, the day was made. His favorite deer stand was still clicking, and it would only be a matter of time before it received the respectable visitor he was waiting for.

What is Frank Hanson onto? Literally, a treasure island for big bucks. Hanson's deer spot is indeed an island, but not in the strictest sense. It's surrounded on all sides not by water, but by swampland.

Hunters typically lump all swamps together. They consider them wet, dense, forbidden jungles where deer often go, but which present hunters with limited opportunities for a decent shot at their prey. In reality, however, such generalizations neglect the varieties in terrain and flora peculiar to each swamp. Some hunting techniques exploit these peculiarities better than others.

A swamp island hunt typically targets a lone, dominant buck. Locate his access routes, and you're ready for ambush. Large, breeding bucks can require up to 3 or 4 quarts of water per day—one reason why they gravitate to low-lying swamplands. Photographs by Charles S. Alsheimer

In many swamps, small humps of high ground rise out of the mire much like a reef in a lake, creating what is commonly referred to as "swamp islands." Corresponding to the rise in elevation is a change in vegetation, from marsh to upland cover. Some swamp islands may only be a couple of acres, though others might encompass as much as 10 acres or more.

For all their variety, however, swamp islands have one thing in common: When the hunting season kicks into high gear, they're one of the first places a dominant whitetail buck will seek refuge.

The first time you step onto a buck's swamp island you'll be amazed at the concentration of deer sign. The area will reek of deer musk, and there will be beds, droppings, rubs, and scrapes — more than you'll see on a dozen ridges. Why? Because this is where some bucks spend all of their daylight hours when hunting pressure mounts.

There's no doubt that swamp islands are vital to deer survival in many populated areas of the country. Without them, many bucks would probably never make it beyond their second year. And because of them, more bucks die of old age than most hunters would care to admit.

Nevertheless, swamp hunting is no guarantee for success. No big-buck tactic is. But for the deer hunter willing to do a little extra legwork to get in deep, swamp hunting is as close to a sure bet as any other technique.

A strong statement? Perhaps. Yet no other bedding area meets so many of the fundamental needs a buck has.

Take safety. Many hunters underestimate the concern bucks have for around-the-clock safety, especially while they're rutting. Though bucks make occasional mistakes during the mating season, don't count on it. The older a buck gets, the more experience he has to draw upon to avoid danger zones and to sort out pockets of safety. Merely hunting the rut isn't a "strategy," because rutting whitetails aren't the love-crazed animals some make them out to be. Safety is the first priority for deer. That's why they usually disappear after opening day.

Here's an interesting illustration of how elusive whitetail bucks can be. A friend of mine, Claude

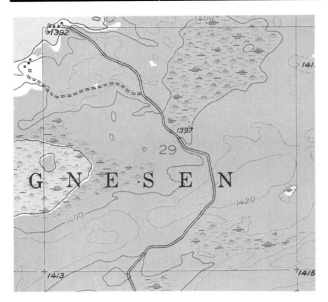

Topographic maps are an invaluable aid to those prepared to go in deep for their buck. As a timesaver, they allow hunters to scout a wider range of territory and to be more selective when choosing potential hotspots to scout on foot. Map: Courtesy of U.S. Geological Survey

Pollington, owns a deer ranch in Michigan. It's heavily wooded, with a mile-square fenced enclosure on one end. After bowhunting both areas, I seriously doubted that there were as many bucks in the enclosure as Pollington claimed. Several yearlings and 2½-year-old bucks had skulked by my tree stand, but I hadn't seen the respectable racks of which he had boasted.

But Pollington was right about how many big bucks lived on his land. Late one evening we drove out to a feeding bin where several heavy-beamed bucks stood in the long shadows of a full moon.

"At the end of each hunting season, I take a little deer census," Pollington whispered as we admired the animals. "We drive the deer from one end of the pen to the other. I know every animal by name, and I know every inch of that pen. Still, each year a big buck I've never seen shows up from Lord knows where. Deer are more slippery than we give them credit for."

Bucks "disappear" because they filter into places that most hunters overlook or avoid, like swamp islands. Even when hunters manage to invade these areas, their approach is hardly stealthy:

horsehair brush and oozing muck telegraph an intruder's every move. Indeed, these moated castles are nearly hunter-proof. It's no wonder big bucks head for them when the heat is on.

Seclusion is another big-buck requirement swamp islands meet. Though many hunters expect breeding bucks to follow does most of the day, in actuality breeding bucks are loners in the autumn. In fact, they're basically loners the rest of the year as well, when they form social groups apart from does. True, you might see an occasional rutting buck on the tail of a doe in estrus, but he's really the exception. A recent hunt in Nebraska illustrated this point perfectly.

My hunt on Dick Minor's ranch, near Gordon, occurred on the second week of the season, coinciding perfectly with the peak of the rut. After getting the lay of the land by pickup, I spent the rest of my time scouting on foot.

Glassing with high-powered binoculars from a downwind position, I probed the most promising side hills and brush pockets on the sprawling, 100-square-mile ranch. Though I counted more than 200 animals (some were mule deer), I saw only two stiff-legged bucks chasing does. Both were near the edge of grainfields, just before sunrise. How many bucks did I see bedding near does? Not one.

Soon I had further evidence of bucks' loner tendencies. The Minors have their own airstrip, and Dick Minor Jr. invited me on a short plane ride to deliver supplies to a neighbor. As we flew over the land I'd just scouted, I continued to count deer. The largest buck I saw (easily 150 to 160 Boone and Crockett Club points) was nowhere near any does. He was hidden in a willow clump within a large cattail swamp—a classic swamp island—that skirted the Snake River.

Minor yelled over the roaring Cessna, "You won't see any bucks bedded with does during the day. They're the opposite of muleys. Whitetail bucks avoid does until it's time to breed them at night."

This thinking doesn't jibe with the mainline whitetail strategy that suggests that if you hunt near does, eventually a buck will appear. The age-old tactic seems to work often enough to perpetuate the idea, but the odds for bagging a big buck favor those who hunt areas that bucks stake out exclusively for themselves. Swamp islands, where available, top the list.

In addition to safety and seclusion, swamp islands attract bucks with their nutritional offerings. Though they typically lose weight during the rut, bucks do eat. And most swamp islands offer the lush browse they crave, evidenced by the nipped-off buckbrush and large droppings I often find in these pockets.

The water available in swamps is another appeal of the islands. A large, breeding buck consumes from 3 to 4 quarts per day. Although deer can survive on water from vegetation, dew, or snow, a reliable source of water in a bedding area is an added attraction to deer—particularly for bucks that bed all day after nocturnal romancing.

With so many amenities available to deer in these concentrated pockets, it's easy to see why swamp islands are buck magnets. Yet, for all their apparent comforts, swamp islands lack one element that is essential to a buck's autumn routine: mating partners.

This deficiency, though it may seem a liability to hunting swamp islands, is actually a hunter's greatest asset. The mating urge guarantees that a buck will leave his daytime lair and return to it *on a regular basis* during the rut, a routine that presents island hunters with high-volume travel patterns and logical ambush sites. Before you can exploit these hotspots, however, you need to find where they're located on your hunting range.

One of the most effective ways to locate swamp islands is by using a common contour or topographic map. A map will allow you to scout a wider hunting range and be more selective in choosing sweet spots to scout on foot.

As mentioned, swamp islands generally provide excellent habitat for bucks. Depending on the surrounding terrain, however, their actual deer activity can vary widely. Using topographic maps can cut your scouting mistakes, and your scouting time, in half.

Serious swamp hunting strategy calls for the selection of anywhere from 15 to 20 stands each fall. Why so many? Three reasons.

First, the wind must be absolutely perfect over the island you plan to hunt. These are bedding areas for bucks, not feeding or breeding areas, so there are no second chances. If disturbed from an island, a buck will leave, and chances are you won't see him for the rest of the season. Therefore, whatever it takes to avoid being winded is worth the effort. If you have to take an out-of-the-way route, portage a canoe, or pack in waders to approach your stand downwind, do so. If these aren't feasible, hunt another stand.

Dave Hartman, an avid Wisconsin bowhunter, has taken his share of big bucks off swamp islands. "I won't go in if the wind isn't strong and steady out of one direction," says Hartman. "If it's light or variable, I just won't risk it. If I have to wait two weeks to hunt a particular stand, no matter how hot it looks or how many bucks I've taken off it, I'll wait."

Second, monitoring multiple stands gives an accurate picture of how many rutting bucks an area supports. Actively breeding bucks make a lot of rubs during the rut (the latest research indicates up to 15 per day). A swamp island that is saturated with fresh rubs suggests that a decent buck is using it. The opposite also holds true. If you're hunting an island without rubs, you're probably wasting your time.

Furthermore, if rubbing activity at your stand decreases as the hunting season wears on, you can bet your buck is spending less time there. Your best move might be to look at other spots you've scouted. That is, if you've scouted elsewhere. Locating backup stands ahead of time goes a long way to avoiding a season of frustration.

Finally, extra stands help eliminate burnout. Some hunters get fidgety and simply can't sit in one place all day. Hartman has learned to overcome this syndrome by rotating stands. Granted, the chances of tipping off a buck increase with additional trips to and from his stands, but by checking out several areas he can concentrate on the hottest one.

When buying a topographic map, select one with a scale of 1:24,000 minimum. A detailed map is especially important for scouting swamp islands because terrain variations of 10 feet or less do not appear on many maps. Remember, all a buck needs for bedding is a rise of a couple of feet above surrounding swampland.

Familiarize yourself with the map's legend, especially the marsh symbol, which indicates swampland. Contour lines connect areas of equal elevation. The closer contour lines are to each other, the steeper the rise in elevation. The map's different colors indicate whether the ground cover is open field (white on the map pictured), wooded (green), or submerged (blue).

Photograph by Jeff Murray

To find swamp islands on a topo map, use the marsh symbol to locate swampland and then look for contour lines that form small circles of elevation within the swamp. The easiest islands to hunt are those up to five acres in size. Any larger, and buck movements become difficult to pattern and hunting with a partner becomes necessary.

For information on where to obtain topographic maps and aerial photographs, contact the U.S. Geological Survey, ESIC, 507 National Center, Reston, VA 22092 (800-USA-MAPS).

Just as no two swamps are the same, neither are the islands that rise up out of these mires. Using a topo map to locate swamp islands with high buck potential is more than mere guesswork. It's pinpointing terrain and cover that bucks find attractive. Here are three examples:

A. Secluded islands: Always the loner, a mature rutting buck can resist mating until night falls. During the day, find him alone in deep cover.

B. Safety islands: Safety is a buck's number-one concern, even during the rut. Look for island groupings that offer him multiple escape routes.

C. Food islands: Islands near open water and a food source, such as cropland or mast-laden hardwood ridges, are especially attractive to bucks.

Map: Courtesy of U.S. Geological Survey

The location and use of access routes to your stands is critical to hunting swamp islands successfully. Remember that swamp hunting is different from hunting a runway or a natural barrier, where a number of deer from different areas may pass by your blind. By contrast, swamp hunting primarily targets individual bucks. I've taken two deer from the same island within days of each other, but by and large, swamp islands are inhabited by a lone, dominant buck. You must exercise great care as you enter and leave the area in order to be successful.

In addition to scent, noise can prove to be a major obstacle to a stealthy approach. Most marshy areas are replete with dense underbrush, making noiseless travel impossible. A sensible solution is to take your time and make the same natural sounds deer make moving through the brush. Still, constantly defending your face from stubborn branches is no fun. The only alternative is to prune a path, but, as I once learned, this plan can backfire if done improperly.

When I first realized how good swamp island hunting could be, I purchased a gas-operated brusher. I thought that a little swath through the tag alders would end all my access troubles. It only made matters worse. Though I made my cuttings in the early spring, the deer started using "my" path to get to the island! And I soon learned that you can't outwit a mature buck if you share the trail he uses to get to his bedding area. No amount of rubber boots or rubber gloves or cover scent is going to help.

The other consideration to make when accessing swamp islands is timing. It's imperative you arrive well before the buck comes back from his nighttime jaunts. Remember, too, that bucks become increasingly nocturnal as hunting pressure mounts, so you should be settled in well before sunrise (be sure to check applicable local regulations first).

Navigating through the woods in total darkness is hard enough without the added burden of fording extra-thick cover. But Hartman has found a way around this. He draws a map for each spot.

"The key is to sketch out prominent features of the area on a blown-up topo map," he says.

"Then, take compass readings off each landmark to get to the next one. That way you won't have to blaze a trail that could attract hunters or deer. Reflective tape tacked on trees with roofing nails also helps."

Finally, two strategies for advanced swamp-island hunters. Suppose you only have mornings or afternoons to hunt a certain hotspot. How do you know if the buck is already on the island? If he is, you don't dare go in, but if he's still on the prowl, you wouldn't want to miss out.

If the buck enters the swamp from one or two trails, one method is to supervise his comings and goings with an electronic game trail monitor. Another trick is to ambush the buck from a funneling area on high ground bordering the swamp.

Two years ago, Hartman arrowed a dandy 10-point buck that taught him the virtues of the latter tactic.

"From the size of the rubs," Hartman recalls, "I knew a decent buck was using one of my islands, but the knoll was so small I could never sneak onto it without the buck pegging me if he was there. So I perched on top of a finger that pointed into the swamp in hopes of surveying the area and possibly intercepting him on the way in or out.

"One afternoon I got a big break. I heard him come off the island, sloshing through the swamp like a dog retrieving a duck. He managed to get around me as he headed straight for the cornfield. I figured he'd be gone most of the night, so I got in there early the next morning before work. Sure enough, he showed up just after sunrise."

What would Hartman have done if he hadn't connected? "I had a backup plan that I might have to use some day," he said. "I would set up an ambush site downwind from one of the buck's entrance trails right in the middle of the swamp. It wouldn't be easy waiting knee-deep in muck, but when it comes to big bucks anything is worth a try."

If it's a buck you're after, swamp islands are more than worth a try. They provide all the secluded comforts bucks crave and all the promise of a trophy that hunters dream of.

Rattling Whitetails

By Jim Zumbo

If you're like most whitetail hunters, you've probably had your fill of rattling articles. After all, the technique has been so thoroughly discussed in hundreds, perhaps thousands, of magazine stories that it's old news these days. What's so tough and complicated about banging together a set of deer antlers and waiting for a whitetail to come dashing in to check out the ruckus?

Rattling appears to be the simplest of strategies. All you need is a pair of antlers. If you don't have a set of real antlers, several manufacturers offer fake horns that they claim sound better than the real thing.

I've done my share of rattling and have some opinions that may or may not jibe with accepted techniques. I don't believe anything until I've seen it and tried it myself. If a new trick works for me, I'll pass it on—but not until I've actually tested the method.

When I *do* try something new, I like to observe veterans in action, the pros who know what they're doing. That being the case, I set my sights on Murry Burnham to teach me about smacking antlers together. Burnham is often called the father of rattling, a well-deserved title.

I've had the good fortune of hunting with Burnham many times in his home state of Texas and in the Rockies. As one of the founders of the Burnham Brothers game call company, he's as knowledgeable about animal communication as anyone I know.

According to Burnham, the rattling strategy came to light about 40 years ago. No one knows precisely who tried the technique first; perhaps Native Americans were the first rattlers.

Burnham's best guess as to the originator of rattling is the late Paul Young, a car dealer from Laredo, Texas. Young was one of a group of old-timers from deep south Texas who rattled successfully, though secretly.

"Those old boys kept their mouths shut," Burnham told me. "They didn't tell any outsiders about rattling, and it wasn't until a couple of writers started hearing about the technique that rattling got some attention.

"Young and his pals didn't use stands in those days to rattle from," he continued. "They'd just climb up a mesquite tree, bang the antlers together, and the bucks would come running."

Several years ago, Burnham introduced me to rattling in a brushy little valley somewhere in south Texas. I was hidden under a bush on the top of a sloping hill, sitting quietly where I could watch the master. He was about halfway down the slope, behind another bush.

As Burnham began rattling, I looked on with skepticism and curiosity. I'd been reading about rattling for years, and though I believed the technique could work, it hadn't been put to the supreme test—in front of my own eyes.

About two minutes after Burnham began rattling, I saw movement in the brush some 200 yards away. Presently a buck trotted into view, headed straight toward the rattling sound.

I was amazed. The buck seemed to be drawn to the noise as if it were a magnet. I became an instant believer in rattling.

Shouldering my rifle, I followed the buck as he drifted in and out of the vegetation. When I finally got a good look, I saw 8 points on his rack, but his antlers weren't quite what I was looking for.

Putting the rifle down, I watched as Burnham continued to rattle. He'd also spotted the buck, and he was working it in closer. Burnham knew that this was a learning experience for me, that I wanted to see everything there was to see about the technique. Actually, I was more interested in observing deer behavior than shooting a buck. But I'll admit that if a bruiser buck had come

busting out into the Texas countryside, my .30/06 would have been quickly put to work.

The deer stopped about 70 yards out and stared. It appeared to be a standoff. But then Burnham did something interesting. He kicked a big rock loose near his foot, causing it to roll noisily down the slope.

I had to smile at this ploy because it seemed foolish. Yet the buck reacted to the rolling rock and dashed another 30 yards closer. When the deer reappeared, he stopped again, and this time Burnham pulled another trick out of his bag. Rattling the antlers vigorously, he raised them high over his head in full view of the buck. Again I chuckled, and again the buck reacted. Unbelievably, the buck ran within 10 yards of Burnham, seemingly mesmerized by the antlers flashing in the air 7 feet off the ground.

This was too much. I was seeing the master at work, using shenanigans that I'd never heard of. Finally, the buck had had enough, and he disappeared into the brush.

For the next several days, I watched in amazement as Burnham brought in buck after buck. When the hunt was over, I headed north with fond memories and renewed admiration for Burnham's ability as a top-rate hunter.

While I had been with him, Burnham had also debunked a common rattling requirement—namely, the wearing of full camouflage, includ-

Whitetail bucks engage in battle for dominance and the right to breed does. By mimicking these fights, hunters like Gary Roberson lure other bucks in front of the gun. Photographs by Charles S. Alsheimer (left) and Jim Zumbo (right).

A fight between bucks attracts other bucks—and that is why rattling works. Photograph by Leonard Lee Rue III

ing face camo. He'd worn nothing on his face and had made no serious attempt to cover it.

Some rattling experts will tell you to keep the antlers low as you work them so that the approaching buck doesn't see movement and spot you. Burnham had totally ignored this fundamental rule too, bringing in buck after buck by clashing the antlers together as high over his head as he could reach.

Seeing this trick left me spellbound. To me, there is no smarter animal in North America than a whitetail buck, yet these deer were totally fooled by a pair of antlers held by human hands. Not only that, but the antlers were easily 7 or 8 feet in the air in a totally unnatural position. (Of course, I'd use this trick only on private land where I knew there were no other hunters. Safety should always be the foremost concern whenever you are imitating the sounds of game animals.)

The rattling concept is simple. Whitetail bucks commonly engage in battle as they attempt to gain dominance in the herd. The objective of the warring is does, and most biologists feel that by slugging it out, the biggest, strongest bucks will win the right to breed, thus passing on their superior genes.

So why is a fight between two bucks attractive to other bucks? Perhaps male deer are aroused or stimulated by the action and want to challenge battling bucks to ensure their own position in the herd. Or, perhaps they're just curious about what's going on and are attracted merely as spectators—possibly interested in the identity of the combatants, or even in breeding the doe being fought over while the other suitors are preoccupied. Another theory is that a dominant buck who feels superior in his home range might get highly irritated by two rivals skirmishing in his territory, becoming upset enough to dash in and drive away the intruders.

Whatever the reason, rattling works—I can assure you of that. Curiously, many hunters,

especially Northerners, believe that rattling is strictly a Texas strategy, or at least one that works only in the South. That's not true. I think this attitude is based on the fact that few hunters outside Texas give the method a good try.

I know hunters from New York to Michigan to Montana who have successfully rattled in bucks. I've done it in a number of Northern spots, including Saskatchewan—and there isn't much whitetail country farther north than that.

Not too long ago, while visiting a hunting lodge in Georgia, I was surprised when the lodge manager indicated that rattling wasn't done much in his area because it was basically a Texas technique. Even more interesting is the fact that many Texans believe the technique works only in south Texas. Now then, if you aren't familiar with the Lone Star State, you should know that south Texas, also known as the brush country, harbors the biggest bucks in the state. To carry it further, that region produces many of the biggest bucks in the world. That's where rattling started, and that's where many people believe it ends.

In the fall of 1991, I hunted the Texas hill country with Gary Roberson, an affable man who purchased the Burnham Brothers company from Murry Burnham. Burnham was supposed to join us on the hunt, but when extreme flooding closed highways in the area, he was only able to drive within 5 miles of the area before being stopped by a swollen river that raged for several days. Burnham had had high praise for Roberson when we'd arranged the hunt. "He's as good as they get when it comes to rattling," Burnham had told me on the phone. I soon learned that he was right.

After five days of hunting, I collected a whitetail buck from a selection of 20 that Roberson rattled up. The buck was a respectable 9-pointer—not huge by Texas brush country standards, but a nice buck for the hill country, which is known more for its quantity of bucks than for the quality.

Interestingly enough, other hunters on the ranch were amazed at Roberson's success with rattling. Because we weren't in south Texas, most of them assumed the method wouldn't work. Roberson made them believers, however, and by the end of the week most of the others had rattled in bucks of their own.

Roberson's favorite time to rattle is before the peak of the rut. "The bucks seem to have more vigor and are more aggressive at this time," he said. "Once the rut is in full swing, most of the mature bucks are accompanying does; it's tough to pull them away. After the peak of the rut, bucks are tired and hungry. They'll respond to rattling, but they'll approach a little slower and with a bit more caution.

"I prefer to rattle at first light," he continued. "My second choice is last light. If I'm in an area where there's plenty of room and little hunting pressure, I'll rattle all day. I like to start on the downwind side of the spot I'm hunting, rattling and moving into the wind until I either run out of land or shooting light."

Roberson's rattling positions are about 600 yards apart. He claims that a buck may hear him rattle from a distance but might not come in because the "battle" isn't in that deer's territory. If Roberson moves into the buck's area and rattles again, the deer is apt to come in charging.

Originally a skeptic, the author was sold on rattling when buck after buck, including this 9-pointer, was "horned" in. Photograph by Jim Zumbo

Concerning rattling antlers themselves, Roberson uses both real antlers and synthetics that he produces. He disagrees with hunters who saw the tips off the tines of their rattling horns. He leaves the tips intact, but he does saw off the eye guards to prevent injury to himself when he uses the antlers.

"I like to actually twist the antlers more than hit them together," Roberson said. "Once I start rattling I keep on going, stopping only briefly to rest my hands. Many times I've watched approaching bucks stop when I quit rattling. As soon as I start again, the bucks continue their advance."

Roberson doesn't often use a grunt call when rattling, as some other hunters do. He'll use the call only if a buck hangs up and won't exit heavy cover. He'll also use only one kind of scent: that of a buck.

There's a lot more to rattling than what you might think. The most important aspect is to have faith. Don't believe what you hear about rattling not working where you hunt. Give the technique a really good try—a *really* good try. Watch the wind, be cautious not to alert deer while getting to your rattling spot, and rattle from lots of positions.

Don't waver if your pals think you're crazy. Keep up your efforts and trust in the technique. The last laugh will be on your buddies when you drag that rattled-in buck to camp.

Crazy Week Whitetails

By Charles Alsheimer

When I was growing up on a farm, sage hunters always talked about mid-November and the whitetail rut. And I, like so many other hunters, bought into the idea that the best time to hunt whitetails was during the peak of the rut, which in my area was from November 10 to 25. Certainly this is an excellent time to hunt big bucks. But there is an even more productive time to hunt whitetails, especially trophy bucks.

Just before the peak of the whitetail rut, there is a period of time I call the crazy week. It often lasts from 7 to 10 days, and during this time whitetail bucks go absolutely ballistic. When bucks are caught up in the frenzy of the crazy week, all kinds of opportunities open to the hunter who has done his homework.

Technically, a whitetail buck can breed does from the time it peels velvet until its antlers are cast in the late winter. But it takes two to tango, and north of the 40th parallel (which runs through the Pennsylvania/Maryland border in the East and through northern California in the West), the majority of does do not come into estrus until mid-to-late November.

In September, whitetail bucks start rubbing their antlers, and sparring activity increases. As September blends into October, bucks begin making scrapes, and by mid-October, a few whitetail does come into estrus and are bred. This causes what I refer to as a false rut because there aren't enough does in heat to go around. This builds frustration among the bucks and releases a flurry of rutting activity.

Research by wildlife biologist J.M. McMillin has shown that a whitetail buck's testicular volume and serum testosterone level peak around November 1. As a result, bucks are seemingly overflowing with hormones by late October. With few does in estrus, they begin covering as much

In the days leading up to the peak of the whitetail rut, bucks go bonkers, hormones have the animals in a frenzy, and the hunting is never better. Photograph by Charles Alsheimer

ground as it takes to find breedable does. Rubbing, scraping, and doe chasing reach a fever pitch as November arrives. The crazy week begins.

During the crazy week, whitetail bucks, large and small, let their guard down as their sex drive overtakes them. Because does are not yet willing to breed and flee the aggressive pursuit, bucks are often alone as they travel their territory. They also become less nocturnal and more careless as they relentlessly search for receptive does.

The crazy week ends when the bulk of does come into estrus. Almost overnight, rubbing and

scraping activities diminish as the breeding begins. Receptive does are abundant and a buck will often "hole up" with a doe for up to 72 hours.

Several years ago I had a ringside seat to this hole-up phenomenon while shooting photographs on a large estate which was off-limits to hunting. It was mid-November. An inch of snow covered the ground, and the rut was nearing its peak. Around noon, while I was sitting next to a blowdown, a big 10-point buck trailed a doe through a clearing 50 yards from me. The doe was not yet in estrus, so she went under a deadfall to escape the buck's advances. For the next three hours the buck chased off seven different bucks who also had been attracted to the female. Before the day was over, I photographed the buck breeding the doe while all seven bucks watched from a distance.

When I came back the next day, the eight bucks were still near the doe. Their breeding instincts were heated, and the presence of this doe was the driving force in their minds. This is typical behavior during the peak of the rut, and an important factor when hunting. If a hunter does not have a hot doe in his neighborhood during the peak of the rut, there is a high probability the area will be devoid of bucks until a doe in heat moves in.

The key to pinpointing the crazy week is knowing when the whitetail rut peaks. Substantial research has determined whitetail breeding dates across the United States, and the crazy week generally begins 7 to 10 days before peak breeding dates.

A study by wildlife biologist Robert McDowell pinpointed peak whitetail breeding dates based on latitude. McDowell's study revealed that the farther south one goes, the less predictable the whitetail rut becomes.

For the most part, below the 36th parallel (south of North Carolina) the rut is drawn out. Breeding can start as early as August and last until February. There are exceptions, however, and south Texas is one of them. Since 1989, I've killed four whitetails in the 140 Boone and Crockett Club point class in far south Texas, where the peak of the rut is around Christmas. All four were taken during the crazy week phase from December 14 to 20. One I rattled in, and the others were taken while they were on the move.

In the whitetail-rich provinces of Canada, which lie above the 48th parallel, the whitetail rut is late in November and condensed into a short time. In the whitetail's Northern range, the crazy week's peak can fall anywhere from November 10 to 15. So, although rut dates vary from state to state, my experience reveals that the crazy week exists, in varying degrees, throughout the continent.

A tool every serious whitetail hunter should have is the "Whitetail Deer Population Map" published by Information Outfitters (1995 Daniel Lane, Yulee, FL 32097; 904-277-4046). The map shows deer densities throughout the United States and each state's rut dates. Information Outfitters also publishes a "Whitetail Deer Life History Chart," which includes important biological and behavioral data that can be of help to deer hunters.

As a hunter and photographer, I live for the crazy week and plan my photography and hunting around it. I'm primarily a scrape hunter, and I set my stands near these markers. I incorporate a number of techniques to go along with scrape hunting. Buck scent lures, rattling, and grunting are techniques I love. However, scouting and setting up my ambush are what make the other strategies work.

Scraping begins and increases in late October and early November at the onset of the crazy week. During this time, I try to look for two things. I search for areas frequented by several doe groups—the more the better. The does will become buck magnets as the rut approaches. I also look for transition zones, the areas lying between feeding and bedding sites. In the process, I attempt to zero in on the most heavily used scrape—called a primary scrape—in the area's transition zone.

I also try to find the primary scrape (or scrapes) in areas offering a fair amount of cover, because bucks tend to visit them more during daylight hours. Once the crazy week arrives, a primary scrape located in a transition zone will become a hub of activity as lovesick bucks search for breedable does.

From mid-October until the peak of the rut, I try to make the primary scrape as attractive as possible. To keep a whitetail buck interested in a scrape, I place a scent canister above the licking branch. To keep things fresh, I add scent to the can every other day and also put a little scent in the scrape.

I place my tree stand 40 to 60 yards from the scrape and select a tree surrounded by fairly thick cover. The thick vegetation enables me to camouflage my movements better when rattling. I don't try to set up closer than 40 yards from a scrape because most mature bucks merely scent-check a scrape during daylight hours rather than walking right to it. This placement puts me in a better position to intercept the buck as he moves by the scrape.

November 4, 1989 in New York state was the type of day every bowhunter looks forward to: cool, overcast, and no wind—perfect for a crazy week experience. At about 2:30 P.M. I headed for my stand. About 75 yards from it, I applied buck lure to the bottom of my rubber boots and proceeded to make a scent trail through the woods. I quietly walked 50 yards past the stand before backtracking and climbing into the tree stand. About 50 yards away in a grove of white pines was a very active scrape I had been doctoring for more than two weeks.

My plan was to wait about a half-hour, go through a rattling sequence, then wait another

RUT DATA*

STATE	RANGE	PEAK	STATE	RANGE	PEAK
Alabama	Oct.25-Feb.21	Jan.	Minnesota	Sept.15-Feb.	Nov.1-15
Arizona	Nov.-Feb.	Mid Jan.	Mississippi	Nov.20-Mar.15	Dec.5-Jan.15
Arkansas (north)	Oct.21-Dec.17	Nov.5	Missouri	Oct.-Jan.	Nov.10-25
(central)	Oct.15 -Jan.1	Nov.15	Montana	Oct.-Dec.	Mid Nov.
(south)	Oct.25-Feb.6	Nov.27	Nebraska	Oct.-Feb.	Nov.8-Dec.12
Colorado	Oct.15-Dec.15	Nov.15-30	New Hampshire	Oct.-Dec.	Nov.15-25
Connecticut	Oct.-Jan.	Nov.15-30	New Jersey (north)	Oct.-Jan.	Nov.1-17
Delaware	Oct.-Dec.	Nov.1-21	(south)	Oct.-Jan.	Nov.10-30
Florida (north)	Oct.-Dec.	Oct.15-Nov.15	New Mexico	Nov.-Feb.	Dec.21-Jan.7
(northwest)	Jan.-Apr.	Feb.10-Mar.15	New York	Sept.-Jan.	Nov.10-30
(central)	Sept-Nov.	Sept. 20-0ct.20	North Carolina	Oct.-Dec.	Nov.7-15
(south)	July-Oct.	July 20-Aug.20	North Dakota	Oct.15-Jan.20	Nov.20-Dec.10
(Keys)	Sept.-Feb.	Oct.	Ohio	Oct.-Jan.	Nov.1-15
Georgia (coastal)	Sept.-Jan.	Early Oct.	Oklahoma	Oct.-Dec.	Nov.18-25
(north)	Sept.-Jan.	Late Nov.	Oregon (east)	Nov.1-Dec.15	Nov.10-30
(midwest)	Oct.-Dec.	Mid Nov.	(west)	Nov.1-Dec.30	Nov.15-30
(southeast)	Sept.-Dec.	Late Oct.	Pennsylvania	Oct.-Jan.	Nov.5-20
Idaho	Oct.21-Nov.28	Nov.10-15	Rhode Island	Oct.-Dec.	Nov.10-25
Illinois	Oct.-Dec.	Nov.10-20	South Carolina	Sept.-Dec.	Oct.15-Nov.15
Indiana	Oct.-Dec.	Nov.1-20	South Dakota	Oct.-Jan.	Nov.18-Dec.7
lowa	Oct.-Jan.	Nov.2-23	Tennessee	Oct.-Jan.	Nov.15-Dec.15
Kansas	Oct. -Feb.	Nov.15-30	Texas (south)	Nov.-Feb.	Dec.15-Jan.10
Kentucky	Oct.15-Dec.15	Nov.5-20	(central and north)	Oct.-Jan.	Nov.1-30
Louisiana (east)	Nov.-Feb.	Dec.-Mid Jan.	Vermont	Nov.-Dec.	Nov.15-25
(northwest)	Sept.-Jan.	Mid Oct.-Mid Nov	Virginia	Oct.-Jan.	Nov.1-17
(southwest)	Aug.-Dec.	Mid Sept.-Oct.	Washington	Nov.1-Dec.10	Nov.20-Dec. 7
Maine	Oct.-Dec.	Nov.15-30	West Virginia	Oct.-Jan.	Nov.10-23
Maryland	Oct.-Dec.	Oct.21-Nov.10	Wisconsin	Oct.-Jan.	Nov.1-15
Massachusetts	Oct.-Jan.	Nov.5-22	Wyoming	Oct.-Dec.	Nov.15-Dec.7
Michigan	Oct.-Jan.	Mid Nov.			

Table: Courtesy of Information Outfitters, Inc.

* Range and peak periods can vary due to complex and interrelated factors of population dynamics: sex ratio, herd density, and buck age structure; and nutritional influences: forage, mast crop, weather, and carrying capacity.

CRAZY CONDITIONS

Although rut dates are fairly predictable from a biological standpoint, the whitetail's coat, the moon, and the weather can play an important part in pinpointing the peak of the crazy week.

By the time late October rolls around, whitetails have their winter coat. If the first of November arrives and it is unseasonably warm, bucks will move very little during daylight hours because their system simply cannot stand the heat. It's kind of like a person wearing a down coat in 90 F temperatures.

During periods of warm weather, the craziness will take place only during the coolness of night. Because of this, I've become a weather watcher. Wherever I hunt the crazy week, I hope for cool temperatures and a rapidly rising or falling barometric pressure. When cool weather fronts dovetail with the whitetail's peak hormonal level, the result is sheer excitement in the woods

My experience has shown that the effect moon phases have on the crazy week depends on where one hunts. In the North, where the whitetail rut is condensed, a full moon seems to have little effect on a buck's movement during daylight hours. Once Northern whitetails start their breeding frenzy, the only thing that seems to affect their movement is warm weather, which will decrease their daytime activity, and heavy rainfall, which can slow down rutting activity.

But in the South, where the rut is drawn out, a full moon can increase the deer's nocturnal activity. On days following a moonlit night, hunting tends to be slow in the morning and evening. However, it has been my experience that buck activity during midday is considerably higher in such areas during the full moon phase.

hour before rattling again. At 3 P.M. I rattled aggressively for about five minutes and then hung the antlers on a branch. Nothing responded.

For the next hour only chickadees and gray squirrels kept me company. At 4 P.M. I stood up and rattled again. I didn't have to wait long for action. To my right I heard a twig snap in the nearby pine thicket. I wasn't sure what it was but felt confident it was a deer or coyote responding to the rattling. Slowly I raised my grunt tube and grunted softly once.

A beautiful 8-pointer walked out of the pines with his nose on the ground and tail outstretched. He was following the scent trail I had laid down more than an hour before. About 25 yards from me he stopped and curled his lip to enhance his sense of smell. He walked 5 yards ahead into an opening. In one motion, I came to a full draw and released my arrow. My aim looked true, and on impact the big buck bolted and ran back into the pines.

After calming down, I climbed from the stand and went to where the buck was standing when I

shot. From the blood-covered arrow lying on the ground, I knew the hit was good, and after a short tracking effort, I came upon the 8-pointer. The buck had gone less than 75 yards before going down.

Preparation played a big part in the hunt's success, and my use of rattling, grunting, and buck lure techniques made the experience very special. But the real key to my success was the crazy week.

A mature whitetail buck is no pushover and requires all the hunting savvy a hunter can muster. For roughly 50 weeks a year, a buck lives on the edge and cannot survive by making mistakes. But once a year his body chemistry overtakes him and his urge to breed becomes overpowering. During this time, whitetail bucks are on a mission and in the process create the crazy week.

For the serious whitetail hunter, the crazy week is the ultimate. From south Texas to Alberta, it provides hunters one of the most exciting hunting situations on earth, the chase phase of the whitetail rut.

Pushover Deer Drives

By Gary Clancy

Over the years, I've read dozens of articles that have gone into detail on how and where to conduct drives for whitetail deer. Some of these stories have been complete with diagrams indicating the positions of drivers, posters, and deer. A few of the blueprints for whitetail action that I've seen would confuse Gen. Norman Schwarzkopf. Most of these militarylike maneuvers designed to outwit the whitetail deer are a total flop. Complicated drives usually result in confused and disoriented (a nice way of saying lost) drivers, posters left to wonder what happened to the rest of the crew, and deer that must be snickering just a bit as they watch the circus unfold.

So what do I offer you? Yep, another article on deer drives complete with diagrams on how they should work. The difference is that the four drives I'm going to discuss are simple. These drives work with small groups, consisting of two to four hunters. There are no complicated maneuvers, which only serve to confuse party members and make the drive ineffective from the start. These are the drives that my friends and I use when we drive deer.

But a discussion of specific drive plans is worthless without a basic understanding of why drives succeed and why they fail. We need to look at three points: when to drive, where to drive, and how to get posters and drivers into position without alerting every deer in the drive area. Once you have these three points down pat, you can use the four drive plans that I've included in this article—or drives of your own concoction— to help you and your hunting partners get your sights on more deer.

WHEN TO DRIVE

Drives are the answer when deer are not moving naturally or are being forced to move because of hunting pressure. If there are other hunters in the woods, you are better off sitting on a good stand and letting them push deer past your position. Likewise, it is a good idea to stay on stand during those times when deer are typically moving about—namely, during the early morning and late-afternoon feeding periods and all day long when the rut is in progress.

Weather is also a factor to consider. When it is

In drives involving three or more hunters, it pays to have a drive captain who is familiar with the hunting area. Photograph by Charles Alsheimer

very windy, deer are reluctant to move because they know that all of their senses will be impaired. Wind scatters scent, creates a racket in the woods, and is constantly whipping brush and leaves into motion. This leaves deer feeling vulnerable as their senses of sight, smell, and hearing are greatly handicapped. Under such conditions, most deer will be tucked deep in heavy cover waiting for the wind to die down.

Whitetails are extremely nervous when the wind is howling, and instead of sneaking out of cover ahead of drivers, they will frequently burst forth at full speed and will remain on the move when they go by the posters. Shots at stationary deer are rare on drives conducted during windy weather.

Unseasonably warm weather during the hunting season also will greatly decrease natural deer movement. Once a whitetail is all decked out in that gray winter coat, the animal doesn't handle heat very well. When the temperature rises, deer will seek shaded areas and simply bed down, moving mostly at night until the hot spell breaks. Because being out and about in very warm weather is uncomfortable for hunters, too, many choose to hunt only a short time in the morning and perhaps an hour in the evening. The absence of other hunters in the woods means that you

cannot depend upon deer being disturbed and sent past your stand. Stillhunting, too, is a poor choice in hot weather because the footing is usually dry and crunchy, making it nearly impossible to sneak undetected within range of a deer.

All this combines to make driving your best choice in hot weather. But be forewarned: Driving is hard work, and hot weather quickly saps the energy and enthusiasm from most hunters. When driving deer in the heat, plan short drives, take long breaks between drives, and make sure that there is plenty of cold water available. Even with all of these precautions, chances of seeing a lot of deer during hot weather—even on a finely executed drive in super cover—are slim. This is because whitetails are so reluctant to expend energy when it's hot that they're much more likely to hold tight and let drivers pass by. A hunt in southeastern Ohio one recent fall provides the perfect example.

The rugged hill country of this corner of the state is home to good numbers of deer, as well as some real bruiser bucks. On the eve of the firearms deer season opener, a small group of us had gathered at the farm home of our friend John Weiss. Despite what it said on the calendar, a record shattering heat wave made it feel more like a Fourth of July celebration than a deer camp. The next day we found that natural deer movement was being

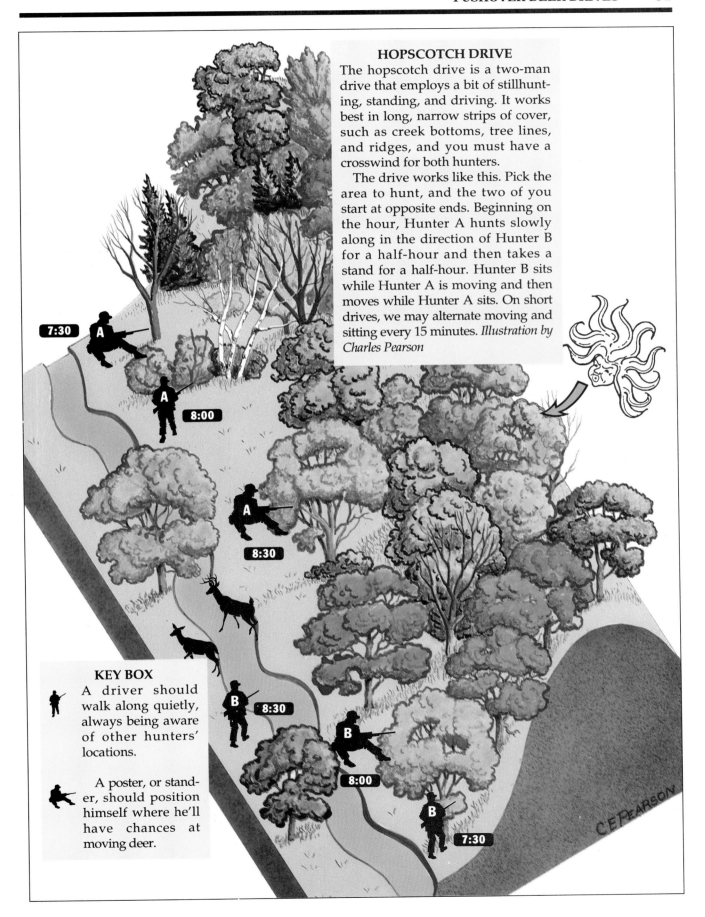

HOPSCOTCH DRIVE

The hopscotch drive is a two-man drive that employs a bit of stillhunting, standing, and driving. It works best in long, narrow strips of cover, such as creek bottoms, tree lines, and ridges, and you must have a crosswind for both hunters.

The drive works like this. Pick the area to hunt, and the two of you start at opposite ends. Beginning on the hour, Hunter A hunts slowly along in the direction of Hunter B for a half-hour and then takes a stand for a half-hour. Hunter B sits while Hunter A is moving and then moves while Hunter A sits. On short drives, we may alternate moving and sitting every 15 minutes. *Illustration by Charles Pearson*

7:30 A

8:00 A

8:30 A

KEY BOX

A driver should walk along quietly, always being aware of other hunters' locations.

A poster, or stander, should position himself where he'll have chances at moving deer.

B 8:30

B 8:00

B 7:30

C E PEARSON

limited to the first few minutes of light in the morning. And as the heat persisted, hunting pressure couldn't even be counted on to move the deer by the second day. It quickly became obvious that if we wanted to find whitetails, we were going to have to go in after them.

Weiss, his son Mike, and their friend Al Wolter were all intimately familiar with the area we were hunting. Together they mapped out strategies for drives through prime deer cover. We worked hard, but moved few deer—the norm when hunting in hot weather. Deer are simply so reluctant to move during hot weather that no matter how well the drive is planned, you are going to walk by more deer than you put on the move.

Cold weather, on the other hand, is the catalyst for more drives than hot weather. This is evidenced by the fact that drives are the norm for hunters in the North Country, where sitting all day on a stand can be pure torture when temperatures dip down into the single digits. The normal procedure is for each hunter in the group to hunt from a morning stand and then meet back at a predetermined site at midmorning. Drives are conducted until mid-afternoon, when once again the hunters split up to take their evening stands.

TWO-MAN RIDGE DRIVE

As I mentioned earlier, bucks tend to bed down just over the crest of a ridge. The two-man ridge drive is designed to take advantage of this fact, and again it is a combination of tactics—this time stillhunting and driving. Hunter A takes the left side of a ridge, Hunter B the right. Each hunter moves slowly along his side of the ridge as if he were still-hunting. Bucks disturbed by one hunter will often cross over the crest of the ridge and drop down the other side—affording the other hunter a shot. A great way to stay in contact with each other without alerting deer is to use mouth diaphragm turkey calls (or crow calls if there is a fall turkey season in progress). A few clucks or caws every few minutes is all it takes to ensure that you and your partner stay in line. *Illustration by Charles Pearson*

WHERE TO DRIVE

The most common recommendation you'll hear is to drive the heaviest cover available. This is sound advice if the deer have been subjected to significant hunting pressure or if the wind is howling. And, yes, you can argue that the best cover in any area will always hold some deer. But don't believe for a minute that pounding through the thickest available cover is *always* the best tactic. Many times I have run into situations that have made driving open timber, or what I like to call secondary thickets (those places that don't look really whitetailish to the hunter), a better bet. Let me explain.

In Wisconsin a few years ago, I ran into a typical midweek situation. There were few hunters in the woods, and the deer were feeding relatively undisturbed on an abundant acorn crop. Deer that are keying on acorns and are not being bothered have a tendency to bed down at the food source, rather than making the trip to thicker bedding cover. Proof came when we switched from unproductive swamp drives to pushes through open hardwoods—we had deer running all over the place.

A similar condition exists during the whitetail rut. When a buck has procreation of the species first and foremost on his mind, he spends as little time as possible holed up in heavy cover. Once hunting pressure slackens, you can bet that bucks will be on the prowl looking for receptive does. And because family units of does frequent more-open terrain, that is where I like to conduct drives during this time of year.

Another thing that I've discovered is that no matter where I've hunted, from Minnesota to Mississippi, bucks in hill country have a habit of bedding down near the tops of ridges. And why not? After all, there they can rest comfortably (if a whitetail ever does) while thermals bring them messages from below, and their high vantage point lets them spot hunters from quite a distance. As a result, my brother-in-law and I have learned to key in on ridges when making two-man deer-hunting drives.

There has been so much written about a whitetail's penchant for heavy cover that in many areas today the best deer cover is liberally sprinkled with orange coats. Drives should never be conducted through cover in which other hunters are hunting. And this is where my secondary thickets come into play. These are the places that most hunters overlook as they search for the best deer cover. These are also the places deer seek out when they find their favorite haunts crawling with hunters.

When I first began to hunt deer, it was with a shotgun in a slug-only zone in southern Minnesota. That part of Minnesota, like much of the Midwest, was comprised mainly of corn and soybean fields. Once these fields were harvested, deer concentrated in the few remaining woodlots and skinny river bottoms. This was also where most hunters focused their efforts. My friends and I, however, avoided these hard-hunted, obvious whitetail strongholds and spent our time driving places the other hunters overlooked—namely, small wet sloughs seemingly better suited for pheasants and mallards. Many of these sloughs had no trees at all, though some had a few straggly willows or cottonwoods. These sloughs ranged in size from 20 acres down to about the size of a three-bedroom rambler. And not only did we always fill our tags while driving these secondary thickets but we also took some very large, cornfed bucks in the process.

I've witnessed the same thing happen where clear-cutting is a common means of harvesting timber. Hunters tend to concentrate their drive efforts in the thicker conifers and hardwoods while ignoring the more open clear-cuts. Where slashing has been left behind and new growth has begun to sprout, clear-cuts provide super cover for whitetail deer. Don't overlook them when planning a potentially successful deer drive.

POSITIONING DRIVERS AND POSTERS

Most deer drives are doomed before they ever get started. The reason is that posters alert deer while moving into position, or drivers get antsy and begin the drives too soon.

The secret is to have posters sneak quietly into position well before the drive is scheduled to begin and then to make sure that none of the drivers approach the starting line until the

THREE-MAN RAVINE DRIVE

Don't ask me why, but no matter where I hunt I find that deer love to bed down in those ravines and fingers that jut out from main valleys and extend into fields or clearcuts. Ravines are perfectly suited for three men to drive, although two can get the job done if the single driver does a lot of zigzagging. The poster should position himself 50 to 100 yards in from the tip of the ravine to ensure shots at deer moving slowly before the animals break over the top. *Illustration by Charles Pearson*

agreed upon time. Some of the most effective drives that I have been involved in were those in which the posters simply remained on their morning stands and at a predetermined time the drivers assembled for the push.

Two hunters can easily work out the details of a two-man drive between themselves, but drives involving three or more hunters need a drive captain. The drive captain should be intimately familiar with the area being driven. It is his responsibility to position the posters, assemble the drivers, ensure that the area to be driven is free of other hunters, and signal the beginning and end of the drive. Drives involving a number of hunters who do not elect a drive captain are often a joke. Most of the time is spent standing

around the tailgates of pickup trucks while everyone draws meaningless lines in the dirt with sharp sticks and argues about where and how to make the next push.

Don't bite off more than you can chew, either. Drives are most effective in small blocks or narrow lanes of cover. I've seen groups try to drive an area the size of the Adirondacks with a half dozen hunters. It typically doesn't work. Because most drives are set up so that deer are pushed into or across an opening, taking up a post position right on the edge of the opening is mighty tempting. The problem with this is that deer tend to run across openings. You will get better shots at stationary or slow-moving deer if you post 50 yards or so deep in the cover.

THE FUNNEL DRIVE

Forced to choose only one location in which to hunt deer for the rest of my days, I would unhesitatingly choose a natural funnel—a constricted area that animals are forced to move through, either because of the terrain or to remain in cover. Funnels are just as effective for drives as they are for stands.

It is important to select an area that the number in your hunting party can cover effectively. Then, the idea is to position posters where the funnel necks down and drive the cover toward the posters. Deer will funnel through the constriction naturally, and the posters will often be afforded shots at walking or standing animals.

Funnels occur naturally in river and creek bottoms, but they abound in other settings as well. *Illustration by Charles Pearson*

What happens is that when a whitetail is faced with the problem of crossing an opening, it nearly always hesitates as if it were trying to make up its mind about whether or not to really dash across. That is when you will get your best opportunity to shoot.

There are still some hunters who believe that the more noise they make the more deer they will move. These groups come screaming through the woods at a half-run, hollering, banging on tin pots and, in some cases, shooting in the air to get deer on the move. You would think they were trying to get a bunch of lazy, half-dead Holsteins on their feet. For every deer that these noisy gangs see, you can bet that a dozen more slipped out undetected as soon as the racket began. It is far more effective to have drivers walk along nat-urally and within sight of each other. This way deer will not be running scared when they go past the posters, but instead will simply be picking their way along, allowing plenty of time for good clean shots.

Drives have a bad (and undeserved) reputation for being dangerous. One simple rule eliminates the possibility of someone getting shot on a drive: Drivers never fire toward posters, and posters never fire in the direction of drivers.

Feel free to experiment with the drives described and illustrated here. Drive plans are like good recipes—they can be made even better by adding just a pinch of this and a half-teaspoon of that. But remember, simple is the key to successful drives.

High-Power Bucks

By Kathy Etling

I'm a fool for trophy whitetails. What's more, I've been this way for a long time. Like many hunters, my dreams of someday taking a Pope and Young Club whitetail, or perhaps even a Boone and Crockett Club-class buck, were fairly well-known among my friends. I would even have been ecstatic to kill a deer that qualified for Missouri's Show Me Big Bucks Club. During the many seasons that I'd been hunting deer, I'd taken plenty of good bucks, but never a really *great* buck—that is, not until 1990.

It was the seventh morning of Missouri's nine-day firearms season, and I had an any-deer permit. Already I'd seen 30 whitetails—four of them bucks—from my stand, but none close to the kind of buck I was hoping for. The biggest antlers up to that point had belonged to an overeager forkhorn, one so brazen that he'd chased several does right past my stand. But by this time I hadn't even seen that buck for a while, which really wasn't surprising. Bucks of any size get scarcer as hunting season wears on. I knew that my odds of taking a buck that year were dropping by the minute.

Finally, I decided to shoot a doe if I didn't see a good buck by noon the following day. I don't feel guilty about waiting for a buck because we try to balance the harvest of deer on our farm by taking several does each year and only one or two bucks. But the longer I sat, the more it looked like a doe was in my immediate future.

My stand is in a pine tree right next to a power line. In almost every direction, Ozark ridges and hollows knife across the landscape. If I look straight ahead, however, my view is of a tall wooden structure that holds aloft huge wires alive with 354,000 volts of electricity. When it's damp, those wires buzz and hum. When they're covered with ice and the skies darken, they'll occasionally glow with an eerie light. If I look to the right or left, the sheared strip that is the power line sluices its way across timbered hills and

Power lines and other rights-of-way provide deer with plenty of edge cover, food, and visibility. They also offer hunters a variety of opportunities, as evidenced by the author and the Missouri nontypical buck she took just under the wire. Photographs by Len Rue Jr. (background) and by Bob Etling (inset).

out of sight. Incredibly enough, this power line is my secret whitetail weapon.

I'd been hunting this spot for four years. Since then, I'd taken a buck there every season, each with bigger antlers than the one the year before. Now, it looked like my streak was about to end.

The morning was frosty cold, a welcome relief from the overly warm weather of the past several days. At 7 A.M. a breeze began to stir, and perhaps that's why I didn't hear the sound. Because without warning, a doe spurted out of the woods 100 yards away, flashed across the power line, and disappeared into a cluster of oaks on the other side.

My internal alarm should have been ringing. I'd never seen a doe run so fast. But because it was a doe, I hesitated before moving my rifle into shooting position. In other words, I was totally unprepared when a heavy antlered 8-point raced out seconds later, hot on the doe's trail. As the buck sped across the opening, his ivory tines gleamed against the bleak gray brush. I tried, but wasn't fast enough to get off a shot.

On the other side of the right-of-way, I envisioned the deer bounding down the weathered rock face that fed into a narrow gorge. My area is rough and remote, one reason why deer use it even late in the season. And though I hoped that the doe might lead the buck past me again, I knew that it wasn't likely to happen. I sat there for five minutes, berating myself for not hearing the deer, as well as for not getting my gun up while I'd had the chance. And can you believe it? At the end of those five minutes, it happened again.

This time, however, when an even bigger buck charged out, I was at least partially ready. As quickly as possible I found the buck in my scope and fired, but by the way the buck acted after the shot, I suspected that I hadn't even come close.

My heart was really heavy now. After almost seven full days of waiting, of craning my neck one way and then the other, of hours spent watching intently, I'd missed chances at not one big buck, but two.

I'd shot. Ethically, I had to check for blood even though I knew it had been a clean miss. As I was unloading my gun to climb out of the tree, I saw a flicker of movement where the buck had entered the woods. Hardly daring to hope, I held my breath, quietly chambered a round, and waited.

I could scarcely believe my eyes when the second buck walked back onto the power line, head held high and every sense alert. He was so much bigger than the first buck that I found it hard to believe that he'd been chased off by the 8-point. Maybe he'd gotten curious about the shot and come back to investigate. Perhaps he was confused, not sure where the noise had come from. But it didn't really matter why he'd come back. All I knew was that I had to make this shot count. And, at a distance of just more than 100 yards, as the buck was quartering toward me, I hit him where I aimed—at the junction of neck and shoulder. The buck crumbled in his tracks.

I was trembling so hard that I could barely make it out of my stand. From where I was, the buck had looked like a big 10-point, possibly in the 130 to 140 Boone and Crockett class. If so, he would have been my all-time best.

But when I got to the buck, I realized that I'd been wrong. If he had been a typical with no deductions, he would have scored 140 points. But I'd missed the 12 extra tines around the bases of the high, heavy antlers that made the rack a nontypical. I'd also missed the double brow tines, as well as a cheater point on another tine. As a nontypical, the buck scored 165⅞ Boone and Crockett points, large enough to qualify for Missouri's Show Me Big Bucks Club—a dream come true.

Experiences like this have sold me on hunting rights-of-ways for whitetails. Electric lines, gas lines, even railroad easements—almost any type of right-of-way—can be a great place for deer. Even when I hunt other states, I'll seek these areas out just as surely as the deer do.

That same year, for example, while hunting in Georgia, I killed a dandy 10-point along yet another power line. This buck scored between 120 and 130 Boone and Crockett points. He sauntered onto the right-of-way just five minutes after I'd climbed into my stand.

This particular right-of-way was a bit different from the one on our farm. It hadn't been cut for

Bill Jordan shown here with buck knows that power cuts are prime places to spot and get shots at whitetails. One reason power cuts are irresistible to deer is because of the abundant supply of browse. In open areas, forbs and grasses grow without having to compete with other larger species as they do in shaded woodlands. During the rut, power cuts become prime places for bucks to meet with estrous does. Photograph by Duncan Dobie

years, and some of the saplings were approaching tree size. Regrowth rates are fast along power lines. Even though the plant is hacked off close to ground level, root systems remain intact. Because these roots have supported a much larger plant, they're able to provide enough nourishment so that tops sprout back quickly.

As I waited in my Georgia stand, I watched the buck's antlers weaving above the bright fall foliage. Every now and then I'd lose sight of the deer completely when he'd step behind a clump of brush. Only rarely could I see even a patch of his silken, gray hide. If he continued on course, however, I'd have a clear shot.

Halfway across the power cut, the buck turned and came my way. I don't like head-on shots, so I hoped he'd switch directions again. Instead, he stopped, his head snapped up, and he stared right at me. I didn't dare move for fear that he'd run. After a few anxious moments, the buck focused on something else farther down the hill. Whatever it was, it had scared him. He wheeled and bolted, white flag waving as he ran.

It was now or never. I whistled, and though it didn't stop the buck completely, he slowed to a trot. As he quartered away, I fired. The 140-grain Remington bullet traveled diagonally through the buck's entire body before exiting the opposite shoulder. I found him where he fell 150 yards away.

The two power lines I hunted that year were especially tempt-

THE QUESTION OF OWNERSHIP

Remember, no matter how tempting a right-of-way may look, landowners usually retain their property rights, according to spokespersons contacted at several major utility companies. A power or gas company will usually pay the landowner for an easement across his or her land—a rental for the placement of poles, wires, or pipe, and nothing more. On rare occasions, a utility will actually own the land itself, a procedure termed "bought in fee." Though some "bought in fee" power lines and gas transmission lines do exist, mainly in the East, they are not common. Inquire as to ownership before you start hunting. To be perfectly safe, you should still get permission to hunt rights-of-way from the private landowner or power or gas company before actually scouting or hunting.

Railroad rights-of-way are a bit different. Railroads actually own these areas until they abandon them. Then, the ownership of the area reverts to the landowner from whom it was obtained. In most areas of the country, it's still fairly easy to get permission to hunt railroad rights-of-way by contacting local rail officials. But, remember: even if you get permission to hunt the right-of-way itself, you'll still often need landowner permission to trail or retrieve game from adjoining private ground.

Of course, many power, gas, and railroad lines are constructed across public ground, too, providing plenty of optimum deer range and hunting opportunities.

---

ing to whitetails because they'd both been built across partially timbered land. That makes a big difference because it provides deer with plenty of edge cover—places where two or more ecotones, or habitat types, come together. Studies have proven that when given a choice, whitetails prefer edges. And wherever a forest meets an opening, edge is formed.

Power lines make hunting easier. They allow hunters to analyze a cross-section of an area's topography. Because we can see the way the land lies, it's easier to determine how deer travel along its folds and creases. On scouting expeditions, you'll notice that deer favor certain spots as crossings.

Rights-of-way attract whitetails for other reasons, too. When it's hot, breezes often stir here. At such times, deer bed in the shade near the crests of open hills. When it's cold, deer seek open, sheltered spots where they can soak up the sun's warmth. During the rut, an open area along a right-of-way is a great place for deer to see and be seen. I've watched a number of whitetails walk out, look around, and then make a beeline for any other deer that they see in a cleared opening.

The presence of flexible, young trees also makes rights-of-way ideal spots to scout for rubs and scrapes. And deer often use the paths made by utility trucks when workers patrol their lines. These paths provide easy travel, and deer, like people, can be pretty lazy at times.

Deer use rights-of-way for all these reasons, plus another, even more important reason: Cutover areas produce the types of foods that deer love. In heavily timbered areas, these are foods that resident whitetails usually can't find anywhere else.

I suspected as much during the hours that I'd spent watching the deer near my stand. I'd seen deer almost every time I visited, and they'd been foraging often. But because I'm not an expert on why deer utilize rights-of-way, I'd decided to ask someone who is.

Richard Harlow, a wildlife research biologist from Clemson, South Carolina, has studied whitetail foods and food habits for more than 40 years. And Harlow recently completed a study on why deer use power lines so frequently.

"Any time you mow an area often, plant growth is kept in a young, tender stage," he explained. "Young plants concentrate nutrients, so the quality's better. In open areas, forbs and grasses get plenty of sun. They don't have to compete with larger species like they do in shaded woodlands. When a right-of-way is cut through timbered land, it provides a change of diet that deer can't resist. Deer go looking for Japanese honeysuckle, blackberry plants, and greenbrier. They also like legumes, such as partridge pea. At spring green-up, deer will eat succulent new grass. When it's cold, they forage for basal rosettes of forbs, those parts of perennials close to the root that don't die in winter."

Richard Harlow's research proves what many power-line hunters have known for a long time. Gary LaRose of Saint Genevieve, Missouri, who hunts the same power line that I do—only on the farm next to ours—has a well-deserved reputation for taking good deer almost every year. A few years ago, he connected on a big typical that netted 153 Boone and Crockett points. Both LaRose's deer and mine were taken south of the Missouri River—in Ozark country not known for its good bucks. Can it be that the power line—and the superior forage—make the difference?

Another top hunter who has taken his share of spectacular bucks is Bill Jordan of Columbus, Georgia—the guy who designed Realtree camouflage. I was hunting with Jordan the year I took my Georgia buck on Callaway Gardens land near Pine Mountain. Just a few days earlier, Jordan had taken a tremendous 8-point buck that grossed more than 160 Boone and Crockett points, and netted 156. He'd killed the buck along the same power line that I would later hunt.

"Power lines are often favored spots within a whitetail's range," Jordan stated. And because he's taken 10 whitetails that scored 150 Boone and Crockett points or better, it's safe to assume that Jordan knows what he's talking about.

"Whenever you hunt a right-of-way, you're using a powerful tool to your advantage: the ability to see long distances.

"When you're scouting, keep in mind what types of whitetail food are found on each side of the power line, too," he continued. "If there's a good bunch of acorns on one side and a food plot on the other, deer might lay up nearby so they can travel between the two areas. If you scout an area right, and if you hunt power lines long enough, you'll soon be able to predict where you'll see deer.

"Even if you aren't sure about food sources, you can still get a good idea of how deer use a right-of-way by sitting in a stand along the edge for a day or two.

"Sometimes when power lines get overgrown, the hunting actually improves," Jordan continued. "You might not be able to see as well, but the deer feel safer when they come out to feed.

"I'm fairly sure that's why I got my big 8-point—because the line was so thick with vegetation. Although I'd scouted the area before and seen some good bucks, I'd never seen this particular buck. The first time I even knew he was around was an hour before dark on the first day of the 1990 firearms season. But I couldn't get a shot. Two days later, I returned with a cameraman to try to get some video footage. It was raining pretty hard, and we both got soaking wet and miserable, but we waited, anyway. Almost like clockwork, the buck came out at the same time he had the two nights previously.

"When he stepped onto the power line, he was 130 yards away, browsing as he moved toward me. I let him get 90 yards away before I shot. When I fired, the buck collapsed."

Hunting from stands is only one way to optimize whitetail opportunities along rights-of-way. Gary LaRose took one of his big whitetails while stillhunting through the underbrush on a particularly rugged portion of power line. He discovered that when fallen leaves cover the ground in timbered areas, rights-of-way are often the quietest places for stalkers and stillhunters. As you move silently along, keep alert, not only to what's on the right-of-way itself but also to what's lurking in the adjoining woodlands, as well.

Another good way to hunt rights-of-way for whitetails is to plan deer drives around them. Using a right-of-way to get standers located makes sense—again, because the hunters will make far less noise than if they were moving through timber or brush. Then, organize the drive to push deer onto the power line. You will get reasonably clear shots by doing this. Right before a deer is forced across an opening, it will usually pause at the edge of the woods for a quick look. That's the moment to make the shot.

Rights-of-way are right for deer in very many ways. Try one, and you could be sold for life on this simple, yet effective, "high-power" whitetail hunting technique.

Tree Your Buck

By Tim Jones

It was midday, and I was slow-scouting for buck sign. Slow-scouting is a blend of still-hunting and scouting—you move as quietly as possible, scouting a limited area and trying not to spook deer that might be in the vicinity. The limited area in this case was a New Brunswick hillside. I knew that a big buck was working the territory—and big in New Brunswick means big! I'd found where the buck regularly crossed a brook in the valley below and a rub where he'd completely stripped the bark off a 5-inch-diameter hemlock—enough damage to kill the tree. I'd also found a couple of half-hearted scrapes. What I wanted to find, if possible, was a big, clean, primary rutting scrape. Then I'd have a chance of ambushing the buck in the one evening and morning I had left to hunt.

I was easing along the lower slope, staying among the softwoods (mostly hemlock with some spruce) whenever possible—partly to keep in the shadows, partly to avoid the crunchy carpet of leaves from the hardwoods (mostly big sugar maples with a scattering of beeches), and partly to check for scrapes under the hemlocks. On a bench far above, I noticed a lone beech tree among the maples. As with many beeches, this one had its lower branches sloping downward toward the ground, with the tips about chest height on a man—or antler height on a big buck. I detoured, crunched my way to the beech, and beneath its branches I found what I was looking for—a wash-tub-size patch of clean earth. Even from a distance, I could smell the rich reek of rutting buck.

I set my ambush 80 yards downwind.

The buck never came that afternoon. But in the first light of dawn the next morning, I heard hoofs in the leaves, eased my little Ruger carbine to ready, and waited. I don't know if the swirling breeze betrayed me or if my approach a few minutes earlier had been heard, but the buck stayed in the safety of a sheltering screen of beech whips, snorted twice, and took one huge bound to safety. In my mind's eye, years later, I can still see that one magnificent leap by the biggest buck I've ever seen or hope to see. Back at camp, a 311-pound, field-dressed buck was hanging on the meat pole. The buck I had seen was as big or bigger.

My afternoon detour to that buck scrape was no accident. In northern New England and Eastern Canada, where I do the majority of my deer hunting, deer put most of their scrapes under either beech trees or hemlocks. When I see a beech or hemlock with branches about the right height, I check it out.

Notice that I didn't say that all scrapes are under hemlock and beech trees. I've found scrapes under virtually every species of tree that grows in this area. But the odds say that, where I hunt, if you are going to find a primary scrape,

Knowing the trees in your hunting area will help you find a prime buck like this one. Photograph by Len Rue Jr.

Acorns are a favorite whitetail food, making an oak ridge a prime spot to set up. Photograph by Charles Alsheimer

An area containing hemlocks would be a good place to scout for rubs. Photograph by Charles Alsheimer

Young softwoods allow deer to hide from inclement weather as well as predators.
Photograph by Charles Alsheimer

it's going to be under a beech or hemlock.

No matter where you hunt, it's a safe bet that the deer use some types of trees more often than others. It's also a safe bet that some deer hunters never catch on to this—never see the trees for the forest, you might say. But if you want to stack the odds of deer hunting success in your favor, it pays to learn what trees are in your hunting area and how the deer will be using those trees when you're in the woods.

For hunters, the best way to think of trees is as furniture in the forest. You use the different furnishings in your home to meet different needs at different times. Deer use trees in much the same way.

If, for example, you want something to eat, you head for the refrigerator or the pantry cabinets, because that's where the food is. If you want to get in shape for the upcoming hunting season, you head for the exercise equipment. If you want to relax in comfort, you head for an easy chair or the couch. And if you're interested in members of the opposite sex . . .

It's the same for deer. Certain trees in their world provide food, others shelter. Still others are perfect for building up neck muscles prior to the rut, and

others are just right for rutting behavior. The only thing for which deer don't have an equivalent is office furniture. Their only job is survival.

For a hunter's purposes, there are basically four broad categories of trees that are important to deer. Probably all hunters recognize one category—the *evergreen softwoods*, which are easily distinguished from deciduous hardwoods (most of which have lost their leaves by the time firearms season rolls around). Some softwoods provide food, others are used for rubbing and scraping, and all provide shelter from bad weather and from the prying eyes of hunters.

Among the hardwoods, hunters should be able to quickly recognize three groups. Most important are the *mast-bearing hardwoods*, such as oaks, beeches, and hickories, and the *fruit-bearing trees*, such as apples, cherries, and persimmons. These two groups are important food sources for deer in the fall—the pantry, if you will. The third group is the *rest of the hardwoods*, such as maples, ashes, poplars, cottonwoods, willows, and so on. Some of these, deer use regularly for food and others for rubbing and scraping beneath.

Illustration by Charles E. Pearson

RED OAK OR WHITE?

Every deer hunter knows that whitetails eat acorns. Most hunters know that deer like some acorns better than others. But how is a hunter supposed to know which oak is which?

Unfortunately, *The Audubon Society Field Guide To North American Trees, Eastern Region* lists 32 varieties of oaks, not counting confusing hybrid crosses, which occur frequently in nature. So sorting out the exact species of oak that you are looking at can be difficult, even for professional foresters.

Fortunately, oaks fall into two broad categories—red oaks and white oaks—and

White Oak

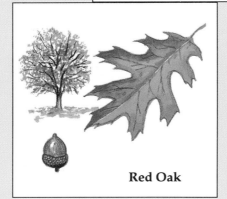

Red Oak

deer generally prefer white oak acorns, when they can get them. White oak acorns ripen in one year and are sweeter than red oak acorns, which require two years to mature.

To tell a red oak from a white oak, look first at the leaves. White oaks usually have rounded leaf tips (called lobes), whereas most red oaks have spiky, or pointed, leaf tips (even though the leaf itself may be rounded, as on the water oak, or elongated, as on the laurel oak). Be careful about leaves that aren't actually on the tree, however, as leaves from one oak can easily blow beneath another nearby tree.

You can also sample the acorns. Red oak acorns are bitter, a result of the high concentration of tannic acid that they contain, whereas white oak acorns taste sweet.

Illustration by Duane Raver

Within each of these categories, some tree species are more important than others. Hunters need to recognize these species both close up and from a distance.

Size, too, can play an important role in how the deer utilize trees. For example, where I hunt, deer browse heavily on young red maple whips, which sprout abundantly in cutover areas. As the maples mature into pole-size trees, the bucks use them for rubbing. But eventually the red maples get too large, their branches are out of reach, and the deer don't use them at all. So it's important to be able to recognize trees at different stages of growth.

To be a better deer hunter you should, at the very least, be able to spot from a distance the mast-bearing hardwoods, such as oaks and beeches, and the fruit-bearing hardwoods such as apples, crab apples, and cherries. A little closer up, you should be able to tell a member of the white oak group from a red oak species. After all, deer can—and do.

For example—and this is true throughout the United States—wherever oaks from the white oak group (white, chinquapin, post oak, and so on) intermix with oaks from the red oak group

(northern red, scarlet, pin, black oak, and so on), deer generally will eat the sweeter acorns of the white oaks before they'll touch the tannin-rich, bitter red oak acorns.

Other groups are important, too, though some preferences are more regional. As the winter comes on in Northern states, deer will browse heavily on hemlocks, cedars, and balsam fir, but a deer with a belly full of spruce would starve to death. Different trees have different nutritional values at different times of year, and the deer instinctively seek out the best available foods in their area at that specific time.

Sometimes it's clear what attracts deer to certain trees. It's easy, for example, to tell why all the local deer are visiting a big white oak that's dropping sweet acorns or an apple tree that's loaded with fruit. It's also easy to tell why pressured deer choose to bed in a thick plantation of young pines rather than among the open understory of mature trees.

Sometimes the connection between deer and trees is not so clear, however, and it takes a little detective work to decipher. In the fall of 1991, every deer on the property that I hunt in Vermont was visiting both apple and black cherry trees. Apples were abundant; so were the tiny black cherries. But the cherry pulp had long since disintegrated, leaving only the pits, which showed occasionally in deer droppings. Apparently, the deer liked these pits enough to detour—perhaps for a little dessert.

It's also hard to tell what's going on when deer are feeding on mushrooms that grow in association with certain types of trees. I've seen times when deer were pawing the leaves under oaks even though there were no acorns to be had. And there were other times when they'd roll over the needle carpet under certain evergreens. In each case I suspect that they were seeking a mushroom that sprouted quickly, then disappeared.

There are other times that the attraction of deer to certain types of trees is even harder to fathom. Why, for example, would deer choose to make scrapes below hemlocks and beeches, as they do in the wooded Northeast?

Of course, no one knows the absolute truth, but it's my guess that the *shape* of the tree is the deciding factor here. Whereas most of the larger trees growing in my area put their branches out slanting upward, which quickly puts them out of the deer's reach, both hemlocks and beeches have lower branches that slant downward from a trunk that's normally clear of branches to nearly head height. These downward-slanting branches are just the right height to catch a buck's antlers, which perhaps stimulates licking, chewing, and ground scraping.

And why would bucks choose certain trees to rub? In my region, for example, bucks rub mainly hemlocks and striped and red maples. Here, I can see several possibilities (or combinations thereof). It might be that these trees offer just the right amount of resistance, whereas others are too stiff or too soft. It might also be that these tree species produce an odor that's pleasant to deer in general or bucks in particular. Or, it may be that each of these species has bark that peels away easily, showing bright white wood beneath—visually advertising the buck's presence. Finally, it may be that these trees grow in places where bucks *want*

to rub—highly visible spots such as along logging trails or on the edges of clear-cuts and fields.

For me, it's not as important to know why deer are using certain species of trees as it is to know what trees they are likely to be using for what purposes in the area I'm hunting, *when* I'm hunting. It's also important to be able to find and identify those species of trees that are important to the local deer.

Take, for example, the New Brunswick buck at the beginning. If I hadn't known that bucks scrape under beech trees—and if I hadn't been able to identify the type of habitat that beeches prefer and pick out a beech from a maple at a distance—I would probably have never found that scrape and gotten a look at that wily old buck.

Fortunately, sorting out the trees from the forest in your regular hunting area is a comparatively easy task, a natural extension of the scouting you already do before, during, and after the deer season. You don't need to know what the deer do in other areas. You don't even need to be able to put a name to every tree that you encounter in the forest—though you may get hooked on dendrology (the study of trees) and *want* to name every tree you see. But for deer hunting purposes, the deer themselves will show you which trees you need to know and why.

The best way to begin your study is with a trip to either the local library or the local bookstore for a pocket guide to the trees of your region. Before you go afield, look for some of the key identifying points of the four groups of trees: softwoods, mast-bearing hardwoods, fruit-bearing hardwoods, and other hardwoods. Then begin to identify the trees that the deer show you are important.

Carry a guidebook with you when you go out scouting and when you stalkhunt. When you find a buck rub or scrape, take a moment to identify the kind of tree it's on or under. If you find a bed or an area where the deer are obviously feeding, check the nearby trees to see if they are part of the reason the deer are in that spot. The better field guides use leaves, fruits, nuts or seeds, barks, flowers, and even sizes and shapes as keys to identification. Once you've identified the trees involved, make a note of them.

	FOOD	RUBS	SCRAPES
NORTHEAST	Northern White Oak, Chestnut Oak, American Beech, Northern Red Oak, Scarlet Oak, Black Oak, Apple (both fruit and twigs), Black Cherry, Red Maple, Sugar Maple, Poplar (twigs and leaves), White and Red Pine (needles), Eastern Hemlock, Balsam Fir, Red and White Cedar.	Red Maple, Striped Maple, Eastern Hemlock, American Beech, Poplar.	American Beech, Eastern Hemlock (these species often have lower branches at buck's antler height).
SOUTH	Water Oak and Willow Oak (both in the Red Oak group, these drop their small acorns early), Live Oak, Chinquapin Oak, Swamp Chestnut Oak, Pecan (domestic), Persimmon, Crab Apple, Red Maple (shoots of young trees).	Red Cedar, Shortleaf Pine, Loblolly Pine, Longleaf Pine, River Birch.	American Beech, Swamp Privet.
MIDWEST	Northern Red Oak, White Oak (where available), Beech, Apple, Black Cherry (during the very early bow seasons).	Quaking Aspen, Tag Alder, Balsam Fir, Jack Pine, random use of all soft-bark species.	Determined by branch height, not tree species.
WEST	Whitetails will key on brush such as Snowberry, Bitter Brush, Mountain Mahogany, Sagebrush, Serviceberry and Chokecherry, and will feed heavily on acorns where available; as a secondary food source, they will eat the tender shoots of tree species such as Willow, White Birch, Aspen and Alder.	Quaking Aspen, Birch, Ponderosa Pine, Lodgepole Pine, Douglas Fir, Engelmann Spruce.	Large Ponderosa Pine, Aspen Thickets.

FOOD images: White Oak, Apple, Persimmon, Water Oak, Black Cherry, Northern Red Oak, Pacific Willow, White Birch

RUBS images: American Beech, Eastern Hemlock, River Birch, Loblolly Pine, Tag Alder, Quaking Aspen, Douglas Fir, Engelmann Spruce

SCRAPES images: Eastern Hemlock, American Beech, Quaking Aspen, Ponderosa Pine, Quaking Aspen

SHELTER

Norway Spruce, Eastern Hemlock, Cedar, Eastern White Pine (particularly plantations of young trees).

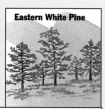

Eastern White Pine

Eastern Hemlock

Norway Spruce

Thick growth of any tree species.

Eastern White Pine

White Cedar, Eastern Hemlock, Balsam Fir, Spruce.

Balsam Fir

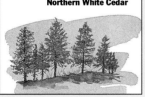

Northern White Cedar

Depends on type of cover inhabited, but prefer thick growth on northern exposures, often bedding on ridgetop or one-third of the way down slope.

Norway Spruce

As you keep scouting you'll probably notice patterns emerging, as I have in my area. Once you've identified key tree species, you can then turn the tables on the deer by using the information to predict their movements. That, of course, can help put you in an area before the deer get there. Or, if you're scouting new ground, it can help you find the deer more quickly.

In the fall of 1991, for example, several friends and I decided to camp in a new area for our annual backpack muzzleloader hunt. My job, seeing as I lived closest to the spot, was to scout out a couple of new sites to find the best concentration of deer. I started on the ridgetops where northern red, black, and scarlet oaks (all members of the red oak group) were growing in confusing profusion. All the oaks had developed huge crops of acorns. In fact, under some trees the footing was downright treacherous—there were so many acorns that it was like walking on marbles. Trouble was, there wasn't a deer track to be found. Squirrels were abundant, but not deer. Strike one.

Sitting on top of a rocky ledge, I pondered the problem. When there are acorns available in my area, the deer usually eat nothing else. Where were the deer?

As I pondered, I looked around me. Down the hill, a mile or so away, I could clearly see an old apple orchard with lots of black cherry trees growing on the fenceline around it.

It didn't take long to walk there. I approached the trees hopefully. No luck. Though both apples and cherries were abundant, there were no deer tracks. Strike two.

The only possible answer was that the deer were eating something else, somewhere else. I didn't know precisely, but I had a hunch. The area I was hunting was on the northernmost fringe of the range of white oaks, which grow here, but only on sunny, sheltered northern sides of valleys—not on the wind and snow-scoured ridges above.

Sure enough, the deer were lower, in a belt of white oaks right behind a row of summer cottages that bordered the sunny north shore of a long, narrow lake. We were able to camp behind the oaks and hunt down on them. And we were close to deer every day—though in our thick woods, close doesn't necessarily count, especially with muzzleloaders!

Only later, when every white oak acorn was gone, did the deer move back up the ridge to the red oaks. They never bothered the apples or the cherries.

That's the way it is with deer and trees. They know which ones provide the best feed at different times of year, which ones are the best for hiding under, and which ones are ideal for rubbing and scraping. If you let the deer show you which trees are important, learn what kind of soils and exposure those trees grow best in, and learn to recognize the various tree species on sight—as the deer do—you just might gain the one piece of information that leads you to the biggest buck you've ever seen in your life. 🦌

Illustration by Duane Raver

How To Take the Biggest Buck

By John E. Phillips

Often, the biggest buck on a piece of property will die of old age. Not only that, but by the time this buck passes on, he will probably have learned more about you than you know about him.

To take a buck like this, you must first understand what this deer knows about you and the other sportsmen who hunt him. You must determine how and why he has been able to elude hunters for years and where he is able to survive undetected. Only when you learn what a buck knows about your habits will you increase your odds of taking that deer.

WHAT A BIG BUCK KNOWS ABOUT HUNTERS

The biggest buck on any property moves in open areas primarily at night for two reasons: First, he realizes that his chances for survival are best under the cover of darkness,

One technique for taking big bucks is to set up early about a mile away from the nearest road and let incoming hunters push deer to you. Photograph by Charles J. Alsheimer

and second, he knows that his best opportunity to scout for hunters is after dark. When an older-age-class buck walks through open woods after dark, his nose lets him know where hunters have traveled during the day and helps him identify their movement patterns. By the time a buck is three years old, he has learned that to survive, he must stay away from the areas that hunters frequent during daylight hours.

The mature bucks on any property also associate the sights, sounds, and smells of hunters with danger. They can detect the sounds of doors slamming and safeties clicking, as well as the noises made by hunters walking through the woods, stepping on sticks and brushing up against cover. The smells of cigarette smoke, chewing tobacco, candy bars, and many other man-made odors put them on red alert immediately.

Most trophy bucks also

• The middle of open fields, where hunter and hunted can easily spot each other.

Older-age-class bucks pattern hunters much better than they get patterned themselves.

TACTICS THAT PRODUCE THE BIGGEST BUCKS

Plain and simple: To take the biggest buck on any tract of land, be in an area that a large buck frequents at a time when he least expects you. Develop a hunting strategy different from that of every other person who hunts that same place.

• Strategy 1: Each morning, once the other members of your party decide where they want to hunt, pick the region where no one else will be. This section of land will be where the biggest buck is likely to live.

• Strategy 2: Learn to use a compass to travel in the woods before daylight and after dark. Reach a stand site about 1 mile away from the nearest road before daylight and then let other hunters coming into the woods at daylight push big bucks to you.

• Strategy 3: Purchase a pair of chest or hip waders and decide that you will live in them during deer season. The most meticulous, productive hunter on any section of land is the trapper. He must be conscious of eliminating human odor and moving in and out of the woods undetected. The trapper, whose livelihood depends on expertise, has learned that rubber waders prevent human odor from escaping from feet and legs, and thus allow for movement through brush and water that will go undetected by a deer's sensitive nose.

By learning the wisdom of the trapper and

have pinpointed the times and places that they expect to see hunters They know that most hunters will

• Arrive in the woods 45 minutes to 1 hour before daylight.

• Take a stand not more than 300 yards from a road where their vehicles are parked.

• Move and change positions several times during the day, with peak movement times typically occurring just before daylight, between 8:30 and 9:30 A.M., at 11:30 A.M., at 2 P.M., and 1 hour before dark.

The largest buck in an area has identified the regions where hunters will not likely set up, such as

• Thick-cover spots where it is difficult to see, move through, or get an open shot.

• Land within 100 yards of camp, where everyone knows no deer live.

• Areas across water that require access by boat, canoe, or chest-high wading.

• Flooded timber, which might result in wet feet or even bodies.

using water as a means by which to move through deer hideouts, you will not alert big bucks to your presence. Also you'll be able to hunt flooded timber—areas where you will be unexpected.

• Strategy 4: Utilize an aerial photo to determine where the biggest buck must be. Aerial photos will show you the lay of the land and can also help you pinpoint sections where trophy bucks must live.

If you are unfamiliar with the land that you are planning to hunt, take an aerial photo of the property to a place where hunters who know that country congregate. Ask the hunters to mark on your map where they will be hunting. Concentrate your efforts in places where no one else is.

As you become more familiar with the land, mark the regions that you and the others most often hunt. By doing this you will then be able to identify the parts of the property not being hunted—one of which is where the biggest buck is likely to live.

• Strategy 5: An hour before daylight, head into a small thicket in the middle of a field that you believe a buck is frequenting. Wait for the buck in his bedding area. If you try to get to this spot during daylight hours, the buck will see you coming. But if you reach the bedding area before daylight, you will have a better chance of spotting the trophy before he sees you.

• Strategy 6: Learn what is inside thick-cover regions. Even in the worst tangles, you will often find a break in the cover such as a small path, a creek, or a ditch. To find these open regions, charter a plane, fly over the area, and look down into the cover. Either that, or you can attempt to walk through it. You may be surprised at the number and sizes of openings you'll find. By taking a stand near one of these thick-cover openings, you may just see and bag the biggest buck on that property.

Small openings in thick tangles can be productive places to take a stand. Photograph by Charles J. Alsheimer

• Strategy 7: Build a trophy buck stand for the last few days of the hunt. At the end of the season, the largest bucks will be buried deep in thick cover during daylight hours. The more hunting pressure exerted on a region, the more certain you can be that the biggest bucks will be in the densest cover. The trick is to set up a stand before the largest bucks retreat to these sanctuaries.

First, determine from which direction the wind most often blows in your area. For example, where I live in Alabama, the wind usually blows from the northwest. If I pick a stand site facing northwest, the chances of my being able to hunt from that stand on most any day are greatly increased.

Next, choose a landmark that you can easily identify before daylight—such as a dead or fallen tree, a ditch, a gully, or any other form of unusual structure on the edge of the lower third of the area that you plan to hunt. Do not use flagging tape or any other type of trail marker that can tip another hunter off to that spot.

About 50 to 60 yards inside the thicket, where no one outside the cover can see what you are doing, use a small saw or pruning shears to make a trail 3 to 4 feet

Racked whitetails have learned that hunters will avoid crossing water, so a good strategy is to don a pair of waders, head out early, and wait for an unsuspecting buck to come sloshing in. Photograph by Bill Lea

Thick cover areas that are tough for hunters to get to, see in, and shoot through provide prime bed and rub sites for big bucks that have learned the habits of those who pursue them. Photographs by Charles J. Alsheimer

wide. Cut this trail to the center of the lower third of the thicket. Then clear an area about 5 to 6 feet in diameter, cutting shrubs down to the ground. Once you have completed your circle, cut three, 4-foot-wide shooting lanes that spoke out for 30 to 40 yards and are close enough together so that when you sit in the circle you can look down the center lane and use your peripheral vision to see down the other two lanes. Then, leave the area, and do not tell anyone about this trophy buck, end-of-the-season hotspot.

During the last few days of deer season when a favorable wind is blowing, return to this thick-cover area with a ground blind that has a top on it. Go into this region long before daylight, set up your ground blind, and plan to stay in the blind until either you bag your buck or darkness arrives.
• Strategy 8: During the rut, hunt funnel areas where two woodlots are necked down because of two converging habitats. For example, if a clear-cut, a pine plantation, or an agricultural field corners into a creek or a road and a small woodlot or thick-cover area is between the creek and the corner of the field, then deer most often will use this natural funnel to go from one woodlot to the other without having to cross the creek or field.

During the rut, the biggest buck on any property will assume the responsibility of breeding most of the does in his region. To find these does, he will utilize these funnels to travel from woodlot to woodlot, and often he will come through these funnels during daylight hours.

The biggest buck on any piece of property has outsmarted all of the other hunters on that land. To bag this buck you not only have to outsmart the deer, but you must also hunt smarter than all of the others who have failed to take the buck in the past.

Three Season Muleys

by Jim Zumbo

I reached the top of the ridge about an hour before sunrise. I leaned back on a limber pine bent by decades of powerful winds and took a well-deserved rest. I'd been climbing for two hours after leaving my pickup truck in the valley bottom.

Moments later I heard a bull elk bugling his soul out. In the brightening skies, I caught sight of him, a lovely 6-point animal with a harem of cows and calves. Nestling into a comfortable position, I watched him through binoculars as he tended his 12 females, constantly keeping them herded in a tight knot.

If I'd had an elk tag in my pocket I'd have been after him instantly. As it was, I was after a big buck muley high in the Wyoming mountains. It was mid-September, and I was hunting alone, hoping to spot the buck of a lifetime. Though I'd taken plenty of good muleys over the years, I was searching for a real bruiser. The mountains I hunted in western Wyoming were noted for big bucks, but getting one wouldn't be easy.

Early in the season, while hunters are scarce, mule deer bucks gather in bachelor groups high in the Wyoming mountains. Photograph by Tom Tietz

During the late hunting seasons bucks become most vulnerable. Snow drives them from the high country, and does drive them wild. Photograph by John R. Ford

I hunted hard the rest of the day but never saw a really good buck. I passed up a half-dozen with modest racks, one of them at least 26 inches wide, but I was looking for something much better. The next three days were repeats of the first. I could have taken a decent buck anytime, but the fantasy deer never showed. Nonetheless, it had been a special hunt—just me and the lofty peaks, where the air was crisp and sweet under incredibly blue skies.

Although I was hunting during a general season, I saw only four other hunters during those four days, and I'd seen them through a spotting scope. I was a nonresident of Wyoming at the time and had to draw a license; resident hunters who could have bought a license over the counter were curiously absent. I assumed that they weren't interested in early seasons and were

waiting for the traditional hunts later on.

A month later I hunted Colorado's general opener in mid-October. Compared with Wyoming it was like night and day. The woods were alive with people; it was almost impossible to hunt for an hour and not see another hunter.

I took a buck on that hunt—not the brute I was after, but a respectable deer with a 25-inch spread. With the crowds everywhere, I was glad to get him.

Later, during the tag end of November, I headed for Montana. Because of the timing, it was a prime period for good bucks. Snow had evicted most big game out of the highest mountains, and the rut prompted many big bucks to push down to winter ranges bustling with does.

I saw my big buck on that hunt, but a last-minute change in wind direction foiled my plans.

After spotting him at the edge of a sagebrush flat in the company of a dozen does, I made a stalk across a brushy clearing. I was about 400 yards away when the wind swapped ends and blew toward the buck. His reaction was immediate. I could only watch as he bolted away, his huge body making 20-foot bounds in the kind of graceful flight unique to mule deer. I'd judged his heavy antlers to be 30 inches wide, but as he ran they seemed much larger. I never saw him again, though I hunted the area for four more days. Other bucks abounded, but none that interested me.

Those three hunts were completely different in every aspect, including terrain, weather, hunting conditions, techniques, mule deer behavior, and competition from other hunters. Over the course of three months, I'd hunted muleys using widely varying strategies, each of them appropriate for the situation at hand. Timing is everything in hunting, and from September to October to November, the changes in mule deer availability are dramatic. My early hunt in Wyoming was typical for the early season. In September, bucks hang out in bachelor groups. Usually the deer are in small groups, but once, in late August, I saw 21 big bucks together. I'd been bowhunting in Utah at about 8,000 feet in elevation, and I watched in frustration as the deer ran by me single file out of range about 70 yards away.

For rifle hunters, the earliest hunts begin in early September in some states, but bowhunters commonly pursue muleys in August in several states. Because of the hot weather, bucks seek higher elevations where the air is cooler and there are fewer insects. That's not to say that big bucks don't remain in lowlands—they do—but you won't be able to hunt them there with a rifle that time of year. States with special September rifle seasons allow hunting only in the high country, usually above 10,000 feet, and only in chosen units. Many hunts are restricted to wilderness areas and are referred to as "high country" or "backcountry" hunts.

September hunting for muleys can be just as rigorous as hunting sheep or goats. On a num-ber of occasions I have seen big muleys above 13,000 feet in Colorado's high country while hunting ptarmigan in mid-September. The place I hunted birds wasn't open to early deer hunting, but other similar areas in Colorado offer September deer seasons.

If you aren't having success seeing good bucks during the early season but are locating plenty of does and fawns, leave the area and try elsewhere. Most bucks will be apart from does, usually at higher elevations. Most hunters tend to hunt a spot when they see plenty of game, hoping the bruiser will eventually show up. In September, he probably won't show up because he's a mile or more away, hanging out with other bucks.

Another suggestion is to use binoculars extensively, looking in shaded areas under rimrock or in and around patches of brush just under ridgetops. Because of lighter pressure, bucks may bed in the open where they can spot danger from below, but they'll tend to stay in the shade because it's cooler. In the middle of the day, glass for deer moving about because they'll commonly re-bed when the sun lights their sleeping quarters. As always, your binoculars are vital in locating bucks.

Once the October general season opens, you can forget about solitude in the deer woods. A few days prior to the opener, hunters begin arriving, setting up camps in choice spots, cutting firewood, driving roads looking for animals, and hiking around scouting for sign.

Wary old bucks know exactly what's happening long before the first shot is fired on opening day. They quickly abandon their normal feeding and bedding patterns and head for nasty country that offers good security cover. Favorite spots may include a huge chunk of thick oak brush that blankets an entire mountain slope, a deep canyon or plateau choked with pinyon and juniper trees, or a spruce-fir blowdown forest impenetrable to all but the most persistent and dedicated hunters.

For years I hunted an area in Utah that was one of the most popular deer spots in the state. Because of the energy boom in the mid-1970s and early '80s, new roads were punched into practically every canyon and atop every ridge. The only reason why some bucks grew old was the presence of thick vegetation. Each year my Utah hunting partners and I managed to take a good buck or two, but we had to work at it. We were in the woods a mile from our parked trucks by first light, and we stayed there all day. While most other hunters were driving roads and hunting close to their vehicles, we slipped through some of the most miserable cover in the West. The smart muleys often stayed holed up until we practically stepped on them.

Hunting in woods crowded with other hunters requires more than just hiking around, looking for deer. If you've read it once, you've read it a hundred times—scouting is an important key to success. Not only do you have to be smarter than the deer, but you also have to outwit the other hunters.

Most hunters never have time to scout before the season, and the ones who do sometimes don't know how to scout. The idea isn't simply to look for deer, but rather to seek hiding and escape cover. Because wary bucks change their habits prior to opening day, it's vital to find out where they go when they're disturbed.

In October, when most rifle seasons are under way, muley bucks spend most of their daylight hours bedded in the thickest cover they can find. Photograph by Michael Mauro

How to accomplish that? It might be best to determine where they *won't* be. Don't bother looking for them in sparse cover or in places that are popular with other hunters. Avoid hunting within a half-mile of a road and stay away from major horse and hiking trails.

Big muleys become nocturnal when the pressure is on. They move in the dark, and they stay put in daytime beds where they feel secure. Older bucks will lay up in tight cover in which you'd expect to find a savvy whitetail. You'll

need to penetrate that curtain of cover and dig them out.

You don't hear much about driving for muleys, but the technique works much of the time, and I use it as a last resort. Drives are simple to put on, whether there are two or 10 hunters involved. To outsmart a buck, don't set up standers where they can see into wide-open vistas. A big buck will slip through cover, running or sneaking through fingers of brush and trees as he makes his escape.

If there's a steep, rocky draw in your hunt area, which is quite common in mule deer country, be sure someone is watching it. Muleys will hide in canyons and draws at every opportunity, and they will remain in the hidden recesses and pockets until they feel safe enough to come out several days later.

Tree stands also aren't much talked about, or used, in the mule deer woods, but they can be extremely effective, especially where underbrush is thick. Any time you can observe from an elevated position you put yourself at a decided advantage.

Competing with lots of other hunters and being successful involves more than luck. You might get lucky on occasion and see a good deer near a road, or in an open meadow, but to be consistently successful you need to stay one step ahead of the competition. That means getting into the woods before shooting hours, hunting all day and remaining out there until shooting light is over.

If you see lots of does and fawns but few or no bucks, try another spot. It's tempting to stay with an area where you see plenty of deer, but the bigger bucks are apt to be off in tighter cover or in more remote country. Remember that during the October general hunts, the rut hasn't started and big bucks are usually alone or in the company of other mature bucks. Finding them won't be easy, and you won't find them by doing what all of the other hunters do. You've got to discipline yourself to hunt hard and long. Only then will you beat the odds, which typically amount to a 30 or 40 percent hunter-success rate in most mule deer states.

Hunting during the late season offers the best of mule deer hunting, just as it does for whitetails. Bucks become vulnerable because of their interest in breeding, but there's another major advantage when you're hunting muleys. During typical years, snow piles high in the upper elevations, forcing deer to the low country. Big bucks suddenly, often overnight, become accessible.

Mule deer rut usually takes place in mid-to-late November. Because of the deer's vulnerability, most states don't allow general rifle hunting during the mule deer rut, just as they don't offer general hunting during the elk rut in September. Montana is one of the few states that holds the general deer and elk season throughout the month of November. But many other states offer lottery-drawn late-season hunts. If you're lucky enough to get one of these tags, you may be in for the best hunting of the season—perhaps the best in your career.

An interesting situation often develops during the rut. Valerius Geist, a university professor in Canada who is considered to be one of the foremost experts in mule deer behavior, says that the biggest, oldest bucks often spend much of their time bedded and out of sight near a herd of does. Lesser bucks are much more visible as they wander about, seeking does in estrus. Geist says that the older bucks don't move much and are seldom spotted by eager hunters who take the first good buck they see.

When the rut is in full swing, you should assume there's *always* a buck near a bunch of does. A few years ago, while hunting in eastern Montana with well-known hunter and booking agent Jack Atcheson Sr., I saw a dozen or more herds of muleys every day. We were in wide-open treeless country that harbored an unbeliev-

able number of muleys.

Every time we spotted some does and fawns we unlimbered our spotting scopes and almost always found the buck. He'd either be with the does or off by himself, quietly bedded nearby. If no buck was in the group of does, we'd wait awhile, and usually we'd see him show up, often at a trot. Much of our glassing was done at long distances, generally a half-mile to a mile or more away.

I took a nice 4×3 buck on the last day of the hunt. He was with a dozen does and never knew that I was in his world when I squeezed the trigger. He was far too interested in the females around him.

Mule deer breeding habits are vastly different than those of whitetails. Muleys don't make scrapes, and their rubs aren't necessarily signposts, but rubs do tell you where muleys are traveling. I always concentrate my efforts in areas where rubs are plentiful, and I find more bucks in those spots.

Remember that muleys are looking for does in heat during the breeding season, and they'll travel long distances to find females. If you see tracks in the snow that you believe are made by does, follow anyway. Chances are good that a buck may intercept them ahead of you, and he will remain with the does for several hours.

Late hunts require special gear, as well as a willingness to put up with some pain and suffering. You'll probably be dealing with snow and cold weather—sometimes really cold, as in 20°F or more below zero.

When you're planning your mule deer hunt, give priority consideration to the time of year. If you must hunt during the general season, be aware of the surprising competition you'll face on public land. If you can, give some thought to the early and late seasons, too. Above all, don't forget that the buck you hunt puts on three faces in the fall. He's a completely different animal during each of those periods. Learn all you can about him and match your tactics to his. That's the best way to beat the system, and remember that they're his systems—all three of them. ➷

Maximum Security Muleys

By John Haviland

et's take a look at deer No. 1300, a muley buck from an Idaho Department of Fish and Game study. During the carefree summer and early fall, the buck roamed his home range of nearly 4.5 square miles. But as human activity increased during the October hunting season, the buck's behavior abruptly changed. He quit venturing into the open and hid in a dense stand of junipers, which was labeled in the study as his "hunting season home range." Even under cover, the buck rarely moved, reinforcing his security. No. 1300 showed the typical response of a modern mule deer.

As the hunting season progressed, fewer hunters drove the gravel roads and combed the hills in the area of southeastern Idaho where the buck lived. No. 1300 was lulled into a false sense of security. The buck ventured from his juniper patch for the first time in weeks on the evening of the last day of the hunting season. Alas, an unseen hunter waited in the adjacent grain field.

ecil Brown is the Idaho biologist who tracked No. 1300 and many other mule deer via radio collar during his recently completed study, *Mule Deer Security*. During the experiment, Brown examined how stress, disturbance, and security factor into mule deer behavior. The results were surprising. Brown discovered that shelter and escape terrain had even more influence on deer than food and water did.

The report proved what many hunters had already theorized: that the floppy-eared mule deer ain't what it used to be. Increased hunting pressure throughout the West has created a warier animal, especially during the hunting season.

"I guess I wouldn't say individual mule deer are smarter than they used to be," Brown said. "But over the years, the deer that have learned the proper response to the hunting pressure have lived. The ones that didn't were killed."

During his study, Brown monitored nine radio-collared mule deer in summer and early fall ranges of "low security habitat," which consisted mostly of farmland and rolling, open terrain. The deer either moved to more secure habitat within the first days of the hunting season or were shot. Some deer moved as much as 4 miles.

Brown contrasted those deer with 10 others that lived in "secure habitat," which consisted of steep, rocky, broken terrain mixed with dense vegetation such as juniper and mountain mahogany. The second group's daily survival rate was seven times higher during the same period of study. On average, these deer moved only 1/2 mile.

But secure habitat is a relative term. "Primarily you have to look at hunting access to an area,"

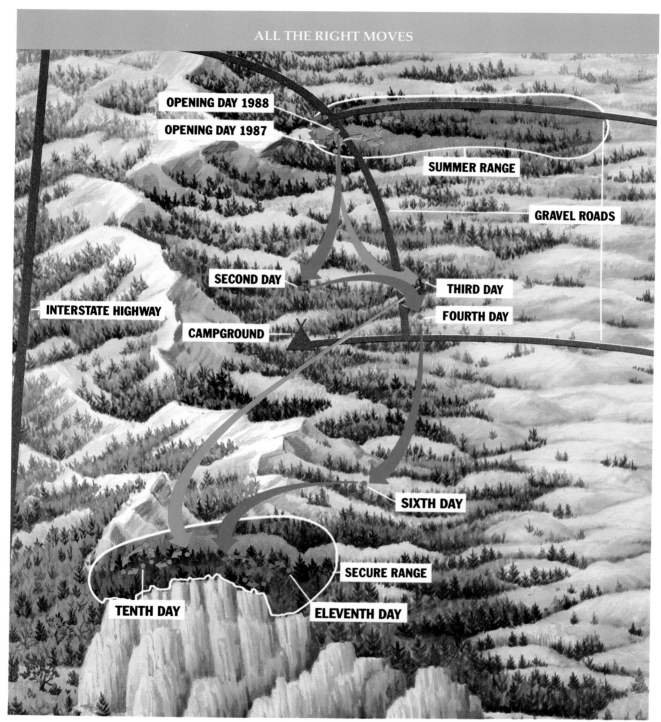

ALL THE RIGHT MOVES

OPENING DAY 1988

OPENING DAY 1987

SUMMER RANGE

GRAVEL ROADS

SECOND DAY

THIRD DAY

FOURTH DAY

INTERSTATE HIGHWAY

CAMPGROUND

SIXTH DAY

SECURE RANGE

TENTH DAY

ELEVENTH DAY

The drawing shows a mule deer buck's travel patterns over two subsequent hunting seasons in a heavily hunted area in southeastern Idaho (red arrows 1987; blue arrows 1988). The buck's movements were recorded via radio collar an average of every two days. Both years the buck started on his summer range, a fairly sparse, relatively flat area mixed with low-growing brush and cropland. During the spring and summer months, the buck traveled and fed throughout this food-rich area. But as soon as opening day rolled around, he began heading for his secure range: high in the mountains, surrounded by broken terrain, rimrock, and dense trees and bushes. Both years of the study, the buck followed a nearly identical migration path and never ventured from the secure habitat during the hunting season. According to biologist Cecil Brown, the deer was a 4×4 with an antler spread of more than 25 inches when captured. By the end of the study, the antler spread extended to more than 30 inches. Illustration by Charles Pearson

When hunting season starts, mule deer head for the thickest, roughest country they can find. Anticipate their movements, and you can take a trophy. Photograph by Jim Zumbo

Brown said. He explained that if roads divide the terrain and make it easy to reach, no amount of rough topography and thick vegetative cover will hide the deer. "Hunters can make drives through these areas and move the deer out," he said.

Large areas of cover uninterrupted by roads are far more appealing to mule deer. Steep, rocky terrain is also appealing because sight distance is limited and even the hardiest hunters have difficulty hunting it effectively.

Jack Atcheson Jr. is an outfitter and mule deer guide in the breaks of Montana's Missouri River. Like Brown, Atcheson has noticed how mule deer react to the pressures of hunting season.

Atcheson and his guides start scouting heavily the week before the start of hunting season.

"If you're going to do some meaningful scouting, you have to get back in the rougher country where the crowds don't go," Atcheson said. "A buck you see back in that rough country is likely to still be there when hunting starts."

Atcheson says that when scouting, you should look not only for bucks but also for the type of habitat mule deer need to survive the hunting season.

Even in snow, a hunter might miss a well-camouflaged buck like this one hidden behind barren trees. Photograph by Jim Zumbo

WHAT'S ON THE RADIO?

During a five-year study on mule deer security by the Idaho Department of Fish and Game, radio telemetry was used to track mule deer throughout a vast area in the southeastern part of the state. Using motion-sensitive radio-collar transmitters, 107 deer were monitored over approximately 1,300 square miles, an area which included six mountain ranges.

The deer were captured in a variety of ways, including box traps, foot snares, and chemical immobilization, as well as by net gunning and drive netting with the aid of a helicopter. After the deer were captured, they were outfitted with radio collars and tracked via radio receivers both from the ground and from airplanes. The deer's positions were recorded every other day during the hunting season, two times a week in the early fall, and about every 20 days throughout the rest of the year. If an animal died, the transmitter sent out a mortality signal. Testing of the radio transmitters revealed that they were 97 percent accurate, and the collars have proved to be one of the most important tools available to wildlife biologists.

"We can accomplish a lot of things with radio telemetry that we couldn't have done without it," said Cecil Brown, who headed the study. "It has really increased our research ability."

And when mule deer are holed up in secure cover, a radio receiver certainly has a better chance of finding them than any man.

Biologists attach a radio telemetry collar to a young mule deer buck that was captured in a drive net (left). A doe captured on her summer range is about to be released with her new necklace (above right).

"In drier country like the prairie, water is critical and it's going to dictate to some degree where the deer will be," Atcheson said. When secure cover, food, and water are found all in one place, Atcheson says that half the work of finding a buck is over.

"When I find places like that, I call them micro-habitats, and I remember them," he said. Many times Atcheson's hunters have killed bucks in one of these micro-habitats, and the next year, he'll find bucks of equal size in the same spots. "The bucks must be moving in to fill up the vacant habitat."

Brown said that during the study he would occasionally find one of his deer hidden in an island of sagebrush or timber. "Hunters would drive right past these pockets because they never thought a deer would be in such an obvious spot," Brown said. "Also, in the lower elevations, deer would often hide in the middle of 2 or 3 square miles of sagebrush. Hunters would take one look and think there wasn't enough cover to hide any deer and move on."

The deer in Brown's study responded in one of three ways to the hunting pressure. The majority of the deer moved to a small portion of their range out of harm's way and sat tight. By reducing their movements, they were further shielded from hunters. Other deer moved completely out of the sparsely covered country until they found a secure home range. The remaining deer kept up a random movement the whole season, often moving more than 30 miles from their summer ranges.

In each case, increased human activity triggered the deer's shift in range. One buck Brown studied started its move just before hunting season because of the commotion from a cattle drive.

"Some deer don't have a pattern and seem to

DAILY MULE DEER ACTIVITY

Source: Idaho Department of Fish and Game, Cecil Brown, Michael McDonald

Cecil Brown, a wildlife biologist with the Idaho Department of Fish and Game, and graduate student Michael McDonald studied three mature mule deer bucks to determine how the hunting season would affect their hourly movements. Using radio collars to track the bucks, the biologists discovered that the deer decreased their activity when hunter activity was highest.

The graph shows that one of the most significant variances occurred between 7 A.M. and 11 A.M., when hunting pressure is generally highest. During these morning hours, the deer's activity level dropped 30.3 percent. The muleys' peak morning activity also shifted one hour earlier—from 7 A.M. to 6 A.M.—most likely in response to hunters moving in to set up just before sunrise.

During the hunting season, the bucks' daytime activity dropped an average of 12 percent. The deer showed a brief increase in activity around noon and again late in the afternoon. But as sunset approached, their movement dropped

significantly for a brief period, presumably as hunters reentered the hunting area for the evening. Yet, as is the case with most big-game animals, the muleys were very active around sunset, feeding as the cover of darkness approached.

Although the deer kept different hours at night during the hunting season than they did before the season, the average nocturnal activity was about the same. McDonald surmised in his report that the deer in the study may restrict their activity around the clock. This way the deer can remain close to the most secure habitat in their range, decreasing vulnerability and reducing the possibility of detection.

Of the three bucks tracked during the study, one was killed by a hunter. This buck was a mover. The two bucks that survived the hunting season decreased their daytime activity by 17 percent and 14 percent, respectively; the harvested animal decreased his daytime activity by only 1 percent. After 20 years of heavy hunting in the area, most of the deer seem to have learned to stay put in secure habitat while the season is under way.

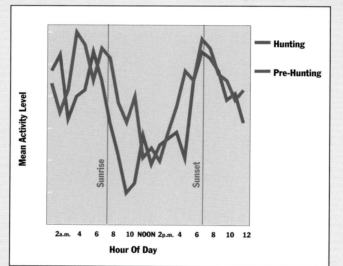

be on the run the whole season," Brown said. "One buck kept moving in a random manner and by the end of the season had made a big circle right back to where he had started.

"Most of the animals moved to areas located on or near their migration routes between their summer and winter ranges where they had been before, so they knew where they were going," Brown said. The biologist noted that some deer faithfully selected the same ranges each year.

Atcheson also noticed a strong territoriality in mule deer. "From year to year, I see the same bucks in the same drainages," Atcheson said. "I remember one buck had been neutered

somehow, and we could tell he was the same buck by his weird antlers. For six years in a row, we saw him in the same draws and often in the same beds."

The deer's daily habits also changed after the hunting season started. After opening day, the Idaho muleys were more active at night, just before daylight, and in the hours around sunset. A study by Brown and graduate student Michael McDonald showed that during the day, muleys were generally most active when hunter movements were lowest.

"The majority of hunters start out at first light and by midmorning they're tired, and if they haven't seen any deer they head for home," Brown said.

With the woods quiet and empty of hunters, afternoon can be a good time to hunt. The deer are up from their beds around 2 P.M. or 3 P.M. to stretch and browse. Brown's charts indicated that the deer had slight increases in activity during this mid-to-late afternoon period. The activity levels generally dropped off around 5 P.M. and then increased dramatically during the last hour or two before sunset.

Mule deer living in the open use the lay of the land to hide. Atcheson says that he has watched bedded deer conceal themselves by drooping their ears and by lying flat on the ground. "If there's any tall cover, like sagebrush or dog-hair-thick trees, the deer are going to hide in that," Atcheson said. "Their main cover, though, is getting way away from hunters and limiting their movements."

Because man has successfully suppressed forest fires for decades, much of today's forests are thicker with less understory browse for the deer to eat. As a consequence, deer must move to the edges of the forest to feed. Atcheson sits on vantage points early and late in the day glassing the edges of cover.

One year Atcheson spotted a buck with the magical 30-inch antler spread. The buck showed himself for only a minute and then dropped back into the ponderosa pines. Atcheson and one of his guides went into the pines to move the buck toward two hunters waiting at the far end. "That buck heard us in there, but he held tight until my guide threw a rock in a thicket and almost hit the buck," Atcheson said. The buck jumped up and fled deeper into the forest past one of the hunters, who shot it.

"The buck could have run into the open prairie and we never would have had a chance at him, but he wanted to stay in that cover," Atcheson said.

During the lull of midday Atcheson moves undercover to stillhunt. But sneaking up on a hiding deer is difficult.

"They'll hold tight when they hear you and see you, but if you make eye contact or they smell you, they'll blow out of there," Atcheson said.

However, the same broken country that con-ceals the deer hides the hunter. Atcheson moves along with the wind in his favor, staying in shallow draws with only his head visible above the ground to look for deer. A hunter must search every bit of ground. Any buck he walks past may be the only buck for miles.

"I wonder how many bucks I have sneaked by so carefully and never seen?" Atcheson asked. "In some cases, it might be better to let the buck see you in that thick stuff so he'll bolt out of there and at least you'll see him and maybe get a shot."

Many bucks move only at night to avoid hunters, but the next best thing is a cloudy sky and falling snow. Deer feel more secure moving in the reduced light of a cloudy day and with a curtain of falling snow to screen their movements.

"Deer definitely use the cover of falling snow," Atcheson said. "Without a doubt, all of my best days hunting deer have been when it's snowing."

Atcheson said that many hunters believe deer hold tight when snow is falling; the guide, however, says that is only true when the wind is also blowing.

"Hunting deer in a snowstorm only works when there's no wind and when the snow's pretty much falling straight down," Atcheson said. "The wind messes up their early warning system of hearing and smell, which makes them really skittish." Atcheson said that when the wind is blowing, like in a blizzard, deer bed down in thick cover.

Atcheson sees more mature bucks now on the public land he hunts than ever before. He said that it's partly because a succession of mild winters has caused less winterkill. But, he said that the major reason is that the bucks' adaptive behavior to hunting pressure has allowed them to live longer. When the hunting season starts, the deer head for the thickest, rockiest, steepest terrain in the area. In recent years, the majority of the bucks taken by Atcheson's hunters were in such secluded spots that the deer had to be carried out on packboards.

"If those bucks ever figure out how to read a calendar, we're all in trouble," Atcheson remarked.

Perhaps they already can.

Golden Moments

By Jim Zumbo

According to a fundamental rule in big game species behavior, animals are most active early in the morning and late in the afternoon. This is no deep, dark secret, of course, as anyone who has spent any time in the woods understands this behavioral pattern.

What is surprising, however, is that so many hunters fail to take advantage of these red-hot periods—I mean *really* take advantage of them, rather than merely watching intently from the particular spot where they happen to be during these low-light minutes. Too often hunters are either in camp, in vehicles, or walking in or out of the woods during these two prime times of the day.

To fully capitalize on these productive hours, it's important to first understand some basics in big-game animal habits. Feeding generally begins in late afternoon, often when there's still shooting light. Animals continue to forage on and off during the night and are normally on their way back to bedding areas just as shooting light arrives. They chew their cuds in their beds during daylight hours and begin a renewed feeding cycle as darkness quickly approaches.

How many times have you left camp too late in the morning, arriving at your hunting spot either when the sun is already up or during good shooting light? If this is the case, you've already missed those early morning minutes—that prime period when animals are moving. The same is true during late afternoon hours, which may be even more important. Most hunters are out of the woods before shooting light is gone, again missing that precious time when animals are out of their beds—now traveling toward feeding areas.

This is not to say that hunting during the middle of the day is a waste of time. After all, big-game animals don't just disappear during daylight hours. The trouble is that most animals are bedded and at full alert when the sun is high. Catching them off guard in their beds is one of the biggest hunting challenges that I know of, and jumping an animal from its bed and getting a shot at it is a tough assignment in itself. On the plus side, in woods crowded with other hunters, spooked animals are often active during the day, possibly offering you a shot as they head for security cover. Also, animals sometimes leave their beds during the day to feed lightly, particularly where hunting pressure is light.

All things considered, though, you'll stand a better chance of seeing a vulnerable animal during the very early or very late periods.

Early in the morning, animals will either be feeding or walking to bedding areas, often nibbling on browse as they go. They'll often be distracted when engaged in these activities, allowing you either to move in close for a shot or to take a good rest and shoot when you're comfortable. If you're in a tree stand and have chosen the correct spot to watch, a traveling animal may move within shooting range.

Another plus is that if there are several animals in a herd, you may be given the opportunity to wait and see what materializes. Perhaps the buck you see first isn't the best in the bunch. A bigger one might be hidden nearby. By being patient and observing the animals closely, you might spot the bigger buck before the herd moves out of sight.

To get to your hunting spot in the dark before sunup, you'll probably need a flashlight (where legal). A full moon may allow you to see without a light, but it's always best to carry one. Use a small light, and direct the beam onto the ground directly in front of you. Don't shine the light into the air because you'll risk spooking nearby game—though I don't believe an artificial light will move most animals very far in the dark. (Wise old trophies are the exception, however, and may be long gone by first light.)

It's also a good idea to be at a predetermined vantage point long before shooting light arrives. If you're hunting right, you'll be in position when the eastern horizon turns from black to slate gray. A rosy, bright sky will follow, and you'll then be able to identify objects such as basic topographical features in the dim light.

As you continue to sit, you'll probably begin to wonder if daylight will ever come. It will, of course, but the arrival will seem agonizingly slow, especially if the tem-perature is cold. If you're hunting in the mountains, you can often count on a brisk breeze to chill you thoroughly just before the sun peeks over the horizon.

Some hunters believe that moving through the woods in the darkness before sunup is foolish because you'll spook animals while you walk. If you wait until it's light enough to see and shoot, they say, you'll have an opportunity to look those animals over.

Of course, this is true if you plan on walking through a prime area. However, if you need to get to a specific spot that's some distance away, you won't have any choice but to travel in the dark.

When you spook animals in the dark, they'll seldom leave a particular area. They're comfortable and secure in the dark, and normally they will move away a bit and then resume what they were doing. I've noted this behavior by observing bucks in the moonlight that I'd frightened while walking. After shooting light arrived, I'd spotted the same bucks in the general area that I'd spooked them. Of course, I wouldn't trust a wary old buck to hang around very long once he gets a whiff of a hunter, regardless of the time of day or night. In this regard, there's always a risk that you must take in walking to your stand, but I think that the potential reward of being in a pre-

Big-game animals can sometimes be caught in the open just as the sun is rising or setting. That's why it pays to be in a hotspot early and late in the day. Photographs by D. Robert Franz and Jim Zumbo

scouted hotspot at daylight is worth that risk.

Most hunters are more willing to get to their hunting area in the dark before sunrise, rather than to leave their area in the dark after sunset. That's no surprise, because most hunters want to be out of the woods—or at least out to a familiar area—before dark. In the morning, you have all day to hunt (or find your way back to your starting point). In the afternoon, you must race the waning light, and if you're deep enough in the boonies, you might have to contend with finding your way out in the night.

If I had to pick one time of day to hunt, I'd select the period just before it gets dark in late afternoon. Because of the decreasing amount of light, animals feel secure. They're hungry and want to get on with their foraging, and as a result they may make themselves vulnerable by exposing themselves in open feeding areas or along trails—even though it may be for only a few minutes while shooting light lasts.

In the morning, on the other hand, animals have full bellies. They become nervous as the day brightens, especially when hunters begin to drive about and walk through their habitat. Once daybreak approaches, an animal's primary concern is to get to escape cover where it can hide for the rest of the day.

After spending plenty of time in deer camps around the United States, it's been my observation that the most successful hunters seldom arrive back in camp before dark. Murry Burnham, a Texas hunter and game-call manufacturer, is a good example. Murry is a superb hunter who rarely leaves for home with an unpunched game tag. He's usually the first one out of camp in the morning and the last one to return at night.

Keep in mind that there is a serious disadvantage to late afternoon hunting, other than the possibility of having to find your way out of the dark woods. If you make a fatal hit on an animal, you might have to locate and field dress the ani-

Late afternoon is a particularly good time to hunt. This whitetail buck in rut starts to feel secure as the light fades.
Photograph by Leonard Lee Rue III

mal in the black of night. Following a blood trail when it's black out isn't as futile as it may seem, however. Crimson spots are actually fairly easy to see in artificial light (where legal), provided that you aren't seriously colorblind.

If you hit an animal and are faced with impending darkness, quickly mark the first blood spot you find by tying a length of fluorescent red or orange flagging at the spot. Tie the marker high on a tree branch or tall shrub so that you can locate it again with a flashlight later on. Immediately continue your search for blood, tying more pieces of ribbon as you go. The idea is to try to determine the quarry's direction of escape so you'll have a line of travel to work with. If the blood trail peters out, leave the area immediately and go for help—if help is a reasonable distance away. As soon as you can, return to the spot with your buddies armed with as many lanterns and powerful flashlights as you can find. If blood still can't be found, continue your search by sectioning off the area and thoroughly covering every square yard in the place that you lost the blood trail and in increasingly large concentric circles around that spot. After the search is over, remember to remove any ribbons you may have tied to branches.

As a matter of hunting ethics, you should never take a questionable shot, especially when nightfall is approaching. Many times, however, we're presented with a perfect shot that requires a lengthy follow-up on a blood trail. On numerous occasions, I've shot elk and deer through the lungs, but had to follow a faint blood trail to find them in dark woods. Sometimes there was no blood trail at all. In these cases, locating the animal was a matter of persistence and determination.

Hunting the edges of darkness, either in the morning or afternoon, requires some thought and planning. You must time your movements with that of the quarry's. The objective is to be at the right place at the right time, not a few minutes too early or a few minutes too late.

Everything you do in the woods should be geared to those golden moments of first and last light. As you hunt during the day, look for signs of fresh feeding. Examine security cover—as that's where animals will bed during the day. In whitetail country, a cedar swamp, dense hemlock stand, or laurel thicket will likely be used as bedding or hiding cover. Plan your mornings and afternoons so that you can intercept deer moving into and out of these escape areas. In muley country, check out thick oak brush pockets, quaking aspen stands with heavy undergrowth, or tightly woven pinyon/juniper forests, because these are places where deer will seek shelter during the day. If you're hunting elk, look for signs of active feeding in meadows, grassy parks, and clearcuts—areas that elk will use in the evening. Find a vantage spot, and *be there* when the animals are there.

Some hunters have a good sense of direction—day or night—and can always find their way into or out of an area. Many other hunters, however, are unwilling to walk around the woods in the dark. This is perfectly natural if you aren't an experienced woodsman, but you can overcome your fears by marking a trail out of the area with reflective plastic flagging tied to trees. Your flashlight will help you spot the ribbon. As you leave, remove the plastic material, or leave it if you intend to return in the morning. Be sure to remove the flagging when the hunt is over.

If you're unnerved by the dark woods and figure on returning to a familiar road, ridge, or trail before dark, mark a way out, anyway. You might take a shot just at last light, and you could need some help finding your route out if you took too much time stalking your quarry, following a blood trail or field-dressing an animal.

Hunting the golden moments will require you to get out of your warm sleeping bag earlier than you'd probably like. You might miss breakfast or be late for dinner, and you'll have to deal with the dark woods, too.

In my opinion, though, these discomforts are well worth the effort. Hunting season comes but once a year, and I believe that it makes good sense to squeeze every minute out of every hunting day. That's why I'll be out there in the dark as often as required.

You should be, too.

PART 5

HUNTING BIGGER GAME

Break the Rules for Bulls

By Bob Robb

It had been the most frustrating, and yet the most glorious, week of elk hunting imaginable. The particular section of southwestern Montana that I was hunting was simply crawling with elk. I was into bulls every day—sometimes several a day—and yet by the sixth day I hadn't even drawn my bow.

Oh, a half-dozen smaller bulls had come in, and I could have taken one had I chosen to do so. But I was after a good bull, one of those elk with many winters—and many hunting seasons—under his belt. I had called up a handful of these big boys so far, but each time they wouldn't come in quite close enough for a shot. They'd hang up in the brush 80 yards out and rake their antlers, or stop and peek around a pine tree, or circle the wagons and try to get my wind. There'd been lots of action and plenty of excitement, but no cigar . . . not yet.

That's why I'd decided to try something radical. On this day I strapped a smallish 5-point elk antler to my daypack and went to an area where I'd seen a heavily antlered 5×5 bull two days before. At dawn I was in position, champing at

An elk like this can be yours—if you are willing to ignore all the old rules. Photograph by Len Rue, Jr.

the bit for enough light to see my sight pins. When it was bright enough, I bugled, and a bull responded instantly, not 100 yards down the canyon. I aggressively closed the gap, and we began a verbal sparring match that obviously incensed the bull and sent the hackles on the back of my neck straight to attention. Thrashing and crashing, the bull came in, but, like many of the others, he hung up just out of range, up the opposite side of a small creek. I could see his antler tops above the brush as he raked and chuckled, showing off his muscle. It was the same big 5 X 5 I'd seen previously.

Taking my little 5-point antler, I poked it above the brush pile I was set up next to, bellowed on my bugle, and pawed the ground with my boot. All the while I twisted and turned the antler in a shadowlike imitation of the big bull. I saw my "rival" raise his head, and when he saw the antler above the brush, he was sold. He came rumbling down the creek bank like an antlered tank. As the bull plowed into the bottom, I dropped my antler and readied the bow. He then charged up the other side and paused, looking for the pipsqueak 5-point that had been there just a minute before. My arrow centered the bull's lungs, and 30 minutes later, I was giggling with glee.

If the elk won't play by the rules, then why should I?

Just because you're set up in a nice spot and have a bull answering your bugles doesn't necessarily mean you're guaranteed a shot. Today's elk sometimes require off-the-wall tactics. Photographs by Bob Robb

Today's bull elk are smartening up. Mature bulls—those who have lived through more than four or five hunting seasons—have seen all of the tricks. They've heard bugling good and bad, smelled the woodsmoke of camps large and small, seen the annual invasion of their mountain homes by hunters dressed in everything from total camouflage to pumpkin orange. They've been stalked, driven, chased, bushwhacked, and run around the mountain more than enough times to ever forget. They've done more than read the textbooks on elk hunting—they've written the chapters themselves.

That's why today you need to be ready to give elk something they've never seen before. Not that textbook maneuvers won't work. Of course they will. But nothing works all of the time, and when the textbook comes up with an answer of

"five" to the question "two plus two," you know it's time to throw away the book and try something radical.

Merritt Pride, who runs Lost Fork Ranch out of Cameron, Montana, is a longtime guide and outfitter and one fine elk hunter. He also isn't afraid to try something different to get a bull within range.

"One time I bugled a nice bull in for a bowhunting client who had a fancy bow with an overdraw and all that," Pride recalled. "When the client went to draw, the arrow fell off the rest—*clank!*—and the bull trotted off. The other bulls had been acting funny that week, so instead of cow calling or bugling, I gave the alarm bark of a cow elk. Everyone says that when a bull hears this, he's gone. But this bull came right back in.

"The hunter was so amazed that he let the arrow fall right off the rest again—*clank!*—and

the bull bolted off a second time. I couldn't believe it! But I barked one more time, and the bull stopped and came back—a little more cautiously this time, but he did come back. My hunter finally got it together and made the shot."

Then there was the time Pride and I were hunting as a team. We had gotten a good bull going in a spot so brushy that you could barely see your hand in front of your face. The bull had a small harem of cows with him, and the group was above us on the side of a small timbered ridge across a creek cut. As the crow flies, the elk were 75 yards off. As the hunter walks, they were 200 yards away.

The bull strutted back and forth across the face of that ridge, bellowing and ripping up brush. As he moved, we moved, staying parallel and not letting him get what he wanted—the wind. This went on for perhaps a half-hour,

when finally we heard some rocks clatter. The bull had had enough, and he was going to take his cows over the ridge and away from this noisy madhouse. Pride and I both realized what was happening at the same instant, and when the guide looked at me with bug eyes and an expression that said, "Now what?" I whispered, "Let's charge 'em!"

So I did. As Pride called and raked like a demon, I crashed through the brush as fast as I could right at the elk. I hoped the herd would think the noise was another bull that was lathered up and ready to do battle. When I came out of the thickest brush into a smallish clearing, there was the bull, not 40 yards off—and he was a dandy 6-point. Stunned to find that the Charge of the Light Brigade had worked, I stumbled over a fallen log. That broke the spell, or I'm sure I would have had a good shot at that trophy.

It seems like elk want to see elk, or at least something with four feet that doesn't resemble a hunter. If they can't see another animal, they often get as cautious as a cat stalking a bird on your front lawn. Any little thing that gets them to believe that you are really another elk, and not some bozo straight from the coffee shop in town, is often enough to win the day.

Take horses, for example. I've had more than one bull bugle at the sound of my horse's hoofs as we clompity-clomped down the trail. I can remember one rifle season in New Mexico when my partner and I were riding along through some rolling mountaintop meadow areas dotted by several islands of heavy timber. Com-ing around the corner of one such timber stand, we ran smack dab into the middle of a herd of 30 elk, five of them nice 5-point bulls. The textbook says to stop, slowly turn the horses around, ride into the timber, dismount, and make a stalk on foot.

The only rule to remember with elk hunting is that there are no rules. And when bulls stop playing by the book, it's time to rip up the manual and fight back with some radical moves of your own. Photograph by Don and Lolly Skillman

Not us. Instead we continued to ride right at the elk, who stood their ground trying to figure out just what in the world we were. When we got to within 150 yards, I turned my horse broadside, tossed the reins to my partner, who had moved his mount in between the elk and me, stepped off the saddle, sat down, and as the horses cleared my position, shot the largest bull in the bunch.

Textbook elk hunting? No way. Effective? You betcha.

An elk hunter's worst enemy—after his own clumsiness—is the wind. Bow season, rifle season, muzzleloader season—it doesn't matter. If you don't have the wind in your favor, you don't have a chance. How good is an elk's sense of smell? Jack Atcheson Sr., the veteran booking agent from Butte, Montana, has shot more big bulls with his rifle on public land than just about any man alive. And Atcheson has a pretty strong respect for the elk's nose.

"Elk have a sense of smell like few other animals you can hunt," he said. "Let me give you an example. I spotted a band of elk feeding along in an open meadow a ½ mile from where I was standing. All at once I felt the wind switch, going now from me right to them. The second that breeze—and it was a gentle breeze, not a strong wind—got my scent to those elk, they threw their heads back, noses in the air for just an instant, then bolted into the dark timber. At a ½ mile! How many elk do you think smell most hunters during the season and skedaddle before the hunters ever even know they are in the neighborhood?"

Elk live in swirling-wind country. Many longtime elk hunters—myself included—believe that elk purposely bed down during the day in areas where the wind always swirls as a means of extra protection against attack from all sides. Textbook strategy says to stay out of these unstable wind areas so that you won't spook elk with your evil odor.

But when it's hot, dry, and the ground underfoot is as crunchy as a crumpled-up newspaper, the elk don't move much during shooting light. If you want a bull, you have to go in after him. The way to avoid the swirling wind is to borrow a page from the whitetail hunter's textbook and get above the breeze—in a tree stand.

In hot weather, elk like to live near water holes and/or wallows, which they use to help them stay cool and comfortable. Scout around and find a wallow or water hole that is peppered with fresh sign—usually tracks and droppings. Take a portable, backpackable tree stand and set it up nearby. Try to move in and place the stand when the breeze seems to be blowing steadily in your face, but once the stand is up, plan on spending the entire day there. Take lunch, an empty bottle for "emergencies," and a good paperback book to help fight boredom, strap yourself in with a safety belt, and be patient.

Give the stand two or three days, if necessary. During that time you'll be surprised at what you'll see from your perch. On a recent hunt in Idaho's Selway-Bitterroot Wilderness during the opening week of rifle season, a friend staked out a water hole under hot conditions for three days. He ended up seeing not only elk but also mule deer, whitetail deer, a coyote, a lone black bear, and a mountain lion, plus numerous raptors, songbirds, and small game. In so doing, he shot the biggest bull of the hunt, an eye-popping 6 × 6.

Another trick borrowed from the whitetail hunter's handbook that can be quite productive for elk is rattling.

While hunting in New Mexico in 1990 with U.S. Outfitters and my good friend Archie Nixon, the rattling light bulb went on in my head. With a bow I had taken a huge bull that scored 345 Boone and Crockett Club points two days earlier, and I was now helping Nixon guide another of his clients. One morning we looked down off a hillside and spotted a very large 6 × 6 bull stalking a lone cow. Suddenly, another big 6 × 6 appeared, and it was obvious that we had ringside seats for what was going to happen next.

The bulls circled each other briefly, then locked horns in a for-real, someone's-going-to-get-hurt battle over that cow. They spun in a big circle, clacking their antlers, pawing the ground, and making a ruckus that would frighten a dead man.

Mature bulls that have heard it all may hang up out of range and require a little extra convincing. But for those hunters who have a few radical tricks up their sleeves, rewards can be tremendous. Photograph by R. E. Ilg

As if by magic, out of the brush popped the head of another nice bull. Then another. And another. And still one more. In a matter of minutes, five nice bulls together with a couple of cows had come to the sound of those bulls battling. Why they came—whether it was curiosity, the breeding urge, or whatever—who can say? But come they did.

Elk hunters have often raked and banged trees with limbs cut from other trees in an attempt to mimic a bull raking his antlers. This is fine, except that the sound doesn't carry very far in the dense timber or over uneven ground. The sound of rattling a pair of deer antlers together carries much better, is realistic, and it works. Not all of the time, of course, just like rattling for deer doesn't work every time, but it's one more trick to pull out of your bag when the hunting's tough and the textbook answers don't get the job done.

I'm not through experimenting with off-the-wall, radical elk strategies, either. For example, I have in mind for my next hunting trip a nice secluded little wallow on a small creek that's not far from a logging road. If the elk sign is there the way it has been the past few years, during bow season, I plan on setting up a tree stand nearby and placing a standing elk decoy in the wallow. Decoys have worked for me when I'm hunting whitetails, so why shouldn't they work for elk? Of course, I'll flag the decoy with some fluorescent orange ribbon for safety's sake, and then I'll spray a little commercial elk-in-heat scent around and bugle from my tree stand.

Will it work? Who knows? The one thing I do know is that if the elk won't play by the rules, I'll throw out the textbook and play the game any way they like. When it comes to hunting today's well-educated bulls, it pays to get radical. ✤

Wyoming's Bull of the Century

By Merwin Martin as told to Jim Zumbo

It was just breaking day when I spotted eight bull elk feeding in a drainage that protected them from fierce early morning winds. There was no doubt in my mind that one of the bulls was the biggest I'd ever seen in a lifetime of hunting. I was after mule deer on the last day of the season, but I forgot about muleys and immediately set up my spotting scope. The general elk season was closed, but I'd drawn a late season tag for this particular area, and the hunt would start in a week.

"Is that bull as big as I think he is?" I said to my pal Harold Liner as I focused the spotting scope. A few moments later, with the bull in the scope, I was astounded. I could hardly believe my eyes. When Harold looked at the bull, he had the same reaction. Both of us were overwhelmed at the massiveness of the antlers that sat atop the head of the giant bull.

It was tough to concentrate on mule deer the rest of the day. All I could think about was the incredible bull, hoping he would still be around when the season opened. It would be a long week to wait.

I was born in Wyoming and started hunting when I was 12 years old. At age 49, when I spotted the trophy elk, I still hadn't taken a really big bull, and I had always wanted a chance at one of the monsters that now and then appear in the mountains where I do most of my hunting.

Because my wife is also an avid hunter, she accompanies me on most hunts. Often she'd draw a cow elk tag, and when she'd get her cow, I'd quit hunting elk and try for a big buck muley. One elk in the freezer would be enough meat for the year.

On November 18, 1991, I left my pickup and headed up the mountain, my flashlight showing the way. Opening day had finally arrived, and with it the chance of seeing the huge bull again. This time, however, I had an elk tag in my pocket and a dream in my heart.

It was snowing lightly, and the foot of snow on the ground made for tough walking. As darkness brightened into sunrise, the intensity of the storm picked up, and I was floundering about in a full-blown blizzard.

Visibility was reduced to less than 100 yards. The arctic wind tore at me and my clothes were wet, and I realized that I could easily get into trouble with hypothermia. I reluctantly headed back to camp at about 9 A.M. to wait out the storm.

I was hunting the Sunlight Basin area northwest of Cody, Wyoming. The region is prime country that supports excellent elk populations, including the occasional transients that drift out of Yellowstone National Park, about 25 miles to the west.

After getting into dry clothes and cooking a hot lunch, I anxiously waited for the blizzard to break. Around noon the wind and snow let up, and the skies began to clear. I eagerly headed for the mountain again, but this time I decided to hunt lower than I'd originally planned. Heavy snow up on the ridges made travel all but impossible.

I chained up all four tires of my pickup and drove as far as I could. I left the rig at 2 P.M., bringing with me fresh batteries for my flashlight, waterproof matches, and several candy bars. My destination was a series of drainages that had good cover and plenty of grass, as I knew that both of these elements are important to elk in snowy landscapes.

Later in the afternoon, while slowly moving along in the deep snow, I was shocked to see the huge bull. He was on the other side of a steep canyon—a canyon whose sides were too steep to climb down and too far apart to shoot across. I'd have to hike to the head of the drainage, cross it, and walk down the other side toward the bull. I looked at my watch and noted that I had only 1½ hours to make the stalk.

About an hour later, I eased out on a shelf above where the bull had been. To my dismay, the elk was gone. All I saw were tracks in the snow where the animal had been feeding.

With darkness coming fast, I had to make an important decision. Should I follow the bull and

Heavy snows pushed a number of big bulls out of Yellowstone, including the monster that Merwin Martin took east of the park. Photograph by Jim Zumbo

risk spooking him—if I hadn't already done so—or should I head back to the truck and try for the bull the next day? I knew that if I flushed the bull, darkness could end the day's hunt before I could find him again.

I knew that it would mean a long climb back to the truck—and much of it in the dark—but I had to know which direction the bull had gone.

Slipping up to the track, I discovered that two bulls had been feeding in the spot, not just the lone giant. Closer inspection revealed that the bulls had moved off in the opposite direction from the one I had figured.

I immediately followed the tracks.

Though daylight was fading, I forced myself to go slow and easy. At one point I eased up onto a small rise that had blocked my view and saw movement in the trail directly in front of me. Instantly I recognized the great bull as he raised his head and looked directly at me. He was less than 50 yards away!

With my heart beating wildly, I shouldered my .270 Weatherby Magnum and fired into the bull's lungs. The huge elk flinched but stayed on his feet. I knew that the bull was hit hard, but I wanted to get a second shot into him just in case. Unfortunately, he had taken a step, and now offered a poor target.

I was as excited as I'd ever been while hunting. I started telling myself to calm down. Finally the bull took another step—just enough for me to score another hit in the chest. By the time I chambered a third round, the mortally wounded bull had turned, and he now offered a full broadside shot. Taking no chances, I shot the bull through the top of the shoulders and put him down for good.

I was beside myself with excitement. I couldn't

believe the size of the huge elk lying in the snow, and I shouted my joy into the forests around me. A lifetime dream had become reality.

My little victory celebration was short-lived, however, because I had just a few minutes of light to dress the bull. Then with the chore completed, I headed back to the truck in the dark.

Two hours later, my flashlight beam finally shone on the welcome sight of my truck. I drove home to Powell, Wyoming, with the thought of finding a pal to help get the elk out the next day.

As soon as I got home, I recounted the story to my wife and then called Harold Liner.

"Did you get him?" Harold asked excitedly when he recognized my voice jabbering on the phone.

"I got him," I said, "but I need help getting him out. He's about a mile in."

"Is he as big as we originally thought?" Harold asked.

"I think he's bigger," I answered.

Harold immediately made arrangements to get the next day off from work, and the following morning, Harold, his younger brother Danny, and I went in for the bull. We were equipped with packboards, ropes, and a block and tackle.

We reached the bull just at dawn and had the elk to the truck about six hours later. We drove to Jim Marsico's Taxidermy Shop in Powell, and I asked Jim to take a look at the bull I'd killed.

As we headed out the door, I jokingly asked Jim if the bull was big enough to mount. But when Jim saw the bull, he just stood there in awe and stared.

Finally he broke out of his trance, ran into his shop, produced a tape and measured the bull.

Jim is not an official scorer, but he is familiar with the scoring system, and when the elk taped out at 418⅞ Boone and Crockett Club

Elk bulls grow big because they are allowed to grow old. Simply put, age translates into massive antlers. Nutrition and good genes are also important, but when it all shakes out, a giant bull must have the years on him. There are few exceptions. Photograph by Leonard Lee Rue III

points, it astounded all of the people who had gathered to watch. (An official Boone and Crockett scorer measured the bull at 412⅖ after drying, and the rack is scheduled to be panel scored in 1995.)

My bull will go down in history as the third biggest elk ever killed in Wyoming—the best in the more than a century since the top two were taken. Not only that, but the official score puts the trophy at number eight in the world!

What makes the bull even more special is the fact that I took him on public land and didn't need to spend a lot of money hunting an expensive place that has a reputation for producing big bulls. I did it by first drawing a late season elk tag in an area outside Yellowstone Park that is known for giving up huge bulls, then by fortunately spotting the bull that I wanted and hunting exclusively for him.

Thanks to help from the weather that caused the bull to migrate, I finally have a bull for my wall.

And what a bull he is.

Beat-the-Heat Bulls

By Larry D. Jones

A chill of excitement surged through my body as a second bull's bugle penetrated the darkness. The elk in the area were hot, so I searched the hillside for a flat spot to set up a bivouac camp.

Finding a small depression near a tree, I leveled a spot for my pad and sleeping bag by scraping pine cones and sticks aside. I checked broadheads for sharpness and readied my pack for the next morning's hunt. Satisfied that my equipment was organized, I slid into my sleeping bag. As I lay there that night in New Mexico, I was mesmerized by the sounds of chirping crickets, bugling bulls, and the occasional hoot of an owl.

I was up and ready to hunt as the first rays of light silhouetted the branches of tall firs. Anxious to hear a bull's bugle, I used my metal reed call to pierce the stillness with loud bugles and pleading cow calls. From the depths of the timbered canyon, three bulls answered my challenge.

For two hours I bugled and pursued the bulls to pressure them. The chase led me to a trail that, according to my maps and boundary description, was the northern edge of my unit. I was close to the bulls, but even if I called them within shooting distance, I couldn't legally take one here. I decided to angle away from the trail by contouring around the hill. About 200 yards inside the boundary I located a group of small, bushy firs. The spot would allow me to see approaching

bulls while giving me necessary concealment. I slipped off my pack, nocked an arrow, leaned my bow against a tree and laid my camera on my pack. I bugled several times, carefully listening for a bull's response between calls. Not hearing any, I made a few cow calls, but still received no answer. I knew that there were bulls within hearing range, so I decided to call more aggressively.

For the next 30 minutes I used several different-sounding calls to produce bugles, grunts, and cow calls. Elk are surprisingly vocal animals, so I varied the sounds of each challenge with growls, moans, squeals, and rusty gate-sounding screeches. I created demanding bugles followed by soft and loud cow mews and occasional whines to simulate a bull with his herd. Between each series of calls, I sat motionless and alert to any sound of an approaching bull.

Forty minutes into my attempts, I heard a branch snap. I quickly grabbed my bow as I stood to scan the timber. I didn't see anything, so I made two soft cow calls. Through an opening in the timber I saw a tan flash as a 5-point bull trotted through. He leaped up a steep bank and took a course that would cross the path I had taken earlier.

He slowed to a walk and occasionally dropped his nose to sniff for hints of other elk. Suddenly, he stopped as he crossed my scent trail 30 yards away. He tested the air nervously, and I knew that he was about to retreat. I wished I had my

The author examining a heavily used wallow. Photograph by Larry D. Jones

camera in hand, because I didn't want to shoot this bull. Not only was this the first day of my hunt, but it was also 3 miles to a road, and the hot days and warm nights could cause meat spoilage by the time I packed out the animal.

Finally convinced that danger might be near, the bull turned and trotted back the way he had come.

Once he was out of sight, I eased over to grab my camera, and then I made a couple of soft cow calls. I knew that it would be difficult to call him back, but through the trees I could see him sneaking toward me. He was suspicious, so he circled around me and never stood in the open. The few photos I took were of antlers in the brush.

This hunt was typical of many of my early season hunts. The days were sometimes sizzling hot and the nights were also warm. Hot weather can create more than one problem for elk hunters—the animals are less active, and it can be difficult to call them. Tracking an animal that's been hit can be tough because blood sign dries quickly, and the hard, dry ground doesn't show hoof prints. Meat spoilage can be a problem as well because the elk's thick hide and massive body retains heat. But after three decades of elk hunting, I've learned a few techniques to combat these problems.

HOT WEATHER HUNTING METHODS

Hunting from tree and ground stands near water, wallows, or feed areas can be excellent alternatives to calling, but scouting for the best spot is essential. When the weather is hot, your most promising feature is water. Find out which areas the elk are using. Once you discover a spot with plenty of sign, set up a blind or tree stand where you can get a shot when an elk passes.

Consider wind direction when selecting your ambush spot. Keep in mind the direction from which the elk will approach. Be sure that the wind is blowing from the elk to you. Construct your stand or blind so that you'll have shooting lanes that allow a broadside or quartering-away shot angle. Once in your blind, position yourself in the shadows. Elk have excellent eyesight.

CALLING METHODS

Some of the most successful tricks I've used to call elk during hot weather include calling before daylight, aggressive calling, and using cow calls near bedding areas, water holes, and wallows.

When elk are bugling, they often can be seduced with cow calls. When they clam up, you may have to call aggressively or change tactics. In hot weather, water holes are among the best places to set up. Photograph by Neal and Mary Jane Mishler

Bulls tend to be more active at night, so drive roads or walk trails an hour before daylight and call in different areas. Once you locate a bull, move within a few hundred yards and call again at first legal shooting light. You'll have a better chance of bringing a bull within range if you excite him before dawn and close in before the temperature rises.

If you have an idea where elk are bedding, approach their bedding area from downwind, but don't penetrate their bedding sites. Select a spot in the shadows where you'll have shooting lanes and where you could see a bull approaching. Use a cow call or mouth diaphragm call to produce a series of soft pleading mews. Make 6 to 12 mews and then listen for a mew or bugle. Continue this series for up to one hour. If you don't hear or see any bulls, move to another location and try again. Be persistent, and you can call bulls from their beds even on a sizzling hot day.

John West of Monroe, Michigan, hunted elk with me in Arizona one year. We noticed that the majority of the hunters returned to camp every day around 10 A.M. because of the heat. West and I were confident we could call in bulls throughout the day, so we continued to hunt.

Early one afternoon, West was slowly stillhunting downwind of a bedding area when the strong, musky odor of elk whacked him in the nose. He selected a cluster of small trees to conceal himself and produced soft cow calls with a diaphragm. Within seconds he called a 6×6 bull to within 18 yards, but he didn't have a clear shooting lane. Once his heart quit pounding, he checked his watch: 12:30 P.M.

On another hot day an elk answered my pleading mews. West and I set up, and after 15 minutes of calling, a 4×4 bull walked to within 30 yards. We both wanted a bigger bull, so we let him walk away without attempting to shoot. I wanted to photograph the bull, so we circled and I sat in the shade of a cedar as West cow-called from a cluster of pines. After 10 minutes, the 4-point approached cautiously. I snapped four photos before the sound of my motor-driven camera sent the bull galloping into the protection of the trees.

Although a few subtle cow calls finessed that bull into camera range, some situations call for more aggressive tactics. On days when the bulls are unresponsive, I spend much of my time walking, calling, and looking for sign. When I spot fresh tracks, droppings, rubs, or wallows, I know that elk are nearby yet unwilling to answer my calls. In this situation, I use a combination of patience and aggressive calling to stir up some action.

I start by calling and listening, and I continue this sequence for up to one hour. I build a tempo of excitement through bugling, grunting, cow calling, and scraping a tree with a stick, which sounds like a bull rubbing his antlers. I change

calls often to sound like different elk. Bulls are lazy when it's hot, and they prefer to relax in the coolness of a shaded bed. Sometimes the excitement created through extended aggressive calling will arouse a bull to stand up and answer.

I've also called from a tree or blind at a water hole or a wallow. I prefer to use cow calls, but bugling will also work. I successfully used cow calls at a water hole one evening for one of the most exciting elk hunts I've ever experienced.

After being in my ground blind for 30 minutes, I made two series of cow calls. Shortly after the second series, a bull walked from the timber and approached the pond. His right antler had five points, but the left antler was broken above the first brow tine. He walked into the water and began to paw and splash water with his foot.

He lowered his head and began whipping it back and forth. His antler sent sprays of water right and left, splattering showers up to 20 feet away. As he stopped to look around, water streamed from his long chocolate-colored mane. He tore at the water again and then began jumping and bucking, sending mud and water flying. He twisted and stumbled and almost fell as he frolicked.

I was spellbound as I watched. After a while I decided to practice drawing my bow on this

TRACKING IN HOT WEATHER

A few ideas to help you track your bull once he's hit include paying attention to the length of his stride, the shape of his track, and the way the bull is grouping his feet.

Observe the way the bull places his feet or the shape of his hoof print—anything that makes his track unique. The feet of every bull have their own peculiarities. They may be round or pointed or have spread-out toes or a chunk missing from a hoof. Bulls usually step onto their front hoof, but when they're shot they may favor one leg and leave a cluster of three tracks with one foot gouging the earth. When you find this, you can pick out the bull's track from others. Always follow tracks and identify blood sign to confirm that you're on the right track.

Photograph by Larry D. Jones

Where the bull has slowed to a walk, measure the length of his stride. It's helpful to know his stride when you can't find the next track or when you have to identify the bull's tracks among others. Use a stick, string, or arrow to measure the stride. Lay the end of your measuring stick at the front of one track and mark the stick where it hits the next track.

When you have a hard time finding the next track, place your stick at the front of the last known track and angle it in the direction where the next track should be. There should be a scuff mark or indentation very close to your stride mark. If the bull has turned, all you have to do is swing the stick around to the right or left to discover the next track.

HOT-WEATHER MEAT CARE

Some of the critical factors in meat care start before you shoot, especially in hot weather. An elk is a huge animal. Don't take a shot so far from camp or in such rugged terrain that you can't reasonably pack out the meat before it spoils.

Shot selection is also critical. The last hour of daylight can be one of the best times to excite a bull into range, but it's essential to make an excellent shot, especially in the heat. If you can't recover your trophy that evening, the meat may spoil. Therefore, limit your shot selection: Only shoot if you're within 20 yards with the elk broadside or slightly quartering away. Aim for the lower third of the body just behind the front leg hairline; that should put your arrow through both lungs so that the animal expires within seconds.

Photograph by Larry D. Jones

Once you find your trophy, it's extremely important to cool the meat as soon as possible. This is best accomplished by skinning your elk, removing the meat from the bones, and laying the meat on branches so that air can flow around it. The meat's mass and large bones retain heat, so don't stack the meat into piles or it may spoil even after skinning.

A bull I killed while filming a video in Oregon was a good example of this. I wanted to bone the animal on camera the following morning, so I gutted and skinned him and left his carcass lying on a tarp overnight. There was frost on the grass the next day, so I knew that the temperature had been below freezing that night. But when I stuck a meat thermometer into the neck meat, it registered more than 70 F. Even without the thick hide, the sheer mass of the meat and large bones had retained heat.

If you experience sizzling hot days and night temperatures that never dip below 50 F, you should get your meat to a freezer within three days.

One way to cool your meat if you can't get it to a locker is to quarter the elk and put the meat into a cool, fast-moving creek. Once the meat has cooled, hang it in the cool shade and dry it. Cover your meat with lightweight, fine-knit bags to protect it from dirt and blowflies. Each evening, remove the bags, separate the meat, and place it in an open meadow where it can become as cool as possible during the night. Each morning re-bag it, place it in the shade, and wrap it in sleeping bags. This insulates it from the heat of the day. This process requires some time and effort, but your meat can be stored for a week this way without spoiling.

---

foolish bull. I drew three times before remembering my camera. I eased it from my pack, but he quit his Walt Disney act before I could film it. He sloshed across the pond and onto the bank, where I photographed him as he thrashed a bush.

After he left the area, I cow called again. After three or four series, another 5×5 bull approached. He walked into the pond and stood broadside drinking. The beams and tines of his antlers were long. I was tempted to shoot, but I had my heart set on a 6×6. I let him melt into the trees before pleading with a few more cow calls.

This time a smaller bull came trotting into the pond. He wasn't cautious at all. Without hesitation, he splashed knee-deep into the pond, dropped to his belly and rolled. His legs went flying as water splashed onto his back. After several water-splashing rolls, he stood and walked

from the pond with water dripping from his drenched, mud-coated body.

Cow calls worked great from my blind that evening, to say the least, and the experience was the most eventful and fun I've ever had calling elk. Although you can't expect this kind of action every time you blow a call, hot-weather elk can be seduced if you make the right moves, set up in the best areas, and make the correct calls.

Don't let hot weather spoil your hunt. Be prepared. Carry food and water so that you can continue to hunt when others return to camp. Adjust your attitude and hunting techniques. Use elk calls throughout the day and use aggressive calling to stimulate rutting bulls. Keep a step ahead of the elk—and the weather—and you can get into some sizzling hot excitement.

Recalling Elk

By Jim Zumbo

Every once in a blue moon I make an accidental discovery while hunting, and if my brain comprehends the significance of the event, I'm able to capitalize on the new wrinkle during future hunts.

In 1991, I made such a discovery, and though the technique that resulted is not an earth-shattering one that will make me millions on the lecture circuit or warrant an appearance on a late-night talk show, it nonetheless will help me outwit more elk.

The big enlightenment occurred when I stumbled into a herd of elk while hunting in eastern Oregon. Typically, when elk are spooked, they explode through the timber, making an uproar that only a bunch of animals their size can.

If you've never heard a couple of dozen elk tearing through the forest, knocking down snags, banging their hoofs on logs, and crashing through blowdowns, you're missing an amazing event. They do it all the time, and it's the most frustrating exodus I've ever experienced.

When deer bound away, all is quiet again within a few moments, and you feel like you at least have a chance of seeing what made the rapid departure. Not so with elk. When they go, they go big time.

They leave no question as to where they were; but what many hunters don't realize is that elk will commonly stop a few hundred yards out, trying to figure out what made them run in the first place. Hunters often aren't aware that the elk have stopped, believing instead that the herd has run out of earshot and into the next county.

A hunter's typical reaction is to go tearing after the elk, trying to get a shot at the fleeing animals. This is often a futile attempt, however, because elk usually live in nasty cover that, at best, permits only glimpses at elk hide—often blurred movement behind 15 or 20 trees or 5 solid yards of brushy foliage.

During my Oregon hunt, the elk did not spook as a result of my walking through the woods. It happened quite by chance that as my partner and I were driving to another hunting area, the animals crossed the road in front of us.

Of course, the elk were already busting through the forest by the time I got out of the truck, loaded my rifle, and bid adieu to my hunting buddy. But all was quiet by the time the truck was out of hearing. After traveling 20 yards into the woods, I resisted the usual urge to chase after the elk. I decided to stay put and listen.

Five minutes later I heard a cow chirp. This was good, as the sound betrayed the location of an elk. Soon I heard another chirp from the same direction. Presently a third elk chirped from a completely different spot. I knew then that the elk were now in at least two groups.

When the two sets of elk continued chirping back and forth, I realized that they were calling to each other. Then it hit me. Could the animals be communicating, attempting to regroup into the original herd? What would happen if I blew my cow call? Would the elk respond to me, too?

I chirped softly on my call, and received an answer immediately. I blew the call again, and this time got an answer from both groups of elk.

The talk continued, and 10 minutes later a big

The author's daughter, Judi, was able to take this nice 6 point bull, thanks to her father's calming cow call. Photograph by Jim Zumbo

cow appeared 80 yards out. She was headed straight for me, followed by her calf, three more cows, and two other calves. Then I heard the other bunch coming. When they came into view, I saw 11 cows and calves, but no bulls. When the two groups spotted each other, they chirped continually and soon joined together about 45 yards from my location.

I was most interested in this incident because I had every reason to believe that my calls had helped deceive the elk. Both groups had headed

right toward me until they'd actually made visual contact with each other.

If my hunch was correct, why wouldn't it be possible to use this strategy with a high degree of success any time elk are spooked in heavy cover? To carry the idea a step further, why not purposely scatter elk in the timber—when they've got you pegged—and then call them back, just as you might do with a flock of fall turkeys?

Elk are highly social and gregarious animals, which means that they like each other's company. Cows that responded to a regroup call could very possibly be trailed by one or two bulls, which commonly follow cows as part of their behavior.

I was intrigued with the concept, and I tried it out several more times on that Oregon hunt, as well as again later during hunts in Wyoming and Montana. And it worked! It worked so well, in fact, that I'm amazed I haven't read or heard about it before. Though there are many ways to use the cow call, the idea of busting elk up on purpose and calling them back is evidently a brand-new concept.

By trial and error, I learned a number of things about the method after I tested it under widely differing conditions. For one thing, I learned that it isn't foolproof, and its success depends on a number of skills, including timing and the abilities to see elk, shoot in heavy timber, and use a cow call. Having a knowledge of elk behavior helps a whole lot, too.

An important requirement is that a hunter pay strict attention to the wind. If elk take off because they've smelled you, forget about calling them back. On days when the wind is erratic—frequently switching directions—all you can do is hope to see the elk in the timber before they spot or smell you.

Being seen may not have the effect on elk that being smelled does. Typically, when a bunch of elk in the timber spook because they've spotted you, only a small percentage of the herd has actually seen you. Those alarmed animals bolt, and the whole herd takes off. Most of the elk don't know what they're running from; they're just making an escape because it's an important part of their survival instincts.

If the spooked elk calm down within a reasonable distance, and if the herd has split up, you can almost always get them to at least respond to your chirps. The elk then may or may not come in, depending on how badly they're alarmed.

Basically, there are two types of spooked elk: those that are disturbed and those that are terrified. You can work with disturbed elk; you can't do a thing with terrified animals. The latter group has passed the point where they'll hide and sneak around in the timber. Instead, they'll make a beeline from point A to point B, stopping for nothing and devastating anything in their way that will break. I've seen terrified elk run smack through hunting camps,

taking down small tents, clothesline ropes, and whatever stood before them. In one case, a cow actually jumped over a playpen that a baby was sleeping in!

When I tried my newly discovered technique in the fall of 1991, I found that most of the time the running elk didn't break up into separate bunches. They tended to stay together. I also found that the bigger the size of the elk herd, the greater its tendency was to split up.

But even when the elk didn't split up, I was still able to call some animals back, or at least get an answer. By listening to them and pinpointing their locations, I could then circle and come at them from a different direction, depending on the wind.

When I chirped at the elk, I did so softly, trying to match my calling with their response. Several

Elk like each other's company, and a cow that responds to a regrouping call could very well be followed by a bull or two. Photograph by Richard P. Smith

times the incoming animals were never visible. They approached cautiously and remained hidden in the timber.

It's important to remember that when elk are responding with thoughts of regrouping, there isn't the sense of urgency on their part that there is with a bull coming in to a cow call during the rut. A bull has romance on his mind early in the fall, and he is likely to throw caution aside to check out the new girl on the block.

Another cow-call technique that I discovered to use on spooked elk is to give a sharp blast on the call at the instant the elk flush. I can practically guarantee the response. Spooked elk will stop in their tracks and look at you. They may stop only for a second or two, but that might be enough time for you to get a good rest or just look over the animals. Of course, it's a whole lot easier to hit a standing elk than a running elk.

This method works so well it's hard to believe. It's a technique that's been widely publicized over the last few years, having been tried by many veteran hunters around the West. Personally, I've *never* seen it fail, and though I hesitate to suggest a 100 percent guarantee, for me it has been just that.

To make the strategy work, you must have the cow call instantly accessible when elk explode from cover. My call has a hole drilled in it so I can hang it around my neck with a string. It's always there when I want it; I don't have to frantically search for it in a pocket when elk are tearing away.

A recent Wyoming elk hunt with my 19-year-old daughter Judi illustrates the effectiveness of the method. A 6-point bull crossed our path as we were riding horseback, and Judi instantly dismounted and drew a bead on the running elk.

I gave a sharp chirp on my cow call, and the bull put on the brakes as if he were about to run into a boiling cauldron. He stared at me, and Judi fired. She missed, and the bull made a hurried dash for the timber. I blew the call again. Incredibly, the bull stopped a second time and stared—even after he'd been shot at. The whole episode was repeated after Judi shot and missed again. Finally, Judi connected, but the bull stayed

on his feet, running toward the forest. I called again, and even more incredibly, the bull stopped to look back—despite the fact that he was hit. Judi waited too long to put another shot in him, and the bull disappeared in the trees. We found him some distance away after a long search. (We didn't know it then, but Judi's rifle's zero was off, her scope having been bumped hard when her scabbard hit a tree.)

It was an unbelievable scenario. There was no question that the bull knew we were dangerous. Our horses had danced wildly every time Judi shot, and we were in plain view. The bull, like so many other elk, simply couldn't contain his curiosity.

Cow calling is an amazing concept. It works throughout the entire fall, instead of only during the rut—as is the case with bugle calls. I suspect that 75 percent of all elk hunters are afield when bugling doesn't work, because only a couple of states offer rifle hunting during the rut. Other than in those states, unless you hunt with a bow or during an early wilderness or limited-entry hunt, you're likely to be chasing elk in mid-to-late October or early November, long after the rut is over. That's when the cow call becomes a valuable tool.

Regardless of the cow call you use, if it makes the correct sound, it will work when used properly. There are a half dozen ways to use the cow call, depending on the time of year you hunt, the behavior of the quarry, and the hunting conditions. There are currently several cow elk calls on the market. I suggest that you try them all to find one that works best for you and then become intimately familiar with how to use it.

I wouldn't think of heading for elk woods without a cow call hung around my neck. It provides so many exciting new dimensions to elk hunting that I can't say enough about it. The word is now out on cow calling, and the word is nothing but good.

I can't wait to try the regrouping concept again. There are a big bunch of elk above my house in the Wyoming mountains that are experts at being elusive. I'm betting that the cow call will be just the ticket to do-in one of the sneaky bulls hanging out with this crowd.

PART 6

THIS HAPPENED TO ME

Reprinting the five "This Happened To Me" pages from *Outdoor Life* in this *Yearbook* may surprise some readers. A few people don't like them. During my 23 years of editing for the magazine, this monthly item was criticized several times and once was killed—but not for long. Letters of protest came streaming in from readers—and "This Happened To Me" was soon restored.

The page in the magazine carries the line "We pay cash for all true adventures published." The editors often get submissions in the form of simple letters detailing an adventure and the drawings are developed from that. But—and this is important—all the stories are true. Each story is thoroughly checked, often by calling police, game wardens, hospitals, or other people involved to check out the details.

As stated in the Preface, readership surveys show that 90 percent of *Outdoor Life* readers read the "This Happened to Me" page, the highest readership score achived by any regular feature of the magazine. The pieces are easily absorbed outdoor adventure and ordeal stories—but they are also more: they are hard-hitting safety messages.

We hope you read all of these five typical pieces. Enjoy them—and learn from them.

Breaking the Bank

by Walter E. Sroka
Illustrations by Ken Laager

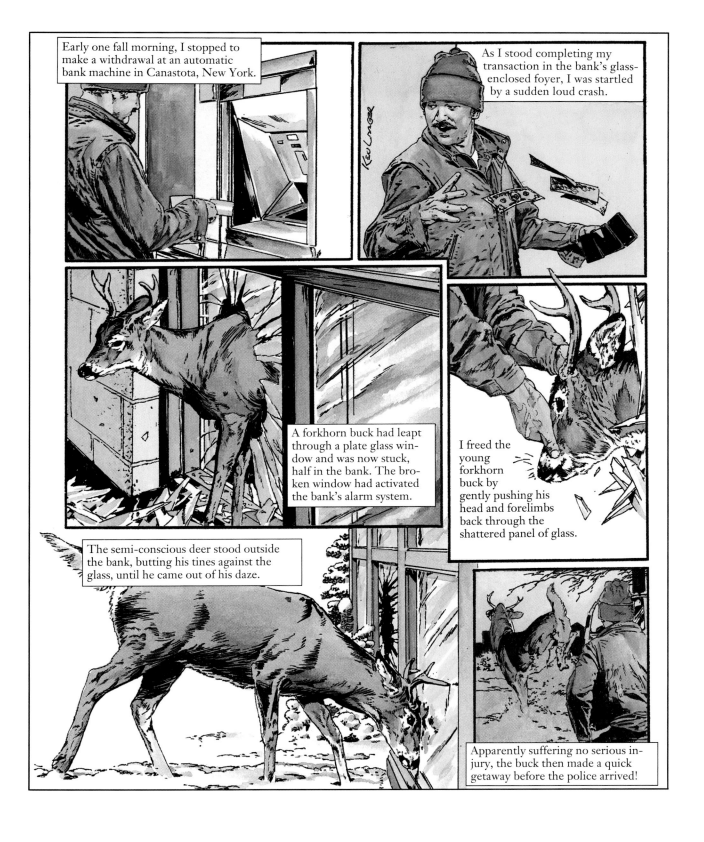

Early one fall morning, I stopped to make a withdrawal at an automatic bank machine in Canastota, New York.

As I stood completing my transaction in the bank's glass-enclosed foyer, I was startled by a sudden loud crash.

A forkhorn buck had leapt through a plate glass window and was now stuck, half in the bank. The broken window had activated the bank's alarm system.

I freed the young forkhorn buck by gently pushing his head and forelimbs back through the shattered panel of glass.

The semi-conscious deer stood outside the bank, butting his tines against the glass, until he came out of his daze.

Apparently suffering no serious injury, the buck then made a quick getaway before the police arrived!

Stuck in a Rut

by Lee Robinson
Illustrations by Ken Laager

On the opening day of deer season, I headed for the deep woods to escape the hunting pressure.

The scraped-up cedar trees proved that I was in deer country, and soon the offending buck appeared.

As I raised my muzzleloader, however, the rut-enraged buck charged.

I fired my .45-caliber, hitting the buck in the flank, but he still came on. Before I could move, the buck struck me in the chest.

The stunned buck went down, giving me time to draw my knife and finally put an end to the ordeal.

Dazed and in pain, I was barely able to stagger to my feet. Snatching up my smokepole, I hit the deer in the neck, breaking the gun in half.

Bruiser Buck

by Bruce Gibbons
Illustrations by Ken Laager

It was the second week of bowhunting season when my brother, my 13-year-old son and I decided to do some scouting.

Just after we split up, I saw an approaching buck. The buck got to within 10 yards before I shouted at him.

The buck's antlers snagged my coat. He simply picked me up and tossed me aside.

Instead of running off, he came at me. The force of the charge knocked me down.

The buck's strength was amazing. My brother, Scott, and son, Tony, tried to get the buck off me, but he relentlessly kept up the attack.

I had been gouged, scraped and bruised. I yelled for Tony to get his knife. He was only 13, but Tony kept his wits about him and had no choice but to kill the buck to save me.

Moose by the Rafters

by Mike Bernard
Illustrations by Ken Laager

Three buddies and I were rafting down a river in Alaska when we spotted a cow moose and her calf attempting to cross the river ahead of us. We slowed the raft to give them a wide berth.

Suddenly, the calf lost its footing in the swift current. Despite nudges from its mother, the calf drifted downstream and drowned.

We pulled the raft ashore opposite the cow, but the moose began to move toward us. We scattered.

Apparently enraged, the cow moose charged us with her hackles raised. I lit out and headed for the nearest tree while my buddies headed up the bank in an effort to avoid the marauding moose coming after us.

After chasing my friends, the cow came after me. I quickly climbed a tree, but the moose circled it for more than two hours.

Finally, she gave up the attack and headed into the brush. We jumped into the raft and fled.

Bulled Over

by Glenn Pless
Illustrations by Ken Laager

It was a late August morning in Alaska as guide Bud Branham and I headed up a grassy slope in search of a big bull moose.

Suddenly, just 100 yards above us, a big bull walked out of the nearby timber and into the grassy avenue. As soon as it saw us, the bull broke into a dead run.

Bud began yelling and waving his arms to turn the charge, but the bull kept coming.

"Glenn, let him have it," Bud yelled. I fired my .30-06. The bull quivered but refused to drop. My second shot slowed him up.

Bud fired as I worked the bolt. At my third shot, the huge animal dropped—a mere five steps from us.

The ground actually shook when the bull fell. The 1,500-pound moose was badly cut up from a previous bout with a bigger bull, hence its bad attitude.

PART 7

BOW-HUNTING

Perfect Practice

By Jeff Murray

S omehow the big whitetail managed to sneak right under Larry Antonich's tree stand. The buck stepped toward a crooked oak branch that would be in the way if Antonich didn't take the shot *now*. The shot was nearly vertical, but as Antonich silently drew his bow, he lined up the 30-yard sight pin behind the crease of the buck's shoulder. The buck didn't flinch until it was too late.

Why a 30-yard and not a 10-yard sight pin? If you practice close-range shots like this one, you'll see why—the arrow flies below the line of sight before it reaches the approximate 10-yard mark. From careful testing and target shooting during the off-season, Antonich knew that the lower pin was necessary.

The old saying "practice makes perfect" is critical in all sports but is especially true in bowhunting. And there's an added hitch. Not only must practice sessions perfect shooting form, but they also must prepare bowhunters for real-world encounters. A perfect practice routine should accomplish three goals: increase accuracy, simulate hunting conditions, and build confidence.

STEP ONE: ACCURACY

Archery is remarkably similar to golf in that getting off a decent shot becomes complicated if one has to think too much, and no two shots are exactly alike. Golfers who can't get the job done on the practice range won't do any better on the course. Bowhunters are no different.

Consistent accuracy is impossible without good form. Strength and dexterity are its foundation, and repetition is the price you must pay to build it. You've laid the cornerstone when the bow hand stops shaking, the grip no longer torques the riser, the release is crisp, and the follow-through is rock-steady.

So the first phase of any practice session, particularly for beginners, should be geared toward developing basic physical and mental skills. As you shoot, shoot, shoot, keep the following in mind:

• Take your time. Approach each shot as though it's your first—and your last.

• Simplify your shooting form. During every shot, I say under my breath, "Draw smooth, pick a spot, follow through."

• It's better to shoot 25 arrows a day than 250 on the weekend. In many cases, a backyard, basement, or garage will make a great informal range (5 or 10-yard shots are more beneficial than no shots at all). If these options are unavailable, join an archery club.

• Shoot rounds of three arrows, then rest. This gives you time to reflect and allows muscles to loosen up and relieve lactic acid buildup. Incidentally, a target with three bull's-eyes instead of just one will save wear and tear on nocks and fletching because arrows will be less likely to hit each other.

• To reduce strain during practice sessions, choose a user-friendly field point target that's self-healing and doesn't require much elbow grease to remove arrows. Morrell

Practicing under hunting conditions is a cornerstone of successful bowhunting. If you hunt with a headnet, practice with a headnet. Also shoot from a tree stand. Many bowhunters hit high when shooting downward. Photographs by Jeff Murray

Manufacturing's Eternity Target, with a total of 54 layers of cotton, burlap, and nylon netting, seems indestructible, yet anyone can easily remove arrows from it, even carbon arrows shot from heavy bows. Saunders' fiber-packed Indian Cord Fiber Matt is another solid choice; the company's Friction Fighter (an agent for coating arrow shafts to reduce drag) and Arrow Puller (for a better grip) are handy target accessories.

Aiming for accuracy on the target range is phase one. Eventually you must aim for realistic hunting conditions. You're ready for phase two when your first shot every day hits where you aim it.

Stump shooting will help you learn to judge distance. Photograph by Jeff Murray

STEP TWO: PRACTICE HUNTING

Faulty range estimation causes bowhunters more misses than any other miscue. Missing slightly high or low on an otherwise "perfect" shot is as common as it is frustrating.

To illustrate the point, imagine a Pope and Young Club whitetail standing broadside 35 yards away. If you hold your 30-yard sight pin dead on, your arrow will sail about 6 inches low—a marginal hit at best. That's assuming the bow delivers arrow speed of at least 220 feet per second (fps) with an arrow weight of 500 grains. Increasing arrow velocity, say, to 240 fps, won't reduce your margin of error by much—only 1½ inches.

Fortunately, this scenario is largely avoidable if you practice at judging distances. Varmints and small game can be an excellent tune-up for big game. If that's impractical, consider the time-honored method of stump shooting. It can be a lot of fun when two or more bowhunters make a contest out of it—taking turns shooting at objects at unknown distances and then tallying up the score. Use blunt points or Judo points as you pick out rotting stumps, pine cones, leaves, and logs (avoid rocky terrain).

Judging exact distances in thick woods compared with open country can be deceptive. Objects appear farther away in dense foliage than in open country, so be sure to practice in both conditions. After enough experience, judging distance becomes second nature.

Calculating distances is one matter, but getting off a shot the way you practiced is another. Big-game animals won't wait for you to ease out of a crouch or step around a tree to draw your bow, so practice shooting from awkward body angles. Shoot from seated, leaning, and twisted positions to learn which adjustments are necessary.

Ever-changing conditions—wind, temperature, precipitation, light, topography, animal position—can drastically affect arrow flight. Consider the following in your mock hunting sessions:

• A stiff breeze in the face exaggerates arrow flight imperfections, such as fishtailing, porpoising, and broadhead planing. Practice shooting into a gusty wind to determine if further fine-tuning is necessary. Also, verify how crosswinds affect the point of impact with your setup.

• Hot weather brings out more than one kind of distraction—biting insects, melting camo face paint, and sweaty palms are a few. If you normally hunt while wearing a camo headnet, by all means practice with it on. A headnet can also replace the paint and keep insects at bay, but make sure that the material doesn't interfere with arrow fletching. Self-adhesive foam padding on the bow grip helps reduce bow torque caused by a slippery bow hand.

• Extreme cold necessitates additional layers of clothing. The extra bulk, however, can cause arrows to fly left for right-handers, right for southpaws. Practice in your hunting duds to know if aiming to the right, adjusting sight pins, or shooting more directly in front of you solves the problem. None seemed satisfactory to me, so I sewed a Velcro strap over the chest area of my insulated coveralls to keep the material bundled tight to my body for better arrow clearance.

• Practice shooting in the rain while wearing raingear. A quiet draw with clothing that crinkles isn't easy. You may elect to substitute plastic vanes for feathers on rainy days, but do so only after comparing points of impact.

• Practice at dawn and dusk. Tests reveal that some bowhunters tend to shoot low when light is low. Additionally, a sight-pin/peep-sight arrangement can cause fits at twilight. If you hunt the deep woods, or if legal shooting hours extend past sunset, consider fiberoptic or tritium sight pins and a magnum peep sight.

• Uphill and downhill angles need negotiating. Gravel pits, gullies, hills, or tree stands are good places to figure distances and sight placement.

Many bowhunters shoot high when shooting downhill. Not coming to full draw is one culprit. Be sure to maintain proper upper body alignment by bending at the waist and concentrate anchoring at full draw. The other common fault is overestimating distances. A simple way around this is determining the *horizontal* distance to game and ignoring the true angled distance.

Similarly, tree-stand hunters tend to shoot high at moderate range. If you hunt from a tree stand, spend plenty of time practicing from one. Set targets at various distances—even directly below you—until you feel comfortable with trajectory angles and shooting distances.

• Before the hunting season, practice on three-dimensional or animal-image targets. These targets aid shot placement by forcing the bowhunter to pick a spot. Some good choices are the lifelike 3-D McKenzie foam targets, which are used at most of the major 3-D bowhunting tournaments, and Ranging's rip-resistant Tyvek paper deer targets.

• Practice with field points but fine-tune equipment for broadheads. Rare is the bow setup with identical points of impact for the two. If you shoot a sight pin that attaches to the bow with a dovetail assembly, a crafty ploy is setting up two sight-pin mounts—one for field points, the other for broadheads. Usually, a single nut or Allen bolt exchanges the two. Some bowsight companies, such as ACCRA 300 and Cobra Manufacturing, produce accessories to accommodate such changes. Beason Bow Sites' bead/bars can also be exchanged easily.

Broadhead target? If you have the space, a pickup load of sand is surprisingly effective. The best commercial target, according to target guru Stanley Hipps, is a 2-pound density,

Practicing with 3-D targets will help you pick out animal's vital areas, and shooting in a crosswind (notice wave action on lake) will help you identify windage adjustments. Photograph by Jeff Murray

closed-cell foam target. He says that thinner 4- or 6-pound foam targets will stop hunting heads, but they don't hold up. "And get a target compact enough to tote along on hunting trips," Hipps advises. "You can't afford to stop practicing when you hunt."

There's no shortcut to confidence in the field. But these pointers should help you avoid the detours and roadblocks. And when the moment of truth suddenly unfolds, you'll know exactly what to do. You won't get rattled because you've been there before. 🦌

Tackling Bigger Game

By Chuck Adams

June 15, 1992. I am writing this from a remote field camp in Zimbabwe, Africa. The past week has been one of the most incredible of my bowhunting career. Seven days ago, I killed a 500-pound waterbuck with one shot from 30 yards. The arrow didn't even seem to slow down as it sliced through both lungs and smacked a tree on the far side. The following day, I shot a 525-pound wildebeest, again through both lungs. My arrow buried in the dirt beyond the animal.

Three days ago, I dropped my most coveted of all African animals—a 1,500-pound Cape buffalo with massive, wide-spreading horns. Cape buffs are considered one of Africa's most dangerous animals, and my guide and I had hunted the big bull for a half-day. When we finally caught up to the animal, I managed to sneak within 40 yards. The broadhead ranged forward at an angle through liver and lungs and punched 6 inches out the other side. The massive animal galloped 250 yards and collapsed.

Yesterday, I finished my Zimbabwe bowhunt by taking a 1,600-pound eland, which I shot in heavy brush. This largest of all African antelope stopped broadside at 35 yards and took my arrow to the fletching through both lungs. He ran 50 yards and dropped.

Most bowhunters don't have the inclination to bowhunt African big game. But lessons learned on the Dark Continent apply equally well to

Adams took this 7×9 point Arizona elk in 1990. Heavy arrows with cutting-nose broadheads provide necessary penetration. Photograph by Chuck Adams

Bowhunting for large game in Alaska is becoming increasingly popular. Photograph by Len Rue Jr.

$$\frac{\text{Arrow weight (grains) X Arow Velocity X Arrow Velocity}}{450,240} = \text{Kinetic energy (foot-pounds)}$$

bears, caribou, elk, moose, and other massive North American animals. First and foremost, you must realize that a bow and arrow suitable for deer will not necessarily do the job on animals weighing more than 300 pounds.

Let's say you want to hunt black bears in Maine, Ontario, or another time-proven bowhunting area. The average bruin in such a place will weigh 50 percent more than a mature whitetail deer, with massive bones and a thicker, more muscular torso. Driving an arrow through the vital chest cavity will require tackle more potent than you might use for deer.

Or perhaps you wish to bowhunt caribou in Quebec, elk in Colorado, or moose in Alaska. Such far-flung adventures are becoming popular with serious bowhunters and are an exciting way to expand yearly outdoor enjoyment. A major key to success on 400-pound caribou, 700-pound elk, or 1,400-pound moose is carrying a bow-and-arrow setup with sufficient horsepower to consistently pass through vital tissue and create an exit hole in the hide. Deep arrow penetration is what kills animals and produces easily followed blood trails.

How can you ensure adequate penetration in game larger than deer? First, you should shoot a higher-energy bow. Second, you would be wise to use arrows of medium to heavy weight. Third, you must utilize a streamlined, low-friction broadhead.

With today's diversity of bow design, it makes no sense to discuss draw weight alone. For example, a 60-pound recurve bow or round-wheel compound bow shoots 10 to 15 percent slower than a 60-pound compound bow with oval speed

The author took this 1,500-pound Cape buffalo in Zimbabwe. Hunting animals this size requires a bow that shoots point-blank arrow energy of at least 60 foot-pounds. Photograph by Chuck Adams

cams. Similarly, a long compound bow measuring 47 or 48 inches from axle to axle shoots 10 to 12 percent slower than a short, 41-inch compound bow of identical peak draw weight.

With such wide variation in equipment, recommending a 60-pound bow for bears, 65-pound bow for elk, or 70-pound bow for moose is meaningless. Such guidelines made sense 20 years ago, when all bows were more or less the same. Today, sophisticated guidelines are required.

The best way to gauge bow power is to shoot arrows through a chronograph at point-blank range (about 3 feet). Most archery shops will evaluate your bow speed for a small fee. If you know your arrow weight in grains, and determine your arrow speed through an archery-store chronograph, you can pinpoint the exact penetrating power of your setup in foot-pounds of kinetic energy. A simple formula to use is given in the box at the top of the page.

A bow-and-arrow combination with a point-blank energy of 40 foot-pounds is adequate for deer, pronghorn antelope, and other species weighing less than 300 pounds. For animals between 300 and 750 pounds—trophy black bears, caribou, and elk, for example—50 foot-pounds or more is preferred. For even larger animals, such as 1,200-pound Alaska brown bears, 1,400-pound American bison, and 1,600-pound bull moose, you should shoot a point-blank arrow energy no less than 60 foot-pounds.

Without exception, a heavier arrow will have more penetrating energy than a lighter arrow shot from the same bow. For example, a very light 400-grain arrow shot from a 60-pound compound bow has about 5 percent less point-blank penetrating energy than a heavy

BOWHUNTING BIGGER GAME

Bowhunting North America's biggest game requires specialized equipment, but preparation must not end there. Every extra-large animal also presents a unique hunting and shooting test. Being an expert at harvesting deer will not necessarily prepare you for setting up shots at caribou, moose, elk, or other over-size targets.

Of this continent's larger animals, black bears most closely resemble whitetail deer in terms of hunting and shooting technique. Most bowhunted black bears are bagged from tree stands over bait. The bowhunter simply waits, as he does for deer, and shoots down-ward at ranges between 10 and 30 yards. If a bowhunter is patient and aims lower than normal to compensate for the flatter downward trajectory, he should nail his bruin.

Virtually every other large animal in North America is best hunted on foot. Shooting requirements vary with the species.

For example, caribou are generally shot from makeshift ground blinds along migration trails, or stalked over broken terrain. Because foliage tends to be sparse, shot length varies wildly from situation to situation. Migratory caribou are often arrowed at 10 or 15 yards; bedded or feeding bulls sometimes require shots beyond 40 yards. If you plan to spot and stalk your animal, spend plenty of time at

Before moose hunting, practice quick releases in heavy brush. Photograph by Chuck Adams

the range beforehand shooting from 40 and 50 yards.

Bowhunting elk is a whole other ball game. Terrain tends to be steep and vegetation dense. A successful elk bowhunter is always in top condition and has the physical and mental stamina to hike 10 or 15 miles per day. Because elk move across a large home territory, fast foot-hunting with a slow final approach is the standard technique. Shots are often well-timed, split-second attempts in thick cover. Fortunately, shots are usually inside 30 yards. Before heading out West, practice shooting quickly, and through brush. Leisurely shooting is common from deer or bear stands, but almost unheard of on elk.

Moose and elk hunting tend to be similar, with thick foliage, fast stalking, and close shots the rule. But moose are usually spotted across wide ravines or valleys and deliberately stalked after an approach route is planned. By compari-son, elk move more rapidly and require consistently changing, relatively blind strategy as they cavort and bugle over hills, valleys, and timber.

Before you try hunting any big North American species, be sure to research the animal's habits, favorite terrain and hunting techniques commonly used. Outdoor books, magazines, and suggestions from outfitters and experienced friends can all steer you toward proper physical and mental preparation.

600-grain arrow shot from the same 60-pound bow. The lighter arrow also loses in-flight energy at a much higher rate. At moderate game-shoot-ing distance—say 40 yards—the heavier projec-tile possesses 10 or 12 percent more penetrating punch. With broadside, chest-cavity hits on elk and bears, heavy-arrow energy produces 3 to 5 extra inches of broadhead penetration. The result can be two lungs punctured instead of one, or an exit hole in the hide for a better blood trail to fol-low. Very light arrows shot from heavy-draw bows often muster high kinetic energy, but arrows in the heavier 500- to 600-grain range pro-duce even better penetrating power—especially at distances beyond 30 or 35 yards.

Broadhead design is crucial to success on ani-mals weighing 300 pounds or more. A stream-

lined, deep-cutting broadhead will maximize the energy of your arrow. By contrast, a high-friction head can compromise a potentially potent bowhunting setup. For bigger big game, I dislike broadheads with conical or pyramid-shaped noses. Such heads can be terrific for deer, but they create excess friction as they pass through a larger animal.

According to the tests I've conducted on cowhides, layers of vegetable-tanned leather, and animal carcasses, broadheads with razor-sharp cutting noses penetrate 25 to 40 percent deeper

Even a large moose like this can be taken with bow-and-arrow—if you have the correct kinetic energy. Photo by Len Rue, Jr.

A chronograph is necessary to accurately determine arrow speed and to compute kinetic energy. Be sure to determine these factors before you start to hunt from any range Photographs by Chuck Adams (left) and Len Rue Jr. (right)

than those with nose cones or pyramid-shaped points. For large animals, strong cutting-nose broadheads such as the Satellite Titan, Hoyt Bow Bullet, Zwickey Black Diamond, Patriot Broadhead, Magnum II, MA-3, and Delta Snuffer are the very best way to go. I prefer three-blade or four-blade models because these penetrate almost as deeply as two-blade heads with significantly more damage to vital tissue.

If you insist on using a nose-cone or pyramid-point broadhead, you will be forced to increase arrow energy to compensate. For instance, the point-blank energy minimum for caribou and elk should be upscaled from 50 to 65 or 70 foot-pounds. For moose and other animals weighing more than 750 pounds, minimum arrow energy should be increased from 60 to 75 or 80 foot-pounds.

Given the excellent selection of low-friction, cutting-nose broadheads currently available, I fail to see the sense in cranking up bow poundage or dramatically increasing arrow weight just to accommodate a nose-cone or pyramid-point broadhead. By using a cutting-nose head instead, you will be kind to your bow-shooting muscles and will also enjoy the flatter trajectory a medium-weight arrow provides.

Any creature in the world can be humanely harvested with bowhunting gear, but large animals require specialized, carefully selected equipment. If you shoot a higher-energy bow, moderately heavy arrows, and deep-slicing broadheads, you will enjoy excellent results on magnum-size big game.

Bucks after the Gun

By Thomas L. Torget

Mark Dulong was as excited as a 5-year-old on Christmas Eve. Which was appropriate inasmuch as this was Christmas Eve. Staring through binoculars at the spectacular buck 300 yards across the Illinois cornfield, Dulong knew that if he was ever to arrow a Pope and Young class whitetail, this was the buck and this was the day.

"He was moving along a hedgerow with three other bucks, headed toward a small patch of woods that led into a bean field," Dulong said. "My buddy and I decided I'd set up in that patch of woods and he'd walk really slowly down the middle of the cornfield, hoping to push the buck past me without spooking him. With only an hour of daylight left, it was our only hope."

Thirty minutes later, the unsuspecting buck tiptoed behind a tree 12 yards from where the 45-year-old bowhunter crouched in the brush. Dulong eased back his bow string, released, and watched his arrow disappear into the deer. As he later stood over the massive 12-point rack that tallied 176 Pope and Young points, Dulong's belief in Santa Claus was never greater.

By December, most bowhunters who began scouting whitetails in August and hunting them in September or October have flat run out of gas. That's easy to understand. As rutting activity fades and temperatures plunge, the compulsion to climb yet another frozen oak loses its urgency. For bowhunters wise enough to persist, however, late-season hunting can yield excellent results.

"A lot of guys suffer from burnout," says Minnesota bowhunter Myles Keller. "December bowhunting can be excellent and it's something I really look forward to. But if a guy doesn't pace himself—if he hunts hard from opening day of bow season through the end of November—it's easy to get physically and mentally worn out."

Keller understands the rewards of late-season bowhunting. Of the 28 Pope and Young class whitetails he's arrowed, *more than half* were tagged in December. Despite such evidence, many bowhunters mistakenly believe "the good hunting" ends with the November rut. They see little merit in scheduling tree stand vigils around other holiday activities. A glance at the Keller trophy room wall hints at the folly of such thinking.

There are three key reasons why late-season bowhunting can pay off: sharply reduced hunting pressure, increased daytime deer movement, and the secondary breeding cycle.

In most states, whitetail gun hunting ends by late November or early December. The popular notion is that any mature buck surviving gun season has become so spooky that he's totally nocturnal and, therefore, nearly impossible to find. Although that may be true during the last days of gun season, whitetails adjust quickly to the abrupt plunge in hunting pressure. Within a week or so, they begin easing back into their pre-gun-season patterns. And because there are so few bowhunters afield—far fewer than in the weeks prior to gun season—deer are under less pressure than at any time since September.

No factor affects whitetail behavior more than hunting pressure. And only when pressure is low do whitetails behave "like they're supposed to." This means that a buck can be patterned in late December almost as readily as he can be in August or September.

Hunters' avoidance of the deer woods in the late season feeds on itself. With almost nobody afield, there are no deer stories passing from one hunter to another, strengthening the view that "nobody's doing any good." Combine that with deteriorating weather and growing demands for family-related holiday activities and it's easy to see why the deer woods can be a lonely place in December.

As wintry weather grows harsher, whitetails feed more actively during midday, a big plus for bowhunters used to seeing bucks only in the first and last minutes of daylight.

"When temperatures plunge, whitetails adapt by staying in sheltered habitat all night and feed-ing more actively at midday because it's warmest then," said biologist Gary Dusek of the Montana Department of Fish, Wildlife and Parks. Moreover, because deer food is less widely available in the late season, feeding activity is concentrated in fewer areas. That not only bunches up the deer but also reinforces the pattern of daytime movement. "Anytime I hunt an area with a limited food supply and heavy snow, I always see more daytime feeding," Keller said. "In really

A doe not bred during the fall rut will come back into estrus 28 days later. The bucks take notice. Photograph by Charles Alsheimer

In their quest for dwindling food sources, mature bucks will often drop their nocturnal behavior and will feed in open crop lands during broad daylight. Photograph by Neal and Mary Jane Mishler

hard winter conditions, I've seen record-book bucks feeding on picked cornfields right in the middle of the day. You sure don't see that in October or November."

Dusek says that scarce food supplies in the late

season can make a whitetail surprisingly easy to pattern. "In doing whitetail research, I've trapped deer in Midwest agricultural areas during severe winter conditions," he says. "It was fairly easy because the timing of their daytime travel was extremely predictable. They used the same trails at the same times every day. If a late-season bowhunter can find such active trails, he ought to be successful."

Keller says that he spends much of his late-season scouting time circling the perimeter of small woodlots searching for large deer tracks leading into or out of the cover. "This is a simple technique and if there's fresh snow on the ground it's even easier," he says. "If I cut a track of a mature buck, I'll analyze where and when he's traveling and that tells me where to place my stand and when to hunt it. This is a late-season tactic that works well for me."

Myles Keller has taken more than two dozen record-class whitetails, the majority of which were taken in December. Keller took this buck in Wisconsin in 1986. Photograph by Myles Keller

Although mid-November is the peak breeding period throughout most of the whitetail's range, some females aren't bred until mid-December or later. A doe is in estrus only about 24 hours and if she isn't impregnated during the first rut she'll recycle 28 days later. Eager bucks will travel the December woods searching for such favored females. As Wisconsin bowhunter Ernie Meinan knows, such prowling can be a buck's undoing. Meinan was in his tree stand on December 17, 1991, when two does raced down a game trail past his stand and stopped in his shooting lane 20 yards away. "They spun their heads around and looked behind them really intently," he said. "So I eased my head back and peeked around the tree limb. A big 10-pointer was watching the does, and when they took off running he did, too." When the buck passed through Meinan's shooting lane he made a perfect shot and dropped the deer. The antlers scored 141 points, easily qualifying for the Pope and Young record book.

Meinan says that the episode is not unusual. "I see bucks chasing does all the time in late December," he said. "Last Christmas I was hunting in Illinois and saw seven bucks chasing does in the middle of a wheat field. Anybody who thinks rutting activity ends in November hasn't spent time in the deer woods in late December."

Bowhunting amid the autumn blaze of October is special. Hunting the rut-crazed days of November is exciting. Being afield in late December is cold and uncomfortable. But bowhunters persistent enough to be there may come home with their best Christmas gift ever.

PART 8

FIREARMS AND SHOOTING

The Ultimate Slug Test

By Jim Carmichel

There was a time, and it wasn't very long ago, when shotgun slugs were a dismal topic. Hunters, who by edict or circumstances found it necessary to go afield with shotgun and slugs, were made to feel like second-rate citizens with third-rate equipment. It was a galling situation made even worse by rifle elitists who looked down their variable-power telescopic noses at any piece of shooting equipment that wouldn't puncture a deer at 600 paces. Sluggish shotgun slugs have been constantly compared to high-performance rifle bullets, and in virtually every category—especially accuracy, velocity, trajectory, and downrange energy—the smoothbore load has always been a distant second best. But suddenly, everything has changed. The portly slug, always a wallflower at the Hunter's Ball, has become a ballistic Cinderella. But this time there was no fairy godmother, and the transformation was the result of a lot of hard work that is just beginning to pay off.

The story of hunting with slugs and smoothbores goes back a lot further than most shooters

Photograph by Jim Carmichel

realize. In fact, it begins with the very first firearms, when rifling hadn't even been invented. But even after the accuracy-enhancing advantages of rifling were widely known, ball-and-smoothbore combinations dominated the shooting scene for many generations. George Washington, like other military leaders, advocated unrifled muskets loaded with "buck and ball," and a surprisingly high percentage of the graceful Kentucky "long rifles" of pioneer days actually had no more rifling than a water hose.

With the coming of breechloaders and smokeless powder, the use of solid balls in smoothbores went into a decline, but still there were hunters who, for various reasons, had a need to shoot large solid balls in a shotgun. From the standpoint of utility, there

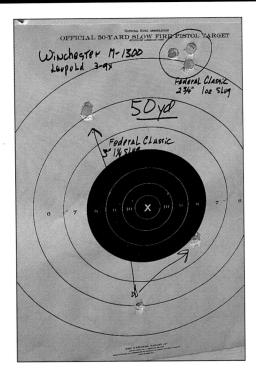

Test results showed the capabilities of the Tar-Hunt rifled shotgun (previous page) at 100 yards, and also illustrated the accuracy difference between 2³/4-inch 1-ounce slug loads and 3-inch 1¹/4-ounce loads Photographs by Jim Carmichel

have always been demands for one gun that does it all. Late in the last century, for example, Holland & Holland introduced its Paradox gun, which was essentially a shotgun, but one with enough rifling at the muzzle to stabilize a projectile so that accuracy was better than with an ordinary smoothbore. Thus, with a Paradox gun, a hunter could drop a charging buffalo or collect a brace of grouse.

Slug shooting in the United States, however, was not nearly so romantic. Here the solid lead "punkin" ball in a shotgun was a matter of economics—a means of launching a solid projectile in the general direction of a deer or other big game without having to invest in a rifle. Though it sounds like a po' boy way to go deer hunting, the punkin ball philosophy of that era made pretty good sense. After all, scientific game management was unknown, and during the half-century from about 1880 to 1930, deer populations in America sank to their lowest ebb. This meant that for most

hunters there was only a remote likelihood of bagging a deer or even getting a shot. Should the opportunity occur, however, a hunter armed with a punkin ball and lots of luck could take home some venison.

Though made of lead, the balls were solid, and if tightly fitted in the barrel, they would no doubt damage a shotgun's choke. For that reason, they were made undersize, and they careened down the bore and exited the muzzle headed on a more or less random course. Fired on at a distance of 100 yards, a deer had a better chance of survival than a pedestrian crossing a street in New York City.

By the 1930s the shotgun slug scene began to change rapidly because of two significant new factors. One of these was the continuing enactment of laws and regulations prohibiting the use of rifles for big-game hunting in certain areas. Thus, hunters who owned and preferred rifles for hunting big game had no choice but to use a shotgun. The other factor was the introduction of the "rifled" slug, patented by Karl Foster in the early 1930s.

Though the flight of Foster's rifled slug has been speculated on in all sorts of ways, the facts are quite simple and can be accurately compared to the flight characteristics of a badminton shuttlecock. Like a shuttlecock, the rifled slug has a skirted cross section with the greater weight forward, causing it to fly nose forward. The "rifling" grooves on the slug should actually be termed "fletching" because the slug's rotation is caused by angular deflection of the atmosphere. There had been some speculation that rifled slugs do not spin at all, but my tests at Briarbank Ballistic Laboratory and other tests conducted elsewhere prove conclusively that they do, and at a rate proportional to forward velocity (for example, when the slug slows down, so does the rate of spin—unlike rifle bullets, which maintain a high percentage of their muzzle RPM).

I recall a time in the late 1940s when a fellow who lived on a farm near ours got word from a relative in Virginia that some deer were to be had there. So he bought a couple of 16-gauge rifled slugs for his L.C. Smith double, put on some clean overalls, and headed his Studebaker for the Blue Ridge Mountains. A couple of days later he was back with a plump buck, and he allowed that bagging a deer was no more trouble than shooting a rabbit.

He must have been nose to nose with that deer, or the poor beast had an especially unlucky day, because squinting over a shotgun barrel at the front bead is a notoriously unreliable means of getting a slug on target. It is a sad exercise in frustration made even worse with double-barreled shotguns because of their converging bores. (Over/unders are not as guilty as side-bys.) Thus, one of the main rules of *serious* slug shooting is to use a single-barreled gun.

Another vital rule of successful slug performance is having a reliable sighting system. It is a phenomenon of unending amazement to me that hunters who would never dream of going hunting with a rifle having no sights will wander off into the wilderness with an unsighted smoothbore and confidently expect to put a slug dead-on target. Perhaps there is a dreamy hope that if the slug's accuracy is as bad as the aiming system, the two will cancel each other out. But alas, seldom do two such wrongs make a right.

Over my years as an *Outdoor Life* editor, I've received hundreds of letters asking if the choke of a shotgun will be harmed by rifled slugs. My standard reply is to stop worrying about the choke and start worrying about how to get some workable sights mounted. Even though the Foster-style rifled slug dates back to the early 1930s (with some stabilized slugs of European origin dating back even longer), it was not until the late 1950s that gunmakers realized that they'd better do themselves and their slug shooting customers a favor by offering smoothbores

with legitimate sights. Before then, conscientious slug hunters had to mount sights themselves. Of course, as soon as one manufacturer offered a smoothbore with sights, others were quick to go after their share of the pie. Which is why slug hunters now have a choice of truly excellent slug guns equipped with sights as good as those on most rifles. This, in turn, has brought about a higher level of hunter confidence in rifled slugs and a significantly improved hit-to-miss ratio.

These improved guns, along with periodic improvements in slug loadings, had hunters reasonably happy, and likely the situation would have remained cozy and content had not an experimenter by the name of Bob Sowash stepped into the slug picture. As director of Ballistic Research Industries (BRI), Sowash ramrodded the development of a solid slug encased in a plastic shoe called a sabot (rhymes with Perot). With rifled barrels, the sabot is spun like a bullet, transferring gyroscopic stability to the .50 caliber (with 12-gauge loads) slug. Upon exiting the muzzle, the two halves of the sabot fall away, leaving the slug to spin on to the target. With unrifled barrels, the slug is held in a more or less point-on direction by its wasp-waisted aerodynamic shape.

I talked to Sowash several times during the development of the BRI slug, and never failed to be impressed by his enthusiasm and the results of his slug experiments. Over the years I've tested a dozen or so slug innovations, mostly of European origin, all claiming to be radical improvements in slug performance, but with none actually being any better, if as good, as the American Foster-style slug. Though Sowash's claims sounded extravagant, he could back them up, and to my knowledge he was the first shooter ever to fire a 1-inch group with shotgun slugs at 100 yards. Suddenly it was a whole new ball game; for the first time ever, shotgun slug performance could be fairly compared to that of rifle bullets. In shotgun slug lingo, the word "performance" refers almost entirely to accuracy. There has never been much doubt about the impact efficiency of a slug; the difficulty has always been a matter of hitting the target at reasonable ranges.

With a sabot-encased slug, a reasonable range now became 100 yards or more.

One key to this dramatic improvement in slug accuracy was the use of rifled barrels. Both Ithaca and Mossberg deserve credit for reacting quickly to a coming demand by offering guns with rifled barrels and cantilevered scope mounting systems attached directly to the barrels. (Receiver-mounted scope systems are less accurate, if the barrel is loosely attached—which many are. By attaching the scope to the barrel, this problem is eliminated.) Winchester quickly followed, and Hastings, a supplier of shotgun barrels and choke tubes, now offers replacement rifled barrels for a wide range of shotguns.

With such radical changes and improvements hitting the market in such a short while, it was not surprising that target shooting competitions for slugs were started, which, in turn, created a market for highly accurate custom guns. The most successful of these has been the Tar-Hunt bolt-action shotgun, which looks, feels, and shoots more like a target rifle than any shotgun you ever saw.

Despite the superior performance demonstrated by the BRI sabot slugs, the sad fact of the matter was that they weren't sold in many gun shops and were not widely available to hunters. This situation ended a couple of years ago when Winchester obtained rights to the BRI slug and began manufacture under the Winchester name. At about the same time, Federal introduced its version of a sabot-encased slug, so now you can buy them anywhere.

A s it so happens, during the birthing of the sabot, several changes and improvements were being made with the traditional Foster-style rifled slug. Federal, Remington, and

The in-depth tests involved firing more than 200 three-shot groups in four representative shotguns at ranges of 50, 75, and 100 yards. Photograph by Jim Carmichel

Winchester offered such changes as heavier slugs in the standard 2¾-inch shell and heavier-yet slugs in magnum cases. On paper these improvements meant higher velocities, more energy, flatter trajectories, and more knockdown power. All at once, slug shooters, who had been treated like orphans for generations, had a key to the candy store. Now, the problem is a matter of which slug or which gun to choose.

This is where *Outdoor Life* magazine steps in with what is probably the most extensive testing of shotgun slugs and slug-designated guns ever conducted by anyone other than the major manufacturers of guns and ammunition. The purpose of these tests was not so much to compare the accuracy of slug against slug, brand against brand, or gun against gun as it was to determine and establish workable guidelines as to which types of slugs work best in what types of shotguns. For example, should you buy a rifled or smoothbore gun? And, if you already own a smoothbore slug gun, will you get best performance with a sabot load or a traditional rifled slug? And, of today's rifled slugs, which will be best in your gun?

The only way to learn these things is by shooting—lots of it—and during these tests, I fired more than 200 test targets (nearly 700 rounds) in four representative types of shotguns at 50, 75, and 100 yards. My findings included several surprises and some solid information that will be mighty valuable the next time you buy a box of slugs or draw a bead on a trophy buck.

I'm not going to bore you with details, but large-scale test programs involve a lot more than just sitting down at a benchrest and popping off a bunch of shots. Test procedures must be established that will eliminate human error as much as possible, and the actual shooting must be carefully controlled so that guns are rotated and cleaned according to a fixed routine. Finally, targets have to be sorted, measured, and statistically analyzed so that the data will have some meaning—all of which takes many hours of tedious work.

Firing a slug from a benchrest is never a particularly pleasant experience because the recoil of a 1-ounce slug fired in a 7-pound shotgun amounts to about 35 foot-pounds. A magnum load with a 1¼-ounce slug generates more than 50 foot-pounds of recoil, kicking harder than a .375 H&H Magnum rifle. Only King Kong could have survived 700 rounds of such punishment, so I devised a shooting fixture utilizing a bench-mounted Zero-Coil recoil absorber along with a front support that provided solid gun positioning. Thus, with scopes of 9× magnification or more mounted on each gun to verify correct aim, the actual shooting was a simple matter of painless trigger pulling, with very little human error to creep in and upset the results.

Three-shot groups with each type of ammo were fired in each of the four guns at the various ranges, and each series of tests was repeated several times so that a reliable statistical average was established. All testing was with the following 12-gauge loads:

Federal
- 2¾-inch sabot hollowpoint l-ounce slug
- 2¾-inch hollowpoint l-ounce rifled slug
- 2¾-inch magnum hollowpoint 1¼-ounce rifled slug
- 3-inch magnum hollowpoint 1¼-ounce rifled slug

Winchester
- 2¾-inch BRI sabot l-ounce slug
- 3-inch BRI sabot l-ounce slug
- 2¾-inch hollowpoint sabot 1-ounce rifled slug

Test Guns
- Browning BPS Game Gun with rifled choke tube extending 3½ inches for total barrel length of 24 inches.
- Mossberg Trophy Slugster with 24-inch rifled barrel.
- Tar-Hunt bolt-action with 21½-inch rifled barrel.

- Winchester Model 1300 Slug Hunter with 22-inch smoothbore and Improved Cylinder Winchoke tube.

It was no surprise that the sabot slugs fired in the Tar-Hunt bolt-action gun delivered the best accuracy. After all, the Tar-Hunt gun is the slug shooting world's version of a target rifle, and it stabilizes the sabot-encased slugs so that they perform more like rifle bullets than shotgun slugs. One string of six three-shot groups fired at 100 yards in rapid succession averaged an incredible 1.705 inches between the centers of the widest shots. This is excellent accuracy even in terms of high-power rifle performance. During another 100-yard test series with the Tar-Hunt and Federal's sabot slug load, one group measured exactly 1 inch—the Holy Grail of slug shooting. The very next group, however, measured 2.866 inches, the widest of the series. So it goes when testing slugs.

Though I expected the Tar-Hunt to shoot well, I was, frankly, more than a little surprised at the excellent 100-yard performance of Browning's BPS Game Gun, which is a smoothbore with a rifled screw-in choke tube. Previous experiments with rifled choke tubes showed no improvement of accuracy over plain smoothbores, but Browning has made it a successful proposition by making the choke tube about three times longer than normal, extending 3½ inches beyond the muzzle. Apparently the additional length of Browning's tube gives the needed spin, because the combined 100-yard group averages of both Federal and Winchester sabot slug loads was only 2.375 inches! Again, this is accuracy good enough to make hotshot riflemen take notice.

Another happy surprise was the 100-yard groups fired with Mossberg's Trophy Slugster with 24-inch rifled barrel. Federal's sabot slug averaged 2.271 inches, whereas the Winchester 2¾-inch BRI sabot load averaged 3.940 inches. Winchester's 3-inch BRI sabot load did better in the Mossberg, with a 2.429-inch average.

Because the 100-yard groups with these guns and sabot loads are so small, there is no need to describe 50- and 75-yard groups except to say that they were proportionally smaller, with most 50-yard groups running around an inch or so. Two 50-yard groups fired with the Mossberg—one with Federal and the other with Winchester BRI sabot slugs— measured almost exactly ½ inch between centers and were the smallest of the test series.

At this point you are probably eager to know how the sabot slugs performed in an unrifled barrel, and what I learned is quite revealing. With the Model 1300 Winchester at 50 yards, the Federal and Winchester sabot slugs averaged 4.445 inches and 3.043 inches, respectively. At 75 yards, group averages were 8.200 inches and 7.335 inches; this represents about the maximum hunting range with sabot slugs in a smoothbore barrel, as target holes indicated serious projectile tipping. Beyond 75 yards there was a rapid decay of accuracy, with 100-yard groups ranging more than 15 inches. In many instances there were hourglass-shaped holes in the 100-yard targets, indicating that the slugs were tumbling in flight.

The old-fashioned Foster-type rifled slugs gave me some interesting comparisons and valuable information. In the Model 1300 Winchester smoothbore, for example, 50-yard-group averages were about the same (3.62 inches) with 1-ounce rifled slugs as they were with the sabot loads. At 75 yards, the 1-ounce rifled slug average of 5.862 inches was notably better than that of the sabot slugs, but at 100 yards, groups were too large to be considered accurate enough for shooting at deer-size game. Thus, when hunting with a smoothbore one must consider 75 yards to be the maximum sure range with either Foster-type rifled slugs or the new sabot-cased slugs. During the tests there were many rounds fired in the smoothbore at 100 yards that hit within an inch or two of point of aim and would have scored good hits. But on the average a miss was more likely.

One of the most interesting and useful pieces of information disclosed by the testing was the greater accuracy of 1-ounce rifled slugs over 1¼-ounce rifled slugs. Though there were isolated contradictions (as

With the right combination of shotgun and slugs, hunters can be confident that they will have a good chance at a nice buck like this Photographs (above) by Charles Alsheimer and (background) by Len Rue Jr.

there usually are in broad-spectrum shooting tests), a 1-ounce rifled slug loading in the 2¾-inch case was the most accurate, followed by the 1¼-ounce rifled slug in the 2¾-inch case, and with the 1¼-ounce rifled slug in the 3-inch magnum case being the least accurate. On the average, groups fired with 1¼-ounce 3-inch magnum loads tended to be about half again larger than groups fired with 1-ounce rifled slugs in the standard 2¾-inch case. This means that slug hunters who buy magnum loads because the slug is heavier or going faster, or because their shotgun has a 3-inch chamber, really don't get anything extra except more recoil and less accuracy. This proved to be true with rifled barrels as well as the smoothbore, and I think that Winchester is doing a good service to shooters by simply not

yards, groups averaged close to 2 inches, expanding to an average 3.943 inches at 75 yards. Winchester's 1-ounce rifled slug averaged a respectable 3.050 inches at 75 yards, but as with the smoothbore, accuracy deteriorated rapidly from there on out. Only the Tar-Hunt delivered what could be considered adequate accuracy for 100-yard shots at game with rifled slugs—that being the combined 5.600-inch average of Federal and Winchester group sizes with 1-ounce rifled slugs.

Though a case-hardened bureaucrat could turn my test data into a weighty 400-page report, the important guidelines are few and simple:

• If you hunt with a shotgun having a rifled barrel, you will get best accuracy with a sabot load.

• If you are considering which slug gun to buy, the smarter choice would be one with a rifled barrel or choke tube such as the Browning. Another option is a replacement Hastings rifled barrel for your present shotgun. But first be sure to check local laws to determine if rifled barrels are legal where you hunt.

• If you hunt with a smoothbore barrel, there is no advantage to using sabot loads. In fact, the traditional rifled slug holds an edge—especially if you avoid magnum loads and stick with 1-ounce slugs.

While I was conducting these tests, a visitor commented that if the new sabot slugs shoot so much like rifle bullets, would not the safety aspect of shotgun slugs in populated areas be diminished? The principal reasoning behind slug-only laws—be the reasoning valid or not—is that the slower-moving slugs will run out of steam quicker than high-velocity rifle bullets, thus posing less of a threat to distant people and livestock. The new sabot slugs as loaded by Federal and Winchester have muzzle and down-range velocities similar to those of traditional rifled slugs, so maximum range will be similar. But don't forget that the safest shot, be it slug or bullet, is one that is well-aimed and accurate. The ones that miss are the ones we need to worry about. 🦌

tempting them with a 1¼-ounce 12-gauge magnum rifled slug. There is no such beast in the Winchester catalog.

Another thing that slug hunters must be aware of is the radical shifts in point of impact that often occur when switching from one load to another. Even at 50 yards the shift can be 1 foot or more; so if you change loads, don't go hunting without first checking your zero. Otherwise you are inviting a miss, and it could mean losing the buck of a lifetime.

The performance of old-fashioned rifled slugs in rifled barrels is nowhere near that of the sabot loads, but somewhat better than that of rifled slugs in a smoothbore. At 50

A New Peek at Peeps

By Jim Carmichel

Though I generally maintain a state of high spirit, I'm forced to admit that for a few weeks in the late spring, I was in a state of declining disposition. This might have been the result of several unfortunate events, such as a cold spring that suddenly turned too hot, the discovery that my favorite varmint rifle needed a new barrel just when woodchuck season was starting, or simply too much office work. I think, however, I can trace my melancholia to a new rifle I unboxed a while back. It is a good model, of reliable caliber, by a famous maker, one of which I've owned dozens of over the passing decades. The model is as familiar to me as the fingers of my hand, which is why, when I slipped the bolt into the receiver, I noticed the absence of two small holes on the left side of the receiver.

These small, lonely holes have been a feature on millions of rifles of all makes, models, and calibers for upward of a century. Their purpose is for attaching adjustable receiver sights, commonly know as "peep" sights. A generation ago (or has it been longer?), any respectable rifle was fitted with a good peep sight. Most usually these peep sights were made by Lyman, though Redfield also made high-quality peeps, and there was the old

Williams adjustable peep that for years sold for only $5 and even today is known as the 5-D model. And, of course, there were other fine brands that are now only relics of simpler times.

Recently, of course, receiver sights have yielded to telescopic sights to such degree that many—if not most—of today's hunters have never aimed a shot through a peep aperture. I also suspect that a like number of today's shooters have no idea as to the purpose of those two little holes in the receiver of their favorite rifle. Because they are anachronisms, I really can't blame a gun manufacturer for a decision to forego them. After all, it costs money to drill and tap holes and fit them with plugs. But still, I am sad to see them go because they are reminders of a time when peep sights represented the best in rifle performance. In fact, if I had my way, a new shooter would have to learn how to shoot a rifle with peep sights before graduating to a telescope, the reason being that an adjustable peep sight teaches a shooter a lot about the mechanics of shooting, marksmanship, and rifle performance that otherwise never gets learned. When my children first began shooting, I started them off with rimfire rifles mounted with adjustable peep sights. If their shots didn't hit where they were aimed I simply told them to "figure it out" and adjust the sights so that their bullets hit the target. Because necessity is the best teacher, they very quickly unraveled the mysteries of how a rifle's sights relate to the trajectory of a bullet.

When my son, Eric, was about 10 years old, he could estimate the distance to a wood-chuck, make the necessary trajec-tory corrections on his peep-sighted .218 Bee, and put his bullet on target. He went on to advanced studies in physics and I like to think that those ear-ly experiences with a peep-sighted rifle, dealing with the abstract relationships of a sight and the bullet's flight, taught him to think like a physicist. A kid doesn't learn to think like that from watching television.

Back when I was a youngster, about my only exposure to sophisticated rifle shooting techniques and equipment was what I read in journals such as *Outdoor Life* or a dusty half-dozen outdated books in the local library. The experts who wrote therein seemed to be unanimous in their agreement that the peep sight was the fastest aiming device one could use on a rifle and was just the ticket for lightning-fast shots at bounding deer. This information, howev-er, was completely at odds with the local experts, who allowed that peep sights might be good for target shooting, but for hunting they were as slow and clumsy as a cow in a rail pile. Unable to understand why there was such a difference of opinion over peep sights, I finally decided that people who hunted with them were probably Yankees or other foreigners who didn't aim a rifle the way we did in the hills of Tennessee.

Finally, I discovered that the reason the gun experts in my neighborhood didn't like peep sights was because they didn't know how to use

them. They were accustomed to aligning both front and rear sights with the target. This, of course, is the way to aim with open sights, but with peep sights you look through—but not at—the rear aperture. This is why a peep sight, if it is to be used efficiently, must be mounted so that it is close to the eye. If the sight is too far from the eye, it is difficult to use and next to worthless. The beloved '03 Springfield, in its early form, had a ladder-type adjustable rear sight that flipped up for long-range shooting. The sliding aperture plate had a tiny peep hole that was all but use-less because it was several inches from the eye. Fortunately, the '03 also had an optional open-notch sight. The M-l Garand of lat-er fame had a peep sight only, but it was positioned at the rear of the receiver, close to the eye, so that aiming was fast and accurate.

Which brings us to the issue of just how accu-rate a peep sight actually is. When you get your eye close to a peep aperture, you see such a large field that there is an impression of rather sloppy, imprecise aiming. Because the peep itself is not seen clearly, there is a sensation of imperfect sight alignment, especially if you are accustomed to using traditional open sights that require careful alignment. But even if you can't see the peep well, or at all, the fact that you are looking through it automatically ensures a highly precise alignment. This is quickly proven by a bit of sim-ple arithmetic.

Let's say that you have a bolt-action rifle with a 24-inch barrel. With a peep sight mounted at the rear of the receiver, this gives you a sight radius of about 30 inches, or a 100-yard error factor of 120. (100 yards=3,600 inches, divided by 30 inch-es=120.) This means that an error in sight align-ment is magnified 120 times on the target at 100 yards. The aperture of a hunting peep is about .080 inches, which means that the greatest error

Author took aim at this elk with a ladder-type folding peep sight. Photograph by Jim Carmichel

you can make, measuring from the center of the hole, is .040 inches. Multiply this .040 by the 120 error factor and you see that the worst possible error in alignment that you can make will cause your bullet to be 4.8 inches from dead center at 100 yards. In actual use, even when making fast shots at moving game, the alignment error is much less because your eye automatically looks through the center of the aperture. Target shooters who routinely use peep sights in rifle tournaments normally have an alignment error of less than one minute of angle. This translates to an error of less than 5 inches at 500 yards, which exceeds the accuracy of most ammunition.

You say this is all well and good for a sharp-eyed young target shooter, but what about us older chaps whose vision is declining? The truth is that peep sights serve us older shooters much better than open sights. As we grow older, it is common for our eyes to lose their ability to rapidly shift focus from one distance to another. Whereas younger eyes shift focus from rear sight to front sight to target and back again so rapidly that all three objects seem to be in sharp focus, older eyes do not change focus so fast, causing both sights or the target, or all three, to look fuzzy. As we become far-sighted, it is the rear sight, in particular, that usually seems the most difficult to see clearly. With peep sights, however, this is less of a problem because your eyes have only to see the front sight and the target.

Some target shooters get miffed if you call their ultra-precise aiming instruments "peeps," preferring more elite terms such as irons (as opposed to scopes) or receiver sights. To most shooters, however, any rear sight that you aim through a small hole is called a peep. So try to be understanding if a target shooter acts insulted when you refer to his prize aperture sight as a peep. After all, it may have cost as much as a high-grade telescopic sight and have micrometer-style adjustments fine enough to divide the direction of a bullet into quarters, sixths, and even eighths of a minute of angle. (Assuming, that is, that rifles and ammunition of such rare accuracy are available.)

By the way, did you know that only peep sights are used on the rifles used in the Olympic games? Likewise, peeps are the rule for NCAA intercollegiate rifle and air-rifle tournaments. Scopes aren't allowed and ordinary open sights simply can't be aimed with the necessary precision.

By now you may be wondering why, if peep sights are so great, they don't come on rifles instead of open sights. As a matter of fact, there are a number of rifles, especially rimfires and air guns, that come out of the box with aperture sights attached. And if you are a student of military or paramilitary firearms, you know that peep sights are standard on virtually all of today's shoulder-fired arms because they are simple, rugged, and accurate .

One longtime reason that gunmakers do not, and have not, provided peep sights on their rifles, other than the fact that open sights are generally cheaper, is because the selection of an aperture sight is largely a matter of personal preference. There are different brands and styles to choose from and, as in selecting a scope, the sight should be matched to the gun, the game, and the shooter.

Up until about 1970, by which time scopes had become the dominant aiming system, most gunmakers cataloged aperture sights as a factory-fitted option. Some makers such as Mossberg and Sako manufactured their own line of peep sights, supplying them as standard on some models, whereas other makers simply fitted a name-brand sight. For example, before the calamitous year of 1964, Winchester catalogs pictured and described the company's Model 70 bolt rifle as being fitted with a Lyman No. 48 sight. In 1950, the company charged $13.75 extra for this option, which required some stock alteration. A pre-1964 Model 70 with a factory-fitted peep sight is much prized by collectors and will fetch a couple of hundred dollars more than an otherwise identical Model 70 with open sights. A good specimen of the now-discontinued Lyman No. 48 sight will have an

asking price of as much as 10 times the 1960 price of $12.50. Of course, Lyman, like other makers of peep sights, offered several different styles and prices, with some retailing for only a dollar or two.

The Lyman No. 48 represented just about everything a receiver-mounted peep sight should be, and during its decades of production, it was made to fit just about every popular rifle, from Krags to Remingtons. My first grown-up target rifle, a Winchester Model 52 Rimfire with a heavy barrel, was fitted with a No. 48 sight, and I still have a match version of the '03 Springfield with a No. 48. The Lyman No. 48 had micrometer-style adjustments that moved the impact of the bullet $\frac{1}{4}$ inch at 100 yards with each click of the elevation or windage adjustment knobs. Like most good quality receiver sights, it also had a calibrated scale that could be set on zero after the rifle was sighted in. Thereafter, even after making changes to allow for different ranges or crosswinds, the setting could be returned to the zero markers with confidence that the bullet would be dead on target at the original sight-in distance. I scratched additional yardage settings on the index scale so that I could make quick and precise sight changes from one distance to another. The sight on my old '03 is so marked in hundred-yard increments out to 600 yards. It has been a third of a century since I scratched the distance settings on that sight, but I'll bet the point of impact is still close enough to make a 300-yard jackrabbit wish he'd stayed in bed. Peep sights are rugged, and once zeroed they tend to keep your bullet on target even after years of rough use.

The Lyman No. 48 came in two versions: one with full-size adjustment knobs and the other a hunting style with rounded, coin slot adjustments. The more streamlined hunting sight was more resistant to brush, saddle scabbards, and other hazards of the hunt that might snag and accidentally cause a change in zero.

The slide fixture of the sight, which held the peep aperture, could be quickly detached from the base, leaving the top of the rifle's receiver completely open. This feature was especially valuable back in the days when scopes weren't as reliable as they are now. With the quick-detachable scope-mounting systems then in vogue, a hunter could take his scope off and insert the peep slide in its base in a matter of seconds. Timed tests have shown that two aimed shots, one with scope and a second with peep, could be fired in about a half-minute. Trapdoor buttplates with a felt-lined compartment in the butt section were perfect for carrying the aperture slide and were almost standard features on high-class rifles made by such spiffy gunmakers as Griffin & Howe. Speaking of which, during that stylish era of rifle making, it was not uncommon on engraved rifles to have the peep sight assembly nicely decorated with matching scrollwork and even gold inlays.

If you're wondering why I've gone into such detail describing a peep sight that is no longer made, the reasons are two: First of all, the Lyman No. 48 was only typical of several other brands and models of receiver-mounted sights having similar features. Some were remarkably small and simple and others were specially designed for specific rifles. Examples of these include the "swinging door" sight that had an aperture arm that pivoted out of the way of the bolt handle on split-receiver rifles such as the Mannlicher-Schoenauer. When the bolt was closed, the aperture snapped back into position, ready to aim. Another style of

specialized peep mounted directly on the bolt of lever-action rifles and rode back and forth as the action was operated. Winchester offered this option on a number of its lever models.

Yet another specialized peep—this one offered by most sight makers—mounted on the rear of the striker or cocking knob of Springfield, Mauser, Krag, and some other bolt-action rifles. This was a very compact arrangement that put the peep aperture very close to the shooter's eye. When the trigger was pulled the sight jumped forward with the striker. This peep arrangement was especially popular with British gunmakers building rifles for the African trade.

The other reason I singled out the Lyman No. 48 is because it just might be once again available. Mace Thompson, president of Lyman Products, tells me that interest in peep sights is booming so much that his company is considering the reintroduction of the 48 and other models of peep sights. At present the company still offers the Series 57 and 66 receiver-mounted sights.

So what has caused the sudden interest in peep sights? Much of the demand comes from blackpowder shooters who want better accuracy from their muzzleloading rifles.

PEEP SIGHTS: MANUFACTURERS AND SUPPLIERS

Beeman Precision Arms Inc.
3440 Airway Drive
Santa Rosa, CA 95403
(Air-rifle sights)

Freelands
3734 14th Ave.
Rock Island, IL 61201
(Mail-order retail; Freeland and other brands of sights)

Lyman Products Corporation
Rte. 147
Middlefield, CT 06455

Outdoor Industries
617 Windsor Parkway
Atlanta, GA 30342
(Folding tang sights)

Precision Sales International
Box 1776
Westfield, MA 01086
(Anschutz sights)

Redfield Gun Sight Corporation
5800 E. Jewell St.
Denver, CO 80222
(Palma target sights)

Shiloh Sharps Arms Company Inc.
Box 279
Big Timber, MT 59011
(Early style vernier sights)

Thompson/Center Arms
Box 5002
Rochester, NH 03867
(Sights for muzzle-loading rifles)

Warner Tool Company
RR 1
Box 8
Keene, NH 03431
(High-quality target sights)

Williams Gun Sight Company
Box 329
Davidson, MI 48423

The author takes aim using the tang mounted peep sight on his Sharps rifle. Photograph by Jim Carmichel

A peep sight mounted on or near the tang of a muzzleloader is fast and convenient to use and can greatly improve bullet placement. Some of the best groups I've ever seen fired with muzzleloading rifles were aimed with peep sights.

Both Lyman and Williams Gun Sight Company offer adjustable peep sights that fit most muzzleloading rifles. One of the nicest sights for rifles of this type is a traditional folding-style tang sight made by Thompson/Center. Made to fit T/C and other muzzleloading or early style breech-loading singleshot rifles, this sight has a vernier-style elevation adjustment like on the peep sights favored by buffalo hunters of the last century. When not in use the tall, ladderlike sight folds down out of harm's way. I used a similar sight made by Shiloh Rifle Company on a Shiloh Sharps rifle for a successful elk hunt. These tang-mounted sights are especially popular with shooters and hunters who want to retain an authentic flavor with their muzzleoaders or early style breechloaders.

Another reason for the comeback of peep sights is the expanding use of shotgun slugs. What with more deer hunting areas mandating slugs-only, plus rifled shotgun barrels and slugs actually accurate enough to hit where they are aimed, there has been a corresponding increase in demand for better shotgun aiming systems.

Some shotguns do not adapt well to scope mounting, but peep sights are available for most pump and autoloading models. Given the accurate range of shotgun slugs and the terrain where they are most often used, a receiver-mounted peep sight is just about perfect for this kind of hunting—especially considering that they mount low on the receiver, allowing the shooter to keep his head down on the stock for fast, accurate aiming. Hunters who have had problems trying to aim a high-mounted scope on a low-comb shotgun will quickly see the advantage of a peep sight on a shotgun.

Another cause of the new-found popularity of peeps is the number of marksmanship training programs for young shooters, along with the increasing number of sophisticated air rifles being manufactured. Nearly all rifles used in training courses are equipped with peep sights, and the increasing number of junior-size or entry level target rifles has not only created a demand for a like number of peep sights but has also created an appreciation for peep sights in general. A young shooter who is taught to use a peep sight for target shooting is more likely to use a similar sight on his plinking and hunting rifles. Renowned marksman Gary Anderson, for example, started his shooting career with peep sights, used them for his world championships and

Olympic Gold Medal winning performances, and now uses them for hunting elk.

Many of today's air rifles are capable of better accuracy than can be appreciated with open sights, which is why scopes or peep sights are necessary for top performance. There are a number of peeps available, from inexpensive models to ultra-sophisticated tournament-grade sights. Most of these clamp on the dovetail rails of most makes of air rifles. Williams Gun Sight offers several styles of peep sights for air rifles, including a no-gunsmithing system that adapts to dovetail rails on foreign as well as domestic makes. Some makers of air guns even offer peep sights as a standard item or as an option, which is a factor worth considering when buying a pellet rifle or even a BB gun.

An all-time classic type of peep sight was the tang sight used on a host of lever-action, single-shot, pump, and autoloading rifles during the early decades of this century. Tang sights fit any rifle with a solid receiver tang extending back into the grip area of the stock and were manufactured by just about everyone in the sight business. The better makes of tang sights were adjustable for both windage and elevation and had a trim, uncluttered shape that added an air of grace to any rifle. Aside from being good-looking and easy to attach (usually by a couple of screws), they had the advantage of being positioned close to the eye and were therefore easy to aim. For storage or carrying, the little tang sights folded down against the grip but could be ready for action in a heartbeat. Even inexpensive little rifles such as the Stevens Crack Shot were improved by a tang sight, but these sights were at their best on high-grade single-shots, and no deluxe-grade lever rifle was properly dressed without one.

By the 1960s, tang sights were out of style and discontinued, but in recent years, a renewed demand has created a seller's market for lucky owners who have a tang sight they'll part with. A good specimen of a Lyman or Marble's tang sight that retailed for $5 in 1950 will now trade even for a pretty good scope. The demand has caused Outdoor Industries in Atlanta to reintro-duce a folding tang peep that looks and works like the originals. This sight is available for quite a few lever and single-shot rifles of current and past manufacture, and I've ordered one for my Model 39 Marlin .22 rimfire. It will make a classy outfit. Speaking of which, a peep sight is a smart and good-looking addition to such stylish rimfires as those made by Browning, Marlin, and Winchester. Peeps are easy to mount and unbeatable for hunting small game or pests.

It seems to me that what with the current trend toward lighter and trimmer hunting rifles, the peep sight offers more advantages than ever. Weighing only a few ounces, a peep sight not only helps keep weight to an absolute minimum but also results in a rifle with a clean, easy-to-carry profile. I do not advocate peep sights as an option to a good scope, but I certainly recommend them as a worthwhile replacement for open sights.

An especially smart mating of peep sights is with lever-action rifles that are primarily used for brush hunting but also for occasional shots across open meadows. This way you have the speed and fast aiming features you need in dense timber plus the more precise aiming necessary for shots of more than 100 yards. Most makes of lever rifles are already drilled and tapped for peep sights, so do-it-yourself mounting is easy. The gold or white bead front sights on most lever rifles are perfectly combined with a peep rear.

Because the rear leaf of common open sights obscures so much of the target, some shooters use a six o'clock hold, with the target perched somewhat indecisively above the front bead. With a peep rear the target is much less obscured, allowing you to sight in so that the bullet hits "behind" the bead. That means that you hold the bead where you want the bullet to hit. It is a very, very fast, reflexive way to fire a rifle. In fact, hunters who have spent a lifetime with open sights sometimes are slow to realize that peeps are so easy. Because there is no rear sight to align, it seems that part of the aiming process is left out. But it only seems that way because when you are looking through the peep the alignment is automatic and the bullet hits where the front sight says it should. And that's about all you can ask of any sight. ✍

The Boom in Blackpowder

By Rick Hacker

What's that you say? You wish you could hunt more than you do, but the season always seems too short? You missed that 6×6 whitetail and you'd like another chance at him, but the cartridge season is over? You finally dropped that weathered old trophy buck with your scoped rifle, and now you'd like to go after something that isn't quite so rutworn, simply for the meat? You want to put more "hunt" in your hunt, and you'd like to get an extra deer? Is that what's bothering you? Well, strike up the band and raise Old Glory because your wishes have been granted. Deer season has been extended, and it's all due to a resurgence of one of the oldest hunting sports in America.

We're speaking, of course, about muzzleloader hunting, a pastime that is finding new favor with sportsmen who want to get a second deer or to make up for the proverbial "one that got away." Muzzleloader hunting is also for the guy or gal who simply wants a challenge and to spend more time in the woods. With the majority of states now offering separate muzzleloader seasons, owning a smokepole is almost like having a second tag. Of course, you're going to have to work for your blackpowder deer, but the poten-

tial for success is there for those who don't mind limiting themselves to a single shot and holding their shooting range to approximately 100 yards.

Getting started in muzzleloading is not that difficult, but it requires you to switch your mental mode of thinking from "cartridge" to "blackpowder." This means that big-game animals must be hunted with big-bore rifles. In muzzleloading, a .36-caliber is a squirrel gun. Deer rifles start at .45 caliber (for the smaller Eastern and Southeastern varieties of whitetails) and go all the way up to .58 caliber for frontloaders that can also adequately be used for elk, bears, and moose. By far the most popular deer caliber is .50, but my own preference is for the .54, as it offers the best combination of accuracy and big-game knockdown power.

There are two types of ignition systems for muzzleloaders: flintlock and percussion. The flintlock system is more susceptible to wind and water, but it is required in some states, such as Pennsylvania. Otherwise, my first choice would be to go with the percussion lock, which is more

Photograph by G. Allan Brown

surefire. After you have harvested a few deer with your caplock, you can always switch to the more temperamental flinter to put an added challenge into your big-game hunting adventures. I have taken deer with both types of charcoal-burners, and although I find it more aesthetically rewarding to bag my buck with a flintlock, when there is a chance of inclement weather I always reach for my percussion.

What kind of muzzleloader should you look for in a big-game rifle? Besides it being well-made (for example, the hammer hits squarely on the nipple, and trigger pull and sights are satisfactory) and having a bore of sufficient caliber, you also want a rifle that is devoid of flashy metal and a shiny lacquered stock. These game-spooking attributes are fine for a gun that will be hung over the fireplace, but not for one to be carried in the woods. Over the years, some of the best rifles I have successfully used for deer hunting include the Kentucky-style .50 caliber Tennessee Mountain Rifle from Dixie Gun Works, the rugged halfstock .50 and .54 Ithaca-Navy Hawken from Navy Arms, and the Lyman Deerstalker, also in .50 and .54 calibers.

Besides these traditionally styled guns, there are some excellent muzzleloaders of more modern configurations. Why a modern-style muzzleloader? Because some cartridge hunters feel more comfortable with a muzzleloader that is stocked and proportioned like a bolt-action, even

ROUND BALLS OR CONICALS
Which to Use?

Round Balls
- Work best in rifles with slow-twist rifling (for example, one-in-66-inch twists)
- Must be patched with a lubricated patch to ensure an adequate gas seal
- Take longer to load
- Are extremely accurate

Conicals
- Work best in rifles with fast-twist rifling (for example, one-in-48-inch twists)
- Are pre-lubed and require no patching to load
- Are quick to load
- Hit with greater striking energy using less powder

BLACKPOWDER STARTER KIT

Depending on the type of frontstuffer you decide to go with, you'll need a number of items to both get started and make things easier in the field. Pictured are a number of accoutrements that you might find helpful.

They are: A) round balls, B) conical bullets, C) speedloaders, D) small powder horn (for priming flintlock pans), E) larger powder horn, F) wedge pin puller (for disassembling some muzzleloaders), G) cleaning jag, H) nipple wrench, I) ball and bullet puller, J) replacement nipple, K) worm (patch puller), L) caps, M) capper, N) short starter, O) powder measure, and P) possibles bag. For round ball users, pictured below are pre-cut and prelubed patches (left side) and uncut patches with a trimming knife. (Patch lube not shown.)

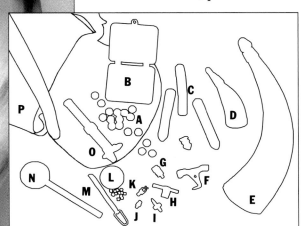

Photographs this spread by G. Allan Brown; Photos on page 178 by G. Allan Brown (top) and Rick Hacker (bottom).

gun that combines the best features of both—sometimes including a camouflage stock, an outside hammer and/or a pistol-grip stock. The fully camouflaged .50 Tree Hawk and the .50 and .54 Scout, both from Thompson/Center, are two of the best examples. Also worth considering is the .50 Shadow Buckskinner Carbine, with its camouflaged synthetic stock, from Traditions.

If your state game laws permit the use of "modern-looking" firearms during the muzzleloading season (not all fish and game departments allow this, so be sure to check the regulations carefully), Mossberg and Hastings both make muzzleloading conversion barrels for pump shotguns such as the Mossberg Model 500 and the Remington Model 870.

Like any hunting rifle, once you have made your selection, the key to success is practice. Plan on allowing enough time at the range to adequately sight in your smokepole and to get used to how it handles and where it shoots. How much powder should you use in working up a hunting load? That depends on what you are hunting and the caliber of your rifle. My general rule is that for deer hunting, most .50-calibers will shoot best with a load of between 65 and 90 grains of powder. For .54s and larger, a load of 85 to 120 grains works best. In all cases, however, follow the manufacturer's recommendations. Generally speaking, hunting loads for conical bullets will require less powder than patched round balls, simply because the heavier conicals hit with more energy.

Unlike a cartridge gun, a blackpowder rifle

though it uses a ramrod and loads from the front. Some of the better known rifles in this category include the .50 and .54 stainless-steel-barreled Knight MK-85 and the lower-priced, synthetically stocked BK-92 from Modern Muzzle Loading; the .45, .50 and .54 GA-87 from Gonic Arms; and the .50 and .54 Apollo 90 Rifle and Carbine from CVA. All of these rifles feature "straight-line" actions; that is, there is no external hammer. Instead, the percussion cap is exploded by the force of a spring-driven boltlike hammer striking the nipple in a straight line. Hence the name.

In addition to the traditional and modern styles of muzzleloaders, there is a new breed of should be cleaned between each shot to obtain the best accuracy. Fouling shots are not what you want. When sighting in your muzzleloader, start out by firing a shot at a 50-yard target, then run a patch lightly moistened with solvent down the bore, followed by two or three dry patches (moist powder won't burn!), load and fire again. Once you have a good group, adjust your sights until your shots are clustered around the center of the target. Then fire a three-shot string at 100 yards so that you'll know where to hold at that range.

When reloading between shots, try to use the same technique as you will when out in the field. That is, load from your pockets or shooting pouch, not from the bench. This will make you more proficient during hunting season, should you need a fast follow-up shot at a wounded or missed deer. Even though you only have one shot, a skilled muzzleloader hunter should be able to reload and fire within 30 seconds.

Although all you really need to get started is a rifle, powder and ball, there are numerous accoutrements on today's market for the

---

BLACKPOWDER VS. PYRODEX: WHAT'S THE DIFFERENCE?

There are only two types of propellants you can use in any muzzleloader: blackpowder and Pyrodex. Anything else will blow up the gun and parts of your anatomy. What's the difference between the two popular powders?

Blackpowder

- Is the traditional propellant that has been used in muzzleloaders for more than 500 years, even though the ingredients have changed somewhat
- Is highly explosive
- Can be used in both flintlock and percussion rifles
- Offers more reliable ignition in inclement weather
- Comes in four grades:
    4FG—used only for priming the pans of flintlocks
    3FG—used for rifles up to .50 caliber
    2FG—used for rifles of .54 caliber and larger
    1FG—only used for cannons, so unless you're hunting with a howitzer, forget it

Pyrodex

- Is a synthetic blackpowder
- Is not as volatile as blackpowder and can therefore be transported by common carrier
- Gives more shots per pound

- Requires a hotter flash to set it off; therefore, specially designed hot caps should be used
- Cannot be used with flintlocks
- Comes in the following grades:
    RS—for rifles/shotguns
    P—for small-caliber (less than .50) rifles and handguns
    CTG—for blackpowder cartridge guns
- Is adequate for general hunting in the regular RS grade, but the new Pyrodex Supreme RS grade provides greater accuracy and consistency of ignition

Both Pyrodex and Blackpowder...

- Are measured by volume, rather than weight
- Must be firmly compressed by the ball for adequate ignition
- Will start to cause rust if your muzzleloader is not cleaned the same day it is fired

LEGAL CONCERNS FOR MUZZLELOADING HUNTER

The following items may be regulated or prohibited by your fish and game department. In all cases, be sure to read and comply with all current muzzleloader hunting regulations.

- Scopes—in keeping with the tradition of close-range muzzleloader hunting, most states prohibit the use of scopes during the blackpowder season.

- Conical bullets—some states only permit round balls to be used on big game, even though conicals are effective game-getters.
- Sabots—these plastic-sleeved encasements for lead bullets are not legal in many states.
- Type of ignition—straight-line actions are not permitted in many states, and a few states, such as Pennsylvania, only allow flintlocks.

muzzleloading hunter. Not all of these items are practical, but some of them are extremely helpful and worth acquiring. First and foremost is a capper, which will make loading your percussion rifle much faster and easier than simply using your fingers. Those little No.11 caps can become mighty elusive in wet or cold weather. Next on your list should be speedloaders, which will enable you to carry pre-loaded charges of powder and ball with you in the field, and to reload in record time without having to measure your powder for every shot. Unbreakable ramrods and special nipples (such as Uncle Mike's Hot Shot and Mountain State Muzzleloading's Magnum Spitfire) that are designed to emit a hotter flash with any type of cap are two other items worth checking into in order to ensure more reliable shooting under field conditions.

Then, of course, there are always the basic tools such as a powder horn or flask (should you elect not to use a speed-loader); powder measure; lubricant; short starter; cleaning jags, tips and worms; and a "possibles bag" or shooting pouch to keep everything together. All are designed simply to make things easier and keep your smokepole in working condition in the field.

When hunting in wet and

inclement weather, always remember to keep your muzzle pointed down; you don't want water trickling down the bore and into your charge. Remember, the only way moisture can get into your powder is either through the muzzle or the nipple/touch-hole area of your rifle's breech. Be sure to keep these two areas protected, either by carrying your muzzleloader under an Army-style poncho or by utilizing tape over the muzzle and a waterproof "cow's knee" leather or plastic covering over the lock and breech.

I s all this extra shooting and loading and cleaning and preparation worth it? I think the answer can best be found during the "muzzleloading-only" season, when you are one of the relatively few hunters in the woods. Maybe you'll be stalking up to a well-traveled game trail, or perhaps you'll be stoically waiting, rifle shouldered and cocked, in a tree stand. A wary whitetail gingerly steps out into the open, not more than 50 yards from your front sights. You never would have had this extra opportunity had it not been for the blackpowder rifle you are now holding. As you nestle the front blade into the rear notch and gently squeeze the trigger, you'll have your answer.

Some hunters use their muzzleloaders to make up for the proverbial "one that got away." Photograph by Charles Alsheimer

HOW TO LOAD A BLACKPOWDER RIFLE

1. *After popping two or three caps on an empty gun to dry out any oil in the nipple and breech areas, a pre-measured charge is poured into the bore. (Try loading from your pockets or a pouch to best mimic field conditions.)*

2. *A pre-lubed conical bullet, which requires no patching, or a round ball centered on a precut and pre-lubed patch is then placed into the bore of the rifle. (Speed-loaders will quicken these initial two steps, in that they contain both powder and projectile.)*

3. and 4. *Finger-pressing is sometimes sufficient to seat a lubed conical into the bore (left), but a patched round ball will require the use of a short starter (right). (A short starter may also be necessary to help seat a tight-fitting conical bullet.)*

5. *The ramrod is then held close to the muzzle to prevent breakage, and the conical or round ball is firmly rammed down against the powder charge. (Making a line on the ramrod at muzzle height will help you tell when the projectile is seated.)*

6. and 7. *For caplocks (left), the nipple is then capped with either a No. 10 or No. 11 cap. For flintlocks (right), the pan is primed with 4FG powder and the frizzen is snapped closed over the charge. Always remember to keep the powder as dry as possible.*

Photographs by Rick Hacker

Handloading Hand Guns

By George H. Haas

The photographs that follow aren't intended to show exactly how to reload handgun cartridges. Excellent equipment is shown in the pictures, but it will probably differ from the gear that you own or buy. Reloading equipment varies from very simple hand-held tools, such as the Lee Loader kit and the Lyman tong tool, all of the way up to semi-automated, power-driven equipment, and because of this, procedures vary. With any kind of equipment, follow the detailed instructions that are given by the manufacturer.

The following pictures and captions are only intended to tell you what kind of work you're getting into so that you can decide whether or not you want to try it. The work is painstaking and very repetitive. Unless you can do that sort of thing with unflagging attention, don't get into it. Unlike model making or stamp collecting, handloading mistakes can be hazardous to your health.

On the other hand, if you can exercise care with every round, despite the onset of boredom toward the end of completing a batch, you'll save

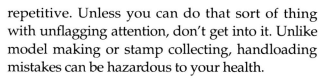

1. Three dies are used to reload straight-sided handgun ammunition (cases without bottlenecks). They are shown disassembled with removable interior parts alongside each hollow die. At top is the resizing die with the decapping (depriming) stem and pin that is screwed into it when in use. The hollow die squeezes a fired case back down to its original dimensions. The second die (expander) with the expander stem expands the case mouth and slightly "bells" the forward edge of the case mouth so that the new bullet will enter easily. Third is the bullet seater with the bullet-seating stem. These are RCBS dies, but other companies make similar ones. For bottlenecked cases—rifle and handgun—only two dies are needed: the resizing die, which sizes the case, decaps it and expands its neck; and the bullet seater, which handles the rest. All photographs by Mary Haas

from 50 to 70 percent on ammunition costs. You'll also be able to vary your loads to suit your changing needs more than you can with purchased factory cartridges. You can load very light target rounds, very powerful hunting rounds and everything in between.

In general, the photos and captions here apply only to handgun cartridges—in particular, to powerful revolver loads, though any straight-sided rifle or handgun case can be loaded by taking the major steps shown here. Reloading bottle-necked cartridges differs quite a bit. With semi-automatic handgun rounds, forming the crimp (securing the case mouth around the bullet) is the only part of the procedure that differs from the ones shown here. Semi-auto cartridges take a gradual-taper crimp rather than the abrupt-roll crimp used for revolver cartridges.

Use a good reloading manual in addition to the instructions given by the equipment and component manufacturers. The following pictures do not show every step, but the manuals do in some detail. For instance, inspection and preparation of cases before reloading is not covered here, and trimming cases back to the original factory lengths isn't covered either, though both are essential to safe reloading. There are several good reloading manuals, but two that are very good on handgun rounds are *Speer Reloading Manual No.11.* (published by Omark) and *Lyman Reloading Handbook No.46.* These manuals also list safe, tested loads for almost every handgun cartridge.

Reloading manuals describe a large number of errors that can lead to accidents, but there are other, more basic errors that are not mentioned. How does one handle an interruption? Suppose you are halfway through charging your cases with powder when you are called to the telephone. When you sit down at your bench again, never assume that you know where you left off. Take a good look at the equipment and the partially loaded rounds to make sure that you know exactly what you did last. If you rely on memory, you may, for instance, dump another full powder charge on top of one that's already in a case. When you return after any interruption, you are courting disaster if you don't take a few minutes to determine exactly what you should do next.

2. *After carefully inspecting all your fired cases to eliminate those with defects, the first step is to resize the cases down to original factory dimensions and remove the fired primers. Here the sizer die is being screwed into the bench press. With the reloading ram and shell holder raised to the topmost position, the die is screwed down until it almost touches the shell holder. This die has a tungsten-carbide sizing ring in its mouth. The tungsten-carbide is slick and very hard, but it is brittle and must not be touched by the shell holder. With these carbide dies, it is not necessary to lubricate the cases to prevent them from sticking in the die. This eliminates a lot of mess and work. Tungsten-carbide sizing dies are so convenient that old-fashioned steel dies are really obsolete for the reloading of straight-sided cases*

It's also an awful thing to reload a batch and then have the sudden thought that something might have gone wrong. For instance, if you ran out of powder halfway through a run, did you really get the right powder needed to continue, or did you mistakenly use the wrong powder? If you are in any doubt, pull all of the bullets with a good bullet puller and inspect for trouble so that it can be corrected. If the bullets are slightly mangled by the puller, you can always reload them in cases and use them for practice shooting

But handloading is very safe if you follow correct procedures and keep your mind on what you are doing.

One important benefit to handloading is not mentioned in reloading manuals. Because handloading greatly reduces the cost of ammunition, you will inevitably shoot more—not while hunting, but at the range when testing your reloads, sighting in and just for the pleasure of it. That leads to real familiarity with your firearm and also improves marksmanship. In the field, this makes it possible to avoid wounding game—and that may be the most important thing that can be said about handloading.

3. *With the ram lowered, a fired case is placed into the shell holder. Shell holders and dies are available for every standard case. The .357 Magnum revolver case shown here will be loaded with a 158-grain hollow-point bullet. These .357 dies can also be used to reload .38 Special cases. The die must be locked in place with the large locking ring, and the decapping pin must be locked with the smaller locking ring on the stem The decapping pin should protrude from the die's mouth just enough to push out the old primer.*

4. *Depressing the operating handle raises the ram and drives the case into the die. Here the ram is shown almost at the top of its travel. The dead primer drops out through the hole in the shell holder and the ram. Run all your empty cases into the sizer die before going on to the next step.*

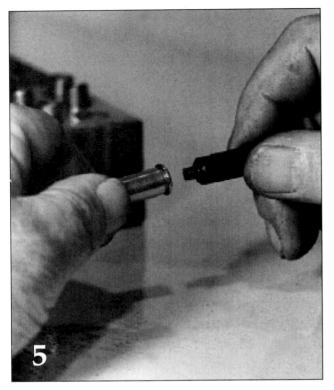

5. If the shell's empty primer pocket contains accumulated ash, it could prevent seating the new primer deeply enough. Inspect for this, and remove ash with a hand-held primer-pocket cleaner, which is available from many suppliers. Normally, however, there is so little residue that this step is not needed, except for precision target shooting.

6. With the sizer die removed, the expander die is screwed into the press. Place a sized case into the shell holder and raise the ram to the topmost position. Screw the main body of the die into the press until it protrudes a few screw threads below the press arbor. Lock it in position with the large locking ring. As shown here, the next step is to screw the expander plug into the die body until you feel it contact the mouth of the case. Lower the ram and screw the expander stem down a few threads more. Run the case into the die. Repeat this process until the first $1/16$ inch of the case's mouth is slightly expanded or belled.

7. Try a new bullet in the case mouth. If the base of the bullet—no more than $1/16$ inch—easily enters the belled mouth, the expander plug is deep enough. If not, screw the die down a quarter turn at a time until it is properly adjusted. Then, lock the small locking ring on the expanding stem by tightly screwing the ring down.

8

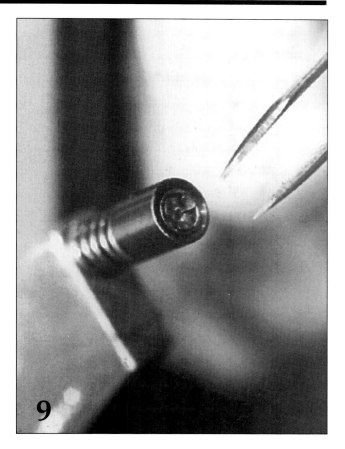

9

10

8. *Priming the cases is done on the downward move-ment of the ram after the case mouth has been expanded. Small handgun primers are used for the .357—not small rifle primers—in all primer brands except Federal. That company's small rifle primers are specifically recommended for use in magnum handgun rounds. Any handgun primer is very small indeed, and if you drop one on the floor, it is then almost impossible to find. One way to avoid this problem is to place the par-tially open box of primers in a plastic dish or container lid so that the rim of the container will catch a primer that gets away from you when you try to pick it up. Remove each primer from the box with a pair of tweezers. Special rubberized "primer flipper" dishes are available, but by using a plastic dish or container lid you can avoid even that moderate expense.*

9. *Here a primer has been inserted—mouth up, natu-rally—in the primer assembly of the priming arm, which is mounted on the press. The spring-loaded primer plug will force the primer into the primer pocket in the base of the case.*

10. *With the case still in the expander die after the case's mouth has been expanded, the primer arm is pushed into the slot in the ram. Make sure that the arm "bottoms" in the slot, or the primer will be off-center and will not enter the primer pocket when force is applied. The primer could also go off if it is not properly centered.*

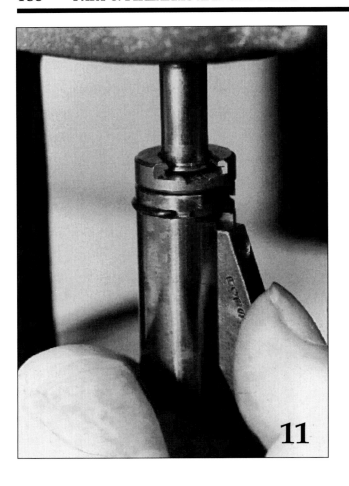

11 *With a smooth stroke of the operating arm, lower the expanded case onto the primer. Here the case is at the bottom of its travel. Expand and reprime all your cases in this operation, and then you are ready to charge your cases with powder. Primers should be seated so that they are just below flush with the case head. Feel with your thumb to make sure. Handloaders soon learn how much strength to apply to achieve the proper depth.*

12 *Here all items needed to charge the case with powder have been laid out. From right to left in order of use: powder measure (by volume, not weight), powder trickler to bring metered charge up to full weight a granule at a time, balancing scales to determine final weight of the charge, and a loading block. A one-pound canister of powder and a funnel are in the background. If you're new to reloading, weigh all your powder charges to avoid mistakes that could cause accidents. Always weigh maximum or near-maximum charges as listed in reliable manuals. After you gain experience, you can meter out light charges with a powder measure only, as long as you check every fifth charge or so with good scales to make sure that the measure's setting has not become inaccurate.*

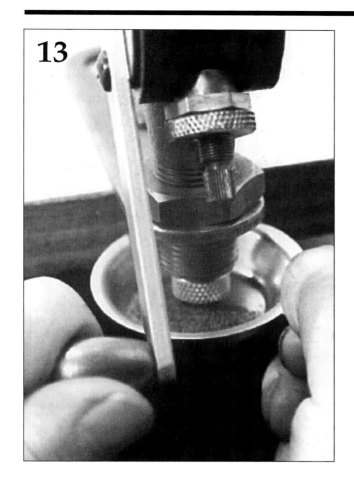

13. *The powder measure is easily adjusted to throw the correct charge by bulk, minus a few granules. The aluminum pan from the scales is held under the powder spout, and the operating handle is lowered to drop the charge into the pan.*

14. *The upper half of the wasp-waisted powder trickler holds several ounces of powder. The horizontal hollow stem has a screw tread cut into its interior and a small hole in its center. Turning the stem counterclockwise causes powder to enter the hole and then trickle a granule at a time into the pan of the scales until the correct weight is reached. Good scales make it possible to weigh powder to within $1/10$ of a grain (avoirdupois). Do weigh to that degree of accuracy at first and always when loading heavy charges. Be sure to set up your powder scales in accordance with the manufacturer's instructions. Erroneous readings can trigger disaster. Make absolutely sure that you understand the graduations marked on your scales. One way to check is to weigh several bullets of a previously known weight. For instance, if the bullet is known to weigh 158 grains and you read 79, you are badly and dangerously mistaken.*

15. *The correct charge is then funneled into the cartridge cases in the loading block. The handy Lee Precision funnel has an inner spout and an outer skirt that goes over the case mouth to prevent spillage. After charging all of the cases, look into the case mouths held in the loading block to make sure that powder is at the same level in all of the cases. It is possible to load a double or even triple charge in handgun cases when using some powders, and even a few grains can wreck a gun, at the least.*

16. *All cases have now been charged with powder. The next step is to seat the bullet and crimp the case mouth in one operation. The bullet must be seated to the correct depth, and the case mouth must be crimped into the cannelure (ribbed crimping groove around the bullet). This is done to ensure that the bullets in the shells remaining in the gun will stay in place despite recoil from previous shots. With the ram in the uppermost position, screw the seater die into the press arbor until it touches the shell holder Then back it out two complete turns. Lock the die in place with the large locking ring Then back off the seating stem and its small locking ring as high as they will go. Place a charged case in the shell holder. With one hand, hold a bullet in the mouth of the case. With the other, raise the ram as far as it will go.*

17. *Screw the seating stem down until you feel it not only touch the bullet but also push it slightly into the case .Then lower the ram. Screw the stem down a few turns more and raise the ram again. Repeat this procedure until the mouth of the case is in the middle of the cannelure around the bullet. The photo shows the halfway point at which the case mouth and the cannelure are still too far apart. Only use bullets with cannelures around their midsections. The cannelure determines the seating depth of the bullet.*

18. *The bullet is now seated at the correct depth*

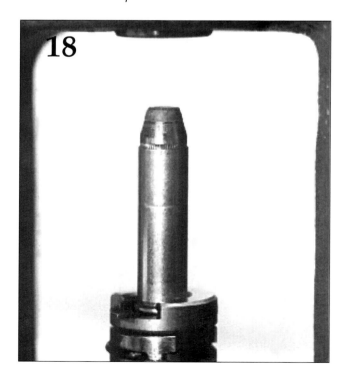

19

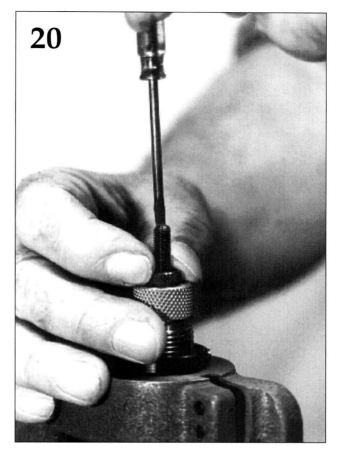

20

19. *After the proper depth has been found, back out the seating stem five or six turns to completely disengage it from the bullet. Then unlock the die body because the whole die must now be lowered until the case mouth contacts the crimping shoulder inside the hollow die.*

20. *To do this, raise the ram to its highest position and screw the entire die body down into the press until you feel the case mouth meet the crimping shoulder inside the die body. Lower the ram and turn the die in no more than one-quarter of a turn. Lower the ram and inspect. The first 1/64 inch of the case mouth should be lightly squeezed into the cannelure. If not, raise or lower the case body accordingly until the desired crimp is achieved. Then lock the die firmly in place with the locking ring. Avoid too long of a crimp because it works the metal too much and shortens the case life. After the right crimp is achieved, screw the seating stem down into the die with the ram raised until you feel it contact the bullet. Hold the stem in that exact position with a screwdriver (as shown here) and screw the small locking ring down firmly so that the stem cannot move. The die body and seating stem have now been adjusted so that crimping and bullet seating are achieved in a single operation with one movement of the ram. After this precise adjustment, load all your cases with bullets.*

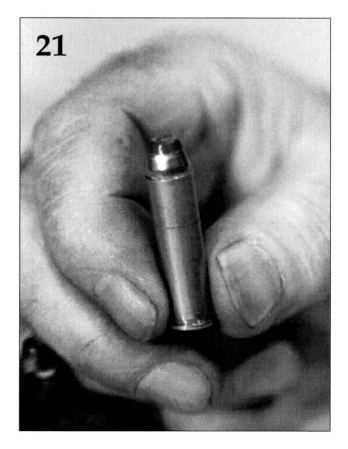

21

21. *Inspect all loaded rounds for case bulges, distorted, or split case mounts or mutilated bullets. Discard all defective rounds in a safe manner. Crimping is inherently the step that causes the most damage, and it must be carefully controlled. Once the die is correctly adjusted, make up a dummy round with no primer and no powder. In future reloading sessions, place the dummy round in the press and adjust the die by screwing its body down to touch the case and its stem down to touch the bullet. With a correctly assembled dummy round, correct adjustment takes about one minute.*

Index